Re-Making Teaching

Dramatic, profound and far-reaching changes are being visited on schools worldwide that have their genesis a long way from the classroom but which impact heavily on teachers and their work. Most of this reform has been achieved with little or no involvement of teachers themselves. This book sets out to survey the contemporary context of what is happening to the work of teaching, and focuses on Advanced Skills Teachers. It shows how teachers are 'speaking' the changes that are occurring to their work in protracted economically rationalist times.

Arguing against the discourses of economy as the major shaping force, the authors present a persuasive case for focusing on the discourses of teaching itself as the only feasible and adequate basis on which to make sense of teaching. And by presenting a range of voices of practising teachers — allowing them to speak for themselves about the difficulty of trying to translate policy-makers' intentions into words and actions — the book graphically illustrates the devastating long-term consequences for the future of schools of poorly-conceptualised reform policies.

John Smyth is Professor of Teacher Education and Director of the Flinders Institute for the Study of Teaching, where **Geoffrey Shacklock** is a Research Associate.

Re-Making Teaching

Ideology, policy and practice

John Smyth and
Geoffrey Shacklock

London and New York

First published 1998
by Routledge
11 New Fetter Lane, London EC4P 4EE

Simultaneously published in the USA and Canada
by Routledge
29 West 35th Street, New York, NY 10001

© 1998 John Smyth and Geoffrey Shacklock

Typeset in Sabon by Routledge
Printed and bound in Great Britain by Clays Ltd, St Ives PLC

British Library Cataloguing in Publication Data
A catalogue record for this book is available from the British
Library

Library of Congress Cataloguing in Publication Data
Smyth, John. Re-making teaching: ideology, policy, and practice/
John Smyth and Geoffrey Shacklock.
Includes bibliographical references and index.
 1. Teachers – Case studies. 2. Teaching – Case studies.
 3. Teacher participation in administration – Case studies.
 4. School supervision – Economic aspects – Case studies.
 5. Teachers – Australia. 6. Teaching – Australia. 7. Teacher
 participation I administration – Australia. 8. School supervision –
 Economic aspects – Australia. I. Shacklock, Geoffrey. II. Title.
LB1775.S59 1998
98–15142
371.1–dc21
CIP

ISBN 0–415–18690–0 (hbk)
ISBN 0–415–18691–9 (pbk)

Contents

Acknowledgements   vii

1 **Preliminaries**   1

2 **Scoping the wider landscape**   11
   Setting the scene: sketching out the bigger picture 11
   What kind of perspective, what kind of research? 26
   Advancing on skills formation in teaching 31

3 **Teaching under (re-)construction**   42
   How is teaching being constructed? 42
   *Critiquing the canon: genesis of reform and school
      restructuring 56*
   'Moral panic' as the basis for educational change 65
   Teaching as gendered work 73

4 **Teachers doing their 'economic' work**   77
   An ideology of production or the production of an ideology? 77
   Developing a 'reading position' on teaching 84
   Discursive pedagogical skill construction in teaching 90
   Marketised relationships in schools 96
   *Management for all seasons: managing teaching through market
      consent 101*

5 **Managing the 'preferred' teacher**   107
   Good teacher/bad teacher: managing 'docile bodies' 107
   Organising the icons of the 'preferred' teacher 116
   Deforming educational reform 120
   International perspectives: does anyone else have the answer? 123

'Low-trust' policies for teachers 130

6 Interrupting the dominant view   134
   Keeping alive alternative discourses about teaching 134
   The missing voices of teachers 144
   ASTs and the remaking of teachers' work 147

7 Letting the 'preferred' teacher speak   154
   Speaking about the pain of reforging skills into words 154
   Speaking about the AST and teachers' work 158
   Speaking about the discursive formation of skill in teachers'
      work 167
   Speaking about the skill and the ideological work of teaching 179
   Speaking about gender 190

8 Conclusion   192
   Rejecting economic palimpsests of teachers' work 192

   Bibliography   203
   Index   218

Acknowledgements

Writing a book can be an incredibly solitary process, but thankfully in this case I had the unstinting support of a range of people.

I was extremely fortunate, in the first instance, to receive a research grant from the Australian Research Council. Flinders University made available a period of sabbatical leave that enabled me to write the first six chapters, and during that time Edith Cowan University at Bunbury kindly provided me with a Visiting Fellowship and the peace and tranquillity within which to write. To Barry Down, in particular, Carol Hogan and Phil Clift, I express my gratitude for the generous hospitality and warmth extended to me during my retreat to Bunbury. Talking to teachers can be a very interesting but nevertheless demanding and time-consuming activity – Lorraine Johnson-Riordan and Adrian Rudzinski as research assistants did a marvellous job of capturing in a nuanced way the storied accounts that appear in this book, and many more we did not have the space to include. To my patient doctoral research students – Alastair Dow, Kenn Fisher, Robyne Garrett, Rosalie Kuhlmann, David Lee, Peter McInerney, Robyn Parkes, Breton Prosser, Alan Reid, Trudy Sweeney, Nick Sorenyi-Reichl and Noel Wilson – who all had to endure the difficulties of making 'an appointment' to see me, I hope that this book compensates a little, and furthermore that it reflects something of the many discussions we had during its formulation. Rob Hattam and Kym Brown deserve thanks just for being great intellectual colleagues, and Bob Lingard read and made many helpful suggestions on the draft manuscript. Helen Fairlie of Routledge had confidence that the book would all come together.

Solveiga deserves singling out, because without her emotional support, cheerful disposition and incredible organisational skills, the referencing, formatting and other aspects would be in total disarray.

Geoff Shacklock, my co-author, was a willing collaborator at all stages of the project. He did a magnificent job of making the teachers' stories come to life, and reacted helpfully to all of my writings.

Some parts of Chapter 2 appear in J. Smyth, 'Some global economic forces affecting school supervision', in G. Firth and E. Pajak (eds) *Handbook of*

Research on School Supervision, New York: Macmillan, 1998; parts of Chapter 4 appear in J. Smyth, G. Shacklock and R. Hattam, 'Teacher development in difficult times', *Teacher Development*, 1(1), 1997; some parts of Chapters 6 and 7 appear in G. Shacklock, J. Smyth and R. Hattam, 'The effects of an Advanced Skills Teacher classification on teachers' work: from storied accounts to policy insight', *Journal of Curriculum and Supervision* (in press).

Finally, this book would not have been possible without the active and willing participation of the many anonymous teachers, principals and school officials who gave generously of their time and insights. I dedicate this book to them in the hope that it may make a small contribution to the creation of a more socially just educational world.

John Smyth
1998

Chapter 1

Preliminaries

The HOPI Indians inhabit the mesa or plateaued mountains of Arizona. They have a centuries-old ritual of rising before dawn and 'praying the sun up'.

Some American anthropologists came along and suggested that just for one morning they might sleep in and miss their prayers and see what happened.

Incredulously the Hopi replied: 'What, and plunge the whole world into darkness for the sake of your stupid experiment?'

Over the past decade we have undergone a cultural experiment at the suggestion of economic scientists. Simply stated, they proposed that an increasingly competitive global economy required the floating of our dollar, the deregulation of our financial system and the reduction and removal of tariffs.

Public employment and public spending had to be cut drastically and much sharper inequalities of income or salaries embraced.

Higher levels of national unemployment were necessary for low inflation and a growing economy, and, in private enterprise, contractual, insecure employment had to be accepted.

In short, competition had to replace protection and cooperation as the prime public ethic.

Those who queried this path were denounced as irrational, naive and as foolish as the Hopi.

Tim Costello, *The Melbourne Age*, 16 Jan. 1997

Those of us committed to teaching in public schools are coming to the belated realisation that in respect of school reforms we should have been more like the Hopi Indians and remained true to our instincts and educative ideals. Somehow we lost our nerve and moral fibre at precisely the time when it counted the most. Instead of being indignant and vociferously denouncing recent changes to schools and teaching deriving from an ill-founded economic experiment, we mistakenly believed that if we ignored it for long enough then it would eventually go away. We were tragically wrong, and the consequence has been that our schools and other social institutions have been vandalised almost beyond redemption by those who argue that schools should be the engines for the economic restoration of sagging international competitiveness. We were too readily seduced by glittering prizes on offer from the fiscal snake-oil salesmen – quality, excellence, lean organisations, world best practice, user-pays, multi-skilled workforce – all in the interests of international competitiveness. The realisation that change can be for the worse has been slow to catch up with us, in a context where change is naturalised and few questions are ever asked about 'to what valued social ends'? Schools around the world have been co-opted into the bold new experiment of micro-economic reform, variously described as economic fundamentalism, economic rationalism, or simply the New Right ideology, with barely a thought about what is being lost and expunged (Carr and Hartnett 1996; Goodson and Hargreaves 1996; Lawn 1996; Apple 1996a). The shrinking of the 'imaginative space' (Zaida 1996) that has accompanied this single-minded pursuit of the 'ruthless economy' (Head 1996) has been matched only by the speed by which the shots are being called further and further away from what transpires in classrooms.

The educational policy experiment embarked upon around the world over the past decade of redrawing the boundaries around teaching through educational reform and restructuring, is in deep and possible terminal trouble. Teachers are reeling from the effects of poorly conceptualised reform policies that have literally torn the heart out of their work.

The exclusion of teachers, by and large, from participating in the changes to their work has not only been extremely disappointing, but will likely have devastating long-term consequences for the future of schools. By excluding teachers as active agents in shaping their own identities and those of their schools, we have wasted a valuable opportunity. There are several reasons for this: (a) the alternative to acknowledging and drawing upon the extensive accumulated knowledge and expertise of teachers is that outsiders presume to know 'what is wrong with schools', and proceed to devise inappropriate prescriptions on 'how to fix the situation'; (b) teachers' work becomes devalued, and we get locked into an unfortunate spiral of low morale, declining commitment, undervalued status, teacher burnout, media hype about failing schools – and the whole process impacts upon itself; (c) we need to work instead at creating the public spaces where discussion about the purposes of schooling and its valued social ends can be discussed, and where there is some democratic process for sorting out whose views prevail and whose get excluded, as discussion about teaching widens to include the relationship between schools and society. This is not by and large the case, as the instance we canvass in the book indicates.

This book is about how teachers are 'speaking' the changes that are occurring to the work of teaching in protracted economically rationalist times. It is as much about the changes being visited upon teachers through the broader forces and agencies at work, as it is about how teachers creatively and constructively accommodate and subjugate those changes, while also resisting and reconstructing the alternatives on their own terms (see Smyth 1993a for some examples of how this is happening). We employ the technique of 'mapping' the discourses of teachers' work (see Figure 1) in terms of the 'official' discourses of the educational policy makers, the discourses of 'enactment' as the policy was given practical expression in schools and the school system, and the 'aspiring' discourses of classroom teachers as they accommodated and resisted the introduction of a new career category for classroom teachers in Australia in the late 1980s known as Advanced Skills Teachers (ASTs) – a notion somewhat like 'lead teachers' in the USA, and the proposed 'expert teachers' in the UK. While we make no claims to present an exhaustive analysis of all possible discourses attaching to the work of teaching, we do engage with the major variants as they were expressed in this particular policy, its attempted enactment, and the voices of teachers as they reacted and responded to it. We believe that this is indicative of dramatic charges occurring to teaching elsewhere.

We want to make the point unambiguously at the beginning that this is not a book *about* Australian education, even though the issues we have chosen to focus on are drawn from the description of an Australian case study. In a sense the issues are far too important to have them relegated to the status of being a local exemplar – rather, they are constitutive of a wider set of global tendencies being played out in different ways in a myriad of other specific contexts. Our claim is that the AST is a convenient carrier or relay of the wider restructurings of teaching underway in various parts of the world. Our concern is to represent the AST initiative in terms of its capacity to illuminate the wider arguments about what is happening to the work of teaching, and we are confident readers will be able to identify and locate their own recognisable variants and carriers of ideology. Having said this, we nevertheless feel compelled to offer some comment on why Australia is a particularly appropriate site, and by way of some background to readers unfamiliar with the Australian scene, we offer the following brief set of contextual pointers:

1   Australia is one of the countries to have most comprehensively and consistently embraced the human capital/economic rationalist agenda, from the 1980s through to the present – most notably through a persistent national pre-occupation with international competitiveness, labour market flexibility, productivity, competencies, and skills formation, to mention a few;

2   at the time of the reported case study of the AST, Australia was deeply implicated in 'experimenting' with the corporate managerialisation of the public sector and the accompanying narrowing of policy goals, probably unprecedented anywhere in the world;

3   Australia has stunningly captured the imperative of 'putting education to work' (Taylor *et al.* 1997: 100) through the adoption of a vocation-alist discourse about education that has involved a thorough convergence of general with vocational education;

4   Australia provides an interesting window on what happens when policy is conceived and publicly presented within one set of lenses, and what can happen through the policy text-production process (described by Ball 1994) when compromises, competing interest groups and conflicting agenda have to be worked through practically;

5   in particular, Australia lived through an especially interesting era during which the AST was developed in which there was a stitching together of agenda between 'progressive democratic educators, those seeking greater equity in labour market access, participation and returns, and those seeking fundamental restructuring of the economy based on principles of tripartite planning' (Freeland 1992) – there are important lessons to be learned here;

6   all of this has occurred against a complex background set of state and federal relationships where there is an 'inherent tension' (Taylor *et al.* 1997: 119) exacerbated in the post-World War Two era by an assertion of 'latent power' federally through the constitution (the states have the responsibility for the provision of education) in a context of considerable 'fiscal imbalance' (the federal government has the largest revenue-raising capacity). This has led to an enhanced strategic role for the federal government in education and schooling, legitimated through its finan-cial assistance power to the states. This 'exceedingly complex picture of the working federalism in Australian education' (p. 94) is not some-thing we can pursue here, and authorities like Taylor *et al.* (1997) are worth consulting for further detail. Suffice to say that the crafting of processes like the AST occurred in the complex reworking of the struc-tures, roles and responsibilities for education in these 'changing federalisms' (p. 93).

These framing and underpinning assumptions about Australian education, and how they operated both to shape and be shaped by processes like the AST, need to be kept in mind when reading both our theorising and the storied accounts of how teachers received it here.

From the reading we have been able to give to teachers' voices in this project and the remarkably consistent stories we have heard from other parts of the world, we discerned the existence of a 'palimpsest'. This funny-sounding word of Greek origins refers to the process of rubbing something smooth and then reinscribing it. This seems to us to be an accurate (albeit linguistically obscure) description of what is happening to teachers' work. We are indebted to Gore Vidal (1995) for bringing the notion of palimpsest to our attention, even though his use of the term was in the context of writing his memoirs. Vidal's (1995) etymological exploration led him to conclude that palimpsest meant: 'Paper, parchment, etc., prepared for writing on and wiping out again, like a slate', and 'a parchment, etc., which has been written on twice, the original having been rubbed out' (p. 6).

This is a pretty useful analogy for what is happening to teachers' work at the moment. The idea that something is being expunged or effaced from the professional and historical renderings of teaching through current rounds of educational restructuring, and something qualitatively different posited in its place, has the feel and ring of authenticity about it. It is true that in the past teachers have not always been as forthright, articulate or as coherent as they might have been in conveying the essence of their work to a wider and increasingly sceptical public. One such way is through close attention to teachers' voices about their work. Teacher accounts about teachers' work are 'palimpsestic' (Jacobs et al. 1995) in that they provide a narrative strategy for a deep discursive reading of the erasure and rewriting of teaching through the restructure of the labour process. Notwithstanding, this is still not the same as saying that teachers have not had robust and viable ways of understanding, representing and conveying meaning about the craft of teaching and their political involvement in it. It would be equally inaccurate to suggest that teachers have not remonstrated, very effectively on many occasions, against economic and managerialist incursions into their work – clearly some teachers have been able to use successful strategies of resistance. Our point is rather that there has been an increased tendency for clashes between what Deever (1996a) labelled a 'discourse of transformation' (p. 256) pursued by teachers, with the 'discourse of reification' pursued by economic reformers and others who have had schools firmly in their sights as the machinery for the creation of human capital.

These ideas fit conceptually with Gunter's (1997) contrast between the 'listening practitioner' and the 'listening school' in which the emphasis in the former is upon compliance, dependence and management, versus the 'vocal teacher' and the 'vocal school' in the latter where the hallmark is one of contributing to 'the political, economic, social and technological debates that affect educational processes' (p. 34). Whereas, in the first case, teachers are inducted into and inculcated with an externally defined agenda, in the latter, they actively question the circumstances making them the way they are, and in the process construct an alternative agenda that is more informed by the internal workings of teaching, learning, curriculum and pedagogy.

We were as interested in the counter-hegemonic discourses teachers used to reappropriate their work in the face of a managerialist ideological onslaught, as we were in the way dominant discourses come to attain their position of ascendancy in fields like education and teaching. In the study reported upon here, while we found an abundance of instances indicative of high levels of official distrust of teachers, we also continually encountered the reverse – where teachers had very effectively subverted, circumvented and reinscribed the suffocating discourses of technicist competencies and skills formation with alternative discourses of hope, possibility and probability based on a deep understanding of the moral, political and relational nature of teaching – a process they often did collectively with other teachers.

SOMETHING OF THE STRUCTURE AND ORGANISATION OF THE BOOK

The book is organised into eight chapters, each of which builds on what precedes and follows. In order to provide the reader with a way of both being forewarned about what is to come, as well as to recapitulate some of the territory already traversed, we suggest a reading stance that adopts a process of 'previewing' and 'reviewing'. We encourage readers to move between our arguments in the first six chapters and the case study of ASTs that is presented in Chapter 7. Given that the project of the book is one that seeks to develop a conversation between the macro-forces shaping teachers' work and the specific micro-forces as lived and experienced by teachers in their everyday lives as workers, we believe this is a useful strategy. We feel that an articulative reading that seeks connections between theorising and case study, where each part informs the contextual understanding of the other, helps integrate the wider arguments with the accounts, the voices, the lives and the experiences of the teachers in the study.

In Chapter 2, we survey the landscape of the book at three levels: first, the contemporary context of what is happening to the work of teaching; second, the kind of perspective and research approach we adopt in the book; and third, the particular educational policy initiative which we access to give a more insightful window on what is occurring in schools.

In Chapter 3, we focus on 'Teaching under (re-)construction' by looking at the technical/rational moves to reconstrue teaching so as to resolve, through administrative managerial means, how teachers and schools might be more closely harnessed to the task of economic restoration. In this chapter we critique the basis of what we see as a hastily conceived and ill-founded connection, and explore the genesis of where the claims for school reform and restructuring are coming from and what their undeclared interests are.

Chapter 4 explores a cachet of notions that we find to be indicative of the increasingly shrill cries from some parts of the community for teachers to 'do their economic work'. It is at this point that we also lay out the basis of an oppositional and resistant reading of teaching that provides a very different basis upon which to interpret and make sense of teaching. Our argument is that the failure of political imagination is insufficient reason for allowing the discourses of the economy to prevail in the reframing of teaching. The only feasible and adequate basis upon which teaching can be construed, we argue, is from within the discourses of teaching itself. Arnold (1996) summed this up nicely when speaking about the mutually supportive elements of administration, management, evaluation and structure leading towards the 'high-tech, post-Fordist school', when he said:

> Conspicuously absent . . . is an engagement with traditional educational discourses – learning theory, curriculum theory, pedagogy, and so forth – all of which seem to be irrelevant to the re-formulation now underway.
>
> (p. 226)

Indeed, it is in this section of the book that we show how teachers undergoing selection to enter the AST category developed their own counter-hegemonic, discordant and assertive reading of *their own* discursive pedagogical construction of teaching skill. This rested most uneasily with the increasingly managerialised market consent being engineered in schools by policy reformers.

From the outset we should say that the AST category in Australia had a quite specific if contradictory set of origins. During the period of the Labor Government in the late 1980s, it was to be one of a package of measures aimed at instituting micro-economic reform through a wider process of labour market award restructuring. Across all occupational groups there was to be a national process of renegotiating salaries, wages, and terms and conditions of work. With the rapidly changing international economic conditions, teachers along with all other workers, were to be incorporated into new, more flexible and efficient working arrangements – ones deemed capable of delivering on a range of skills needed to meet the challenge of international competition.

As a policy initiative the AST was 'sold' in different ways (as it had to be) depending upon the audience; in effect there were three, and they all had quite different and sometimes conflicting aspirations for this particular initiative. First, at the official level within departments like the Federal Treasury, the rhetoric behind the principles of award restructuring implicitly in manœuvres like the AST, were industrial notions like productivity, flexibility, responsiveness, efficiency, effectiveness and outcomes. These were seen to be the crucial and strategic linguistic forms necessary for government to be able to sell the wider changes to a less than convinced public; these terms had a ring of authenticity and credibility about them. Second, at the peak level of the teacher union movement, the AST was sold as a way in which to deliver increases in wages, salaries and improved working conditions, to be made possible through the gains in overall productivity secured by efficiency and productivity. This was considered to be a vital part of the overall tripartite consensus process (officially called the 'Accord' between government, employers and peak parts of the union movement) operating in the public policy arena at the time. The unions had to be convinced that there was 'something in it for them' if any change was to be possible. At the third

level, that of classroom teachers, the AST was promulgated differently again
– it was presented as a package that included the following elements:

1   it was to be a new and enhanced career pathway for teachers who were
    seeking promotion but who had no aspiration or ambition to move out
    of the classroom and into administrative positions; in this sense, it was
    an inducement to keep 'good' teachers in the classrooms;
2   it was to be a form of recognition and reward for teachers who displayed
    exemplary skills and improvement in teaching and who were to be role
    models for the rest of the teaching profession;
3   it was to be an impetus for continuing professional development for
    teachers who were committed to teaching and who wanted a set of
    professional reasons for remaining within teaching;
4   it was also seen as a much needed way of affirming, in the public imagi-
    nation, the status and worth of teaching as a worthwhile occupation,
    and as a way of attracting high-quality entrants to teaching (for more
    about the background to the AST, see pp. 31–34).

What we intend showing in the remainder of the book is that even policies
crafted with such an apparently well-meaning and sensible set of agenda in
mind can produce less than edifying results that can ultimately prove
unhelpful.

In Chapter 5 we pursue the manner in which the educational policy
restructuring underway is producing a set of policies and reforms indicative
of what we term a 'preferred' teacher – that is to say, one who conforms to
the new marketised, customer-oriented teacher able to demonstrate government policy through the satisfaction of pre-determined criterial indicators of
performance. Constructions of the 'good' teacher are beginning to coalesce in
the language and the ideals of the 'new public administration' as schools and
teaching are organised in ways that implicitly endorse reforms that deform
and that perpetrate low-trust policies for teachers.

Interrupting this excessively muscular and dominant view of teaching is
taken up in Chapter 6, as discussion focuses upon how alternative discourses
and platforms of teaching might inhere in a rediscovered discourse of
purpose vying to keep alive teachers' own active processes of redrawing the
boundaries of teaching from within the prevailing orientations of competencies discourses. The missing voices of teachers are, we argue, being
reinserted and reinscribed through an insistence upon the relational nature
of teachers' work, especially as this is beginning to be given expression in
and through policy manœuvres to reskill teachers, like the AST scheme
studied here. For reasons of conceptual simplicity, we can lay out the inter-
sections and the overlaps as follows:

Like Deever (1996a), we do not regard the domains characterised by these
discourses as completely rigid or arbitrary. In Deever's terms, in this book,

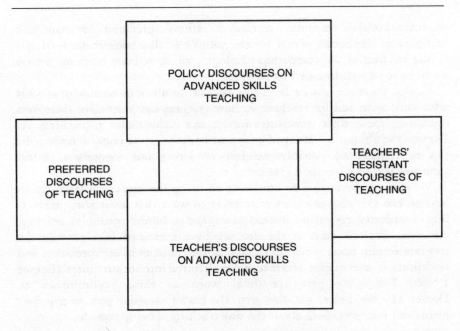

Figure 1 Discourses on and about Advanced Skills Teachers

we seek to 'engage in forays into the various realms and bring back theoretical capital' (p. 255) necessary to explain how teaching is currently being remade. This requires, Deever says, that we 'rethink the notion of borders as overlapping and permeable, rather than abutted and impervious' (p. 255).

Deever (1996a) invokes a useful image of 'poaching' as a way of referring to our own appropriation of theory better to explicate local everyday practices of teachers. Through this means: 'The reader becomes first a co-producer of knowledge through the reading of theory from within, and the authoritative voice by reading against the text of theory' (p. 255). In other words, the 'simultaneous multiple readings upon, within, and against the text of theory . . . produce differing authoritative positions on the part of the writer and the reader' (p. 255). This 'tactical appropriation of theory' becomes a form of 'enlightened poaching' rendered justified because of the way it problematises the whole issue of ownership of knowledge: 'If the appropriation advances the project at the local level, then the raid was justified' (p. 255).

The voice of teachers comes out most noisily, insistently and forcibly in Chapter 7 where we allow the 'preferred' teachers to speak – on a range of levels and issues – about the difficulty of trying to translate policy makers' intentions into words, and of the compromises, contradictions and perplexities of what happened when their teaching was interrupted by a policy reconstrual of their teaching. The clash of 'official', 'preferred', 'resistant' and 'indigenous' discourses which are the subject of this book make for fascinating reading as the competing ideologies vie to reshape teaching within an undeclared and shrouded set of wider interests.

Finally, there are lessons from this project for all of us outside of schools who work with and for teachers on how teachers can keep alive their own discourses about what constitutes robust and viable skills in teaching. As Deever (1996b) put it: 'Many of us appear hesitant . . . to engage in the politics of translation; possibly we fear rendering our theoretical realms somehow less pristine' (p. 173).

We seem to be unable or unwilling to bring our analytical language to bear on the everyday practices of teachers in ways that assist with unravelling complexity, preferring instead to engage in border squabbles amongst ourselves. Projects such as the one we have examined here provide the concrete terrain upon which to engage in the 'politics of appropriation and re-definition' so as to gain 'access to and re-defining interior structures' (Deever 1996b: 178). We give the final word in these preliminaries to Deever (1996b) before we allow you, the reader, to make your own judgements and interpretations about the way teaching is being remade:

> What we must accept, and begin to work with, is a recognition that the basic structures of schooling will continue to exist. We must follow the examples of the opposition in appropriating existing structures for our own uses and our own definitions . . . By treating translation and compromise as evils to be avoided, we position ourselves in a hopeless spot *outside* the area of active conflict. We know how the game should be played, but we refuse to travel to the park where it is happening; we demand that both the game and the crowd come to us. This has not occurred, yet, and I think it is safe to say it probably will not . . . We must be willing to put our theories through the muck of negotiation and compromise that characterise daily practice in contemporary schooling.
>
> (pp. 178–80)

Chapter 2

Scoping the wider landscape

SETTING THE SCENE: SKETCHING OUT THE BIGGER PICTURE

Introductory overview

There are dramatic, profound and far-reaching changes being visited on schools worldwide that have their genesis a long way from classrooms and playgrounds, but they are impacting on teachers and their work. It is important that we understand these underlying forces because without a view of how these are shaping what occurs within education more generally, then solutions will be allowed to hold sway that may constitute ill-conceived resolutions of poorly understood problems.

Lester Thurow (1996) in *The Future of Capitalism: How Today's Economic Forces Will Shape Tomorrow's World* captured the essence of this when he said that unless we look to the 'economic tectonic plates' that are spectacularly remaking the economic surfaces upon which we live, then we are likely to feel the effects but fail to properly grasp or understand their significance.

This emphasis on the economic aspect of what is happening to schools is not to exclude the social and cultural forces at work as well, but we will be concerned here initially with ones that are of an economic persuasion because of the way they are being given greatest force and credence at the moment in policy initiatives and associated discourses. This is an orientation we have more than a few difficulties with, and later in the book, we move to contest this singular driving force.

But, for the moment it is becoming increasingly clear that the dominant or prevailing view of schools is that they are being construed largely as annexes of industry and commerce. Schools as sites of comprehensive intellectual growth; as places that foster and value the wider social good compared with self-interested individualism, and that sustain and maintain local discourses about social justice, are decidedly unfashionable ideas at the moment and are tending to be relegated to the interstices, the cracks and the crevices of discussion, rather than firing the wider public imagination of what schools exist for (Smyth 1998a).

McMurtry (1991) provided an insight as to how this has come about when he said we have become caught up in:

> an international movement towards justifying excellence in education in terms of a goal external to education, namely, 'to compete effectively in the international marketplace', [and] that: (a) this justification of educa- tion has been increasingly presupposed or prescribed by corporate, government and educational leadership, and (b) education as a social institution has been correspondingly subordinated to international market goals, including the language and self-conceptualisations of educators themselves.
>
> (p. 209)

McMurtry (1991) argues that this is not an entirely new phenomenon, but the difference between recent and earlier versions of it is that 'educational process [has] been so pervasively subordinated [on this occasion] to the aims and practices of business that its agents can no longer comprehend their vocation in any other terms' (p. 210). While later in this book we will move to counter this pessimistic portrayal with evidence and alternative possibili- ties, suffice to say for the moment that McMurtry's analysis is a helpful way of establishing the nature and the extent of what is occurring to education more generally. As he puts it:

> Education has always been subject to external pressures that seek to subordinate its practices and goals to vested interests of some kind, whether of slave-holding oligarchies, theocratic states, political parties or merely prevailing dogmas of collective belief. The history of the development of social intelligence is largely a history of this conflict between the claims of education and inquiry, on the one hand, and the demands of ruling interests and ideologies on the other (McMurtry 1988). Today is no different. As in the past, those charged with society's educational function have been disinclined on the whole to challenge the ascendant social power which seeks to reduce learning and reflection to its organ and instrument . . . Senior administrators have increasingly modelled themselves after private sector corporate executives, and [educational] institutions have come more and more to conceive of themselves as serving the needs of corporate capital in a new informa- tion age of global production.
>
> (p. 209)

But this is leaping ahead slightly. Western countries like Australia, New Zealand, the UK, Canada, the USA and some parts of Europe have become caught up in a process of global rearrangement and economic restructuring, in which it is not possible to talk about the work of teaching and what is happening to it without also invoking the backdrop of the wider sets of global forces shaping and moulding it.

In the remainder of this chapter, we intend exploring the relationships between three clusters of ideas: (1) the process of economic globalisation; (2) the effect of global restructuring on the redefinition of education; and (3) the consequences of this for teachers' work (Smyth 1998b).

The process of economic globalisation

Taylor *et al.* (1997) present the case that globalisation is a contested notion and needs to be approached cautiously:

> Put simply, globalisation could be described as a set of processes which in various ways – economic, cultural and political – make supra-national connections. . . . There are . . . two aspects . . . : the facts concerning transnational processes and communication *and* an increasing awareness of this reality.
>
> (pp. 53–4)

Taylor *et al.* (1997) point out, quite rightly, that globalisation is not an amorphous or homogeneous entity. In fact it is a very complex phenomenon in which there is a contradictory 'new politics' at work with the features of 'global integration' and 'national fragmentation'. As to the former:

> New politics associated with social movements such as feminism, green politics and the peace movement operating transnationally have destabilised traditional political organisation within nation states.
>
> (p. 59)

On the other hand, in respect of the latter, there has been:

> the disintegration of some nations into . . . 'ethnic tribalism' . . . In various ways . . . the links between ethnicity and the nation, which forms the artifice of 'the nation' are being challenged and rearranged through these contrary pressures for integration and disintegration.
>
> (p. 59)

Taylor *et al.* (1997) go on to argue that this more complex view of globalisation 'works at both the political and the cultural level, given that the destabilising of relationships between ethnicity and nationhood has also seen some fragmentation of national, group and individual identities' (p. 59). They draw on Giddens' (1994) encapsulation of the simultaneous processes of 'global integration' and 'national disintegration' by way of explaining the 'ethnic diaspora' that Hall (1992) sees as constituting the global emergence of hybrid 'new identities' within nation states. According to Taylor *et al.*, the resulting 'transnational "connectedness"' has profound implications especially in terms of the universalising educational policy tendencies 'which occur across the boundaries of nation states' (p. 60). Their conclusions, in point form, are most apposite in the context of the 'product' emphasis implicit in the policy discourse that was operating to frame the criteria of educational policies like those behind the AST:

- globalisation processes are taken into account in the policy priorities at nation-state level;
- ideological discourses which frame education policies at the national level might already be globalised;
- political structures operating beyond nations are framing national policy options;
- a global policy community may be emerging;
- globalisation processes are affecting the cultural field within which education operates.

(Taylor et al. 1997: 61)

Also arguing for a more complex view of globalisation that acknowledges hybrid identities and the manner in which the technicisation of educational policy works to efface difference, Keyman (1997) proposes that we take a critical reading of postcolonial criticism 'by placing the question of identity/difference at the centre of critical analysis by stressing the importance of culture' (p. 194). According to Keyman (1997) we need 'to dismantle the signifying practices of global modernity' (p. 195) through approaching the question of identity/difference not at an abstract/philosophical level, but rather in terms of the concrete discourse in which it is situated/located: 'This shift is necessary . . . for the assertion and affirmation of a denied, silenced subjectivity' (p. 195). It is, Keyman (1997) argues, 'in this sense that the situated/located notion of difference constitutes a precondition for "engendering" and "decolonising"' (p. 195) the notion of globalisation. Only by doing this will it be possible to 'create an ethical space for the Other *not to be spoken of but to speak and assert its subjectivity*' (emphasis in the original, p. 195). This is especially important in view of the subjugation of teachers' educational voices in the reform process.

Wiseman (1995) put it succinctly when he said that 'globalisation must be the ugliest buzzword of the 1990s' (p. 5). In many respects it is bandied about so freely that its meaning often appears to be completely lost, or at least made deliberately unclear. One thing is clear, however: 'The term globalisation is as much a political term as simply a technical description: it is as much about power as it is about changing technologies' (Spratt 1995: 2).

But, globalisation is not an inevitable fact either, as Spratt (1995) argues: 'Technological change and internationalising capital are changing economic and social relations' (p. 2), and people's capacities to make choices and to decide their futures about work, production and economic exchange are by no means foreclosed.

The short definition of globalisation is that it is the:

> contested trend towards more interdependent, local, national and transnational economies and societies, the expansion of international trade, investment, production, and financial flows, the growing significance of regional trading blocs and trade agreements, more influential roles for international financial institutions and transnational corporations, far greater mobility of capital – particularly financial capital – and the overall spread of highly commodified and individualised economic, social and cultural relations into ever more spheres of human activity.
>
> (Wiseman 1995: 5)

Where globalisation bites hardest is in terms of the rapidity and worldwide impact of decisions taken at a distance, on local actions or events. Or put another way: 'the economic and social consequences of decisions made by financial cowboys in the money markets of New York, London and Tokyo' (Wiseman 1995: 5) – what Giddens calls 'action at a distance'.

It is possible to put this in its most direct form, and Wiseman (1995) does this best of all when he says (and insert your own place-names):

> globalisation is what happens when you lose your job in Brunswick because the company you work for has been bought out by an Australian subsidiary of a Dallas-based transnational that has decided to relocate production of T-shirts to Mexico because of the cheaper wages and lower health-and-safety standards. It is what happens to you when you finally get a new job in Altona but find that your new employment contract has lowered your wages and conditions and your boss explains that this is essential to compete with Mexican – or Indonesian or Chinese – workers. It is what happens to your sister when she gets the chop from the hospital where she works because of the budget cuts by a State government which defends its actions by saying it must meet the demands of international credit-rating agencies for balanced budgets and lower taxes. And it is what happens when you get skin cancer because of the hole in the ozone layer created by chemicals released by refrigerators and aerosols all over the world.
>
> (p. 5)

Clearly, there are worldwide forces at work dramatically changing the circumstances within which we think about and conceive of schooling. Spurred on by vastly improved means of information technology, instantaneous communication, and a capacity of international capital to move around the world at short notice to take advantage of local circumstances (especially, cheap labour), this has meant that corporations as well as governments are faced with unprecedented levels of volatility, uncertainty and unpredictability demanding quite different kinds of responses – both in terms of work organisation as well as workplace skills. Croft and Beresford (1992) summarise this in terms of a set of developments and changes referred to in the literature as the move from 'Fordist' to 'post-Fordist' forms of organisation:

> from *standardisation*, *uniformity* and *universalism* to *fragmentation*, *diversity* and *difference*. At the economic level, this is characterised by a trend towards differentiation in both production and consumption: from the mass production line to semi-autonomous work groups; from standardised to diverse products aimed at diverse groups of consumers and by a move from a production to consumption-led economy. The workforce is now more clearly demarcated as a skilled and relatively well rewarded 'core' of largely white male workers and a 'periphery' of low paid, less secure and often black women workers. At the social and cultural level, there is a greater acknowledgment of heterogeneity and diversity.
>
> (emphases in original, p. 26)

The hallmarks of these tendencies towards restructured arrangements are characterised, among other things, by: flexible forms of production and restructured workplace organisation; greater reliance on market forces as the mode of regulation, rather than rules, regulations and centralised bureaucratic forms of organisation; greater emphasis on image and impression management as a way of shaping consumer choice; recentralisation of control in contexts where responsibility for meeting production is devolved; resorting to increasingly technicist ways of responding to uncertainty; and, greater reliance on technology as the preferred means of resolving complex and intractable social, moral and political problems.

Muetzelfeldt (1995) described the essence of globalisation as residing in the collapse of a broadly based set of social regulatory discourses, and their replacement by a marketised, deregulated, governing-at-a-distance discourse much more committed to supposed forms of individualised choice, autonomy and responsibility. As Muetzelfeldt put it:

> On the one hand, market-like rationality and its instrumental approach to people and to social life has become more global, providing the dominant discourse and organising the dominant public practices of even larger areas of life across more and more of the world. On the other

hand, the capacity of this rationality to provide political as well as social meaning and identity . . . has been hollowed out. We are left with an overarching shell of abstract instrumentalism within which public identity, social institutions and everyday practices are increasingly drained of normative and communal content.

(p. 44)

All of these trends are being played out in education as schooling, and through it the work of teaching is 'structurally adjusted' to accommodate to globalisation.

Changes of this order of magnitude constitute quite a different regulative framework for the exercise of social control. Most noticeably, there has been a dramatic shift of the boundaries of control, from direct, overt and bureaucratic forms of surveillance, to more covert forms that take expression in the way work itself is restructured. For example, the 'just-in-time' (Sewell and Wilkinson 1992; Conti and Warner 1993) and 'total quality management' (Sayer 1986) processes touted in the management literature are a particular case in point. The very success of processes like these relies on somewhat more self-regulative procedures that are predicated on an intensification of work practices brought about by the harnessing of peer pressure through 'team work' and 'partnerships' aimed at responding to 'customer needs', eliminating waste and generally promoting a culture of continuous improvement (Delbridge et al. 1992). We are experiencing the emergence of these same trends in schools through so-called processes of 'empowerment' and the creation of schemes like 'lead teachers' (Ceroni and Garman 1994; Ceroni 1995) and professional hierarchies – matters to be taken up in later parts of the book.

Another way of viewing globalisation is in terms of the way decisions within contemporary capitalism are increasingly removed from the control of national (and democratically elected) governments, and assumed by transnational economic forces which operate largely outside of the scope of any single government, and which are accountable to head offices in London, New York or Tokyo. This process of global economic rearrangement generates unstable social conditions, most notably the changing division of labour whereby full-time jobs are shrinking at the same time as part-time and insecure jobs are expanding (Levin and Rumberger 1983).

For Castells (1989), there are three identifiable aspects to this wider economic restructuring that are important: (1) a fundamental realignment of the relationship between capital and labour, such that capital obtains a significantly higher share in the benefits of production; (2) a new role for the state in the public sector, which is not so much about reducing the role of government intervention in the economy, but a changing of its style; and (3) a new international division of labour in which low-cost labour is profoundly shaping what is happening in the 'developed' world.

As to the first of these contemporary trends, there are a number of outcomes that might best be summarised as: higher productivity through technological innovation; lower wages, reduced social benefits and less protective working conditions; decentralisation of production to regions of the world with more relaxed labour and environmental restrictions; greater reliance on the informal economy (that is, unregulated Labour); restructuring labour markets to incorporate increasing proportions of women, ethnic minorities and immigrant workers; and, weakening trade unions – the single most important factor in restoring the level of profits (Castells 1989: 23–5). Barnet and Cavanagh (1994) in their *Global Dreams: Imperial Corporations and the New World Order* show, through profiles of a number of these major corporations, how a few hundred companies with worldwide connections are exerting a profound influence culturally, financially, economically, and in terms of the nature of work and where it is located globally.

As to the second, the role of the state in the public sector, Castells (1989) argues that what we are witnessing is not the withdrawal of the state from the economic scene, but the emergence of a new form of intervention, whereby new means and new areas are penetrated by the state, while others are deregulated and transferred to the market (p. 25). He sees this emerging redefinition of the role of the state as embracing: deregulation of many activities, including relaxation of environmental controls in the workplace; shrinkage of and privatisation of productive activities in the public sector; regressive tax reform favouring corporations and high-income groups; state support for high-technology research and development and leading industrial sectors; continuing priority and status for defence and defence-related industries; shrinkage of the welfare state; and, fiscal austerity, with the goal of a balanced budget. These changes have significant implications for the way in which schools are organised and administered, and these along with their implications for the work of teachers and the labour process of teaching will be addressed in later chapters of this book.

Thirdly, the opening-up of new markets through global expansion (or 'internationalisation') has been possible as a consequence of several noticeable developments: industry taking advantage of the most favourable conditions anywhere in the world; capital taking advantage of 'around-the-clock capital investment' opportunities; the homogenising of markets, and making up of market loss in one area through increases in another (pp. 26–8).

All of these have pronounced implications for schools, how they are organised, and what transpires within them. While it is not possible in a short space to trace out the precise manner in which these global tendencies impact on schools, it will be sufficient for the moment to say that, as western economies move to position themselves in terms of improved international competitiveness, education and skills formation are major features of this process of structural readjustment (Ilon 1994). Nowhere is this more self-evident than in the USA where schools were roundly condemned in the early 1980s by the business sector through now infamous statements such as those appearing in documents like *Nation at Risk*, which said: 'if an unfriendly foreign power had attempted to impose on America the mediocre educational performance that exists today, we might well have viewed it as an act of war' (National Commission on Excellence in Education 1983: 5).

The negative effect of global restructuring on education

The role and function of education are undergoing dramatic changes in response to these economic imperatives. The notion of a broad liberal education is struggling for its very survival in a context of instrumentalism and technocratic rationality where the catchwords are 'vocationalism', 'skills formation', 'privatisation', 'commodification', and 'managerialism'. In circumstances like these, education 'comes under the gun' as it is simultaneously blamed for the economic crisis while being held out as the means to economic salvation – if only a narrow, mechanistic view of education is embraced.

The best way of seeing this at work is through what Ilon (1994) claims to be a widespread process of international policy 'structural adjustment':

> These policies center around four primary structural shifts: liberalisation, deregulation, privatisation and stabilisation. Together they comprise critical elements of the 'structure' of the economy which affects its external relationship . . . What makes it [a] 'structural adjustment' . . . is that the process is one whereby the national economy is adjusting to a global market . . . so a country cannot afford to veer too far from an equilibrium established by the global capital and free markets.
>
> (p. 96)

Ilon's (1994) argument is that education is affected through this process as funds available to education and the public sector decrease and regardless of whether one is 'an observer of American education, education in the Middle East, or education in Botswana . . . public monies, generally, are decreasing and the amounts needed to maintain real per-pupil expenditures are not available' (p. 97). What we are experiencing is a reduction in the willingness of wealthier sections of the community (who can afford private education for their own children) to continue to fund what they regard as declining quality public education, at the same level.

What we are increasingly likely to experience, therefore, is a set of global conditions that reaches down directly into schools, informing and shaping what goes on. As Ilon (1994) put it, there will be a quite markedly stratified education system:

> Changes wrought by structural adjustment and felt at the national and community levels permeate directly to the schools . . . [where] differential types and qualities of education [will be] offered . . . Globally, the poor will continue to be served by public schools of decreasing quality . . . As the notion that public schools serve a broadly defined national population gives way to the reality that students come from discrete backgrounds and face differential opportunities and problems, a structuring of school curriculum and learning strategies aimed at specific populations will occur . . . For the few that will be educationally equipped for employment at a global level, school curricula will become similar worldwide . . . emphasising information gathering, manipulation, management and creation . . . [But, for the majority there will be] . . . global competition . . . [for] people with limited and low-level skills . . . competing on a world market of others with similar backgrounds. In order to attract businesses which need these types of workers, nations will still have to provide a minimum level of public education, but that education need not go much further than literacy, numeracy and the discipline and tolerance that comes with being in a structured environment.
>
> (p. 99)

These are changes that do not emerge out of the heartland of education, or from strictly pedagogical and curriculum matters. Rather, they are about changing from schools for the betterment of society through a more educated citizenry, to how best to control education by making it do its economic work through greater explicit emphasis on vocationalism, as well as by changing the ideology and the discourse of schooling (where students = customers; teachers = producers; and, learning = outcomes) and through a restoration of the primacy of notions of human capital theory. Coupled with this is a worldwide move towards recentralising control over education through national curricula, testing, appraisal, policy formulation, profiling, auditing, and the like, while giving the impression of decentralisation and handing control down locally. The image of education is also revamped by reconfiguring the work of teaching so that teachers appear more as deliverers of knowledge, testers of learning and pedagogical technicians.

Reality, of course, is that the work of teaching is increasingly routinised and proletarianised as teachers are subjected to the discourses as well as the practices of managerialism – tighter control by outsiders, better forms of accountability, more sophisticated surveillance of outcomes, and greater reliance on measures of competence and performance.

Consequences for teachers' work

In all of this there are a number of quite contradictory tendencies shaping the emerging work of teachers. At precisely the same time external forces are seeking to take a larger role in determining what counts as teaching, teachers are also being exhorted to exercise more control at the local level over what it is they do (Goodman 1994). This recentralisation within a rhetoric of devolution is difficult to reconcile, at least on the surface.

For example, in Australia (and their equivalents exist in other parts of the world, too) there are: National Curricula, in the form of National Subject Profiles and Statements; Key Competencies, Standards and Skills Formation; Performance Appraisal, Performance Management and Performance Indicators. There is daily exposure to educational aerosol words like 'excellence' and 'quality' – the latest bouquet words to be sprayed around over our ever-so-slightly decaying educational institutions; not to mention the formidable armoury of the latest surveillance and control gadgetry being foisted onto schools, teachers and the work of teaching – like curriculum audits; educational review units; school charters; mission statements; strategic reviews; student profiles; benchmarks; line management; leaner organisations; quality assurance; advanced skills assessment; measurement of outcomes; total quality management; corporate managerialism; international best practice; and these are only for starters.

The point to be made in respect of this increasing proliferation of so-called 'educational' (sic) policy initiatives is that they represent technocratic responses to what are in most cases poorly articulated or inchoate problems. In other words, what are offered as technical solutions to our educational (and by inference, economic) ills are not so much coherent responses to carefully thought-through analyses of complex social and educational problems, so much as they are muscular political posturings of a 'can do' type. Their aim is not to resolve complexity, but rather to reassure a doubting public that they are indeed being well served by a political apparatus that is well in control of unstable circumstances. It is a game of smoke and mirrors more than a process of underlying substance. The tragedy is that matters of educational substance get leached out in this stampede for political reassurance. All of this is by way of giving the technical–rational responses to the problems besetting schools a fairly kind and benign treatment.

The harsher version goes something like this. Schools have been put under the spotlight again over the past couple of decades because they represent a convenient and docile scapegoat upon which to deposit blame for the significant shifts in the wider 'economic tectonic plates' (Thurow 1996) afflicting capitalism: namely, 'the end of communism'; 'a technological shift to an era dominated by man-made brainpower industries'; 'a demography never before seen'; 'a global economy'; and, 'an era where there is no dominant economic, political or military power'. These are major global forces

making for high levels of uncertainty, unpredictability and significant insta-
bility – and, schools can be conveniently saddled with the blame for not
having produced a society with the flexible capacity to foresee the massive
changes wrought by the rearrangement of these huge fault lines, or indeed
to be able quickly and efficiently to adjust to change as they became self-
evident.

Our thesis is that one of the major reasons why schools have been the
recipients of such scorn and stinging rebukes worldwide, and the object of
such significant restructuring in the past two decades, is that there are few
other social institutions so significantly placed as schools to produce
educated, trained and informed citizens and workers. Making the argument
stick that schools have 'failed' has not been difficult, especially in a context
where the media is antagonistic and indeed anti-pathetic to analyses of the
wider genesis of complex socio-geo-political problems. Add to this the
public spheres in which there is no longer any opportunity for discussion
and debate about the role and nature of schooling and education, and the
vacuum (fiscally and otherwise) is all too readily filled by the guys from 'the
big end of town' – the corporate multi-nationals who view schools as sources
of compliant labour (part-time, temporary and insecure) for contingent
work, and as convenient sites within which to construct an ideology of
consumption and consumer preference. What this amounts to, when we
distance ourselves from it a little, is a gradual process of making educational
values virtually indistinguishable from those of supermarkets and breweries.

Conclusion

Drawing the argument of this chapter together, somewhat, and without
pursuing these matters in detail, it is becoming clear that schooling, and
through it teachers' work, is increasingly being shaped by a range of forces:

- it is being constrained by the intrusion of external agencies who require
  that schools operate in the 'national interest', a claim that is invariably
  couched in the economic imperative of increased international competitiveness;
- the fiscal crisis of the state is reducing funding to schools, in contexts in
  which schools are exhorted to 'do more with less';
- the breakdown of other social institutions is occurring at the same time
  schools are expected to take on a wider and more complex range of functions;
- control is being recentralised, having the effect of conveying the
  message to teachers that they cannot be trusted and that their work is
  devalued – this happens in contexts in which it is made to look as if
  teachers are being given more autonomy, self-control and decision-
  making power at school level;

- schools are expected to operate more like private enterprises, to market themselves, to compete against one another for students and resources – functions that take them increasingly away from the reason for which they exist, namely, teaching and learning.

Now, all of the matters just alluded to are ones that are obviously ripe with implications for teachers and their working relationships. What we have, as a consequence, are a number of policy initiatives:

- that require teachers to work within more rigidly defined policy frameworks and guidelines, of one kind or another;
- that place greater emphasis on determining the worth of teaching in terms of measurable outcomes;
- that supposedly make teachers more accountable by linking outcomes to the actions and activities of individual teachers, classrooms and schools;
- that move teachers and schools in the direction of processes that are more appropriate to those of the corporate and industrial sector – performance appraisal, curriculum audits, quality assurance, and the like; and
- that preach the virtues of education and schooling being no different to any other commodity – to be measured and calibrated according to quality standards; packaged and delivered to targeted audiences; and haggled over in the artificially constructed user-pays marketplace of education.

On the other hand, there is another set of tendencies and trends appearing to point in the opposite direction. These all have the sounds of pseudo-participation and quasi-democracy about them: devolution; competition; choice; autonomy; collaboration; self-management; liberation management; teamwork and partnerships; networking and collegiality; flexibility; responsiveness.

While the latter tendencies might look and sound as if they are about giving teachers more control over their work, and in some cases it is true they do, in most instances it is more a matter of appearances. There is a substantial contradiction. The work of teaching is increasingly brought under the influence of politicians, policy makers and the captains of industry, at the same time as claims are made that teachers and schools should take greater control of their own destiny – deciding on local priorities; exercising greater self-management; breaking away from expensive and inefficient bureaucratic forms of organisation; and, making schools into leaner organisations able to be more responsive, and so on.

Hargreaves and Dawe (1990) say that teachers are being urged 'to collaborate more, just at the moment when there is less to collaborate about' (p. 228). Their words have a remarkable ring of authenticity about them. As one cynic put it, it feels like 'school-based management emerged just when schools [around the world] were about to go broke'. Introduced in this kind of economic climate, rather than enhancing the work of teaching, processes of self-management can be about what Ball (1993a) has described as 'the self-management of decline'. In the USA where similar processes are afoot:

> School-based resources and decision-making have been narrowed, not expanded. School-based councils feel 'empowered' only to determine who or what will be cut. So fights fall along predictable lines of teachers versus parents . . . administrators versus teachers.
>
> (Fine 1993: 696)

And, all of this is shrouded in confusion and contestation as teachers struggle hard with the ascendancy of management principles that would redefine and control the nature of their work. Little wonder that Taylor-Gooby (1994) describes this as a great policy leap backwards.

How are we supposed to make sense of such contradictions, and what do they mean? How come schools, and the work of teaching, is being pulled in these opposing directions?

Faced with sets of economic circumstances that can only be described, at best, as that of 'overload', governments have had to retreat – mostly, from areas in which they have traditionally been providers, like education (and a range of other public services). Increasingly, they have had to off-load these responsibilities onto the private sector – we can see this worldwide in moves to shift education increasingly into the private sector. Where that has not been possible, they have had to convince the private sector (in order to have it continue to pay the bills) that public enterprises will be organised along the lines of those in the private sector. That is to say, governments have engaged in trade-offs with private enterprise – deals have been struck to deliver skilled (and compliant) labour, in return for a further reduction in already shrinking tax bases. Part of the deal has been government hardening its regulatory functions (directions, guidelines and frameworks), while at the same time appearing to be fair and just, by allowing for autonomy, flexibility, creativity, self-management and responsiveness – and all of this, while maintaining overall steering and setting directions at a distance, as Kickert (1993) has noted.

In schools, this has meant:

- giving schools and teachers responsibility to implement local decisions – but within firmly prescribed guidelines;
- allowing schools discretion over expenditures – but in an overall context in which real resources are shrinking, and where centrally provided services are being wound down through the dismantling of educational bureaucracies;

- fostering the notion that it is fair (and indeed 'good') for schools to compete against one another – that the efficient will survive, and that competition will cause the rest to lift their game or go out of business – regardless of whether they are all operating on a level playing field or not;
- devolving responsibility for achieving learning outcomes – but within a context of accountability, where resources are tied to demonstrating the achievement of guaranteed targets;
- redefining, at a policy level, who are the 'consumers' of education so that there is a much closer connection between education and industry. Industry is now the customer, and in the logic of the marketplace, the customer is always right, and we have to keep the customer happy.

Whether (and in what ways) teachers are losing control of their work, is complicated by the very nature of the work itself. Connell (1989) summarised this nicely when he said, of the task and circumstances of teaching:

> [It] is a labour process without an object. At best, it has an object so intangible – the minds of kids, or their capacity to learn – that cannot be specified in any but vague and metaphorical ways. A great deal of work is done in schools, day in and day out, but this work does not produce any things. Nor does it, like other white collar work, produce visible and quantifiable effects – so many pensions paid, so many dollars turned over, so many patients cured. The 'outcomes of teaching', to use the jargon . . . are notoriously difficult to measure.
>
> (pp. 123–4)

Connell argues that the popular image of teaching as 'talk-and-chalk in front of a class' (p. 124) is extremely misleading. What Connell is saying is that views like this fail to understand that teachers' work is like an 'ever-receding horizon' – it is just never complete. That is to say, there is 'no logical limit to the expansion of an individual teacher's work' (Connell 1989: 125). He takes a concrete example and examines it: a teacher talking at the blackboard (which is far from the standard approach to teaching). Although not apparent to the naked eye, as Connell (1989) suggests, it contains a complex inter-dependency of tasks: time spent preparing the lesson; time spent getting the class settled and willing to listen; time spent supervising exercises and correcting them; keeping order; dealing with conflicts between children; having a joke with them from time to time and building up some personal contact; discussing work with them individually; planning lesson sequences; preparing handouts and physical materials; collecting, using and storing books and audio-visual aids; organising and marking tests and exams; keeping records; liaising with other teachers, and so on.

Most of this has to be done separately for each class – and that's for a conventional form of teaching! What about outside of the classroom? – supervising kids in playgrounds, at the canteen, during sporting events, onto transport, on excursions; planning and arranging swimming, carnivals, athletics days, football and netball matches, geography excursions, biology excursions, and so on; drama workshops, concerts, gymnastic displays, fêtes, speech days, bingo nights; going to parent/teacher nights, parents and citizens association meetings, union meetings, staff meetings, department meetings; organising and getting facilities for, and supervising, the school magazine, the chess club, the camera club, the debating team, the students' council, the end of class disco, the farewell to year 12; making school rules, policing them, administering punishments; being class patron (year teacher, form mistress, house master, team or grade leader) and co-ordinating information about members of the class, doing pastoral work, checking rolls, answering queries; counselling pupils in trouble, dealing with personal crises, with sexual and ethnic antagonisms, with bullying; sometimes dealing with agitated parents, welfare officers, police; modifying curricula, bringing programmes up to date, integrating new materials; getting familiar with new techniques, new machines, new textbooks; attending in-service conferences and courses on new curricula; planning and taking kids on camps, bushwalking, canoeing, swimming; writing end-of-term and end-of-year reports, final references and other official documents. And this, Connell (1989) says, is far from a full tally.

Little wonder that teachers are working as taxi-drivers, insurance sales people, computer consultants, and the like. Ashenden (1989) quipped recently that 'Army recruiters going into schools fishing for students reported catching teachers instead' (p. 9).

WHAT KIND OF PERSPECTIVE, WHAT KIND OF RESEARCH?

There is a sign in our local hot bread shop that provocatively asks: 'What kind of bread are you?' We take this to be a crucial question about being open and declaring our position – indicating what we value, what we stand for and what we ultimately feel is worth fighting for. So much of what is happening to our schools and the work of teaching under the rubric of 'reform' and 'restructuring' is shrouded. There is an opaqueness in that the forces that are shaping what is *really* occurring are not the ones that are openly talked about. Given the current worldwide tendency of regarding schools as one of the primary vehicles by which to put 'economic bread' on the table, we feel it is appropriate that we start this book by telling you what kind of bread we are, in terms of our approach to educational research, what we regard as being important, and where our ideas are coming from.

Our fundamental starting point lies deep in the erosion and corrosion occurring in public schooling, worldwide. We are distressed about the expunging and the progressive depletion of educative values and purposes out of schooling by mean-spirited politicians and their technocratically minded erstwhile policy advisers who have collectively suffered a 'failure of political imagination' (Walter 1996) and who misleadingly believe that schools can be converted into engines for economic growth and consumption. We regard this leaching as being deeply implicated in the process of supplanting educative values with the values, icons, purposes and discourses of transnational capital, and their complicit international corporate compradors – what McLaren (1994) refers to as the 'predatory culture' of the marketplace. We regard this pollution, degradation and subjugation of educational discourses by the anaesthetising lexicon of the market and its accompanying tenets of managerialism as being totally unacceptable. The constantly repeated expectations that schools do more with less, that they accommodate to increasingly muscular forms of accountability and surveillance while being infinitely measured and ranked on performance, outcomes and against each other, is no longer educationally acceptable.

While we have no coherent or instant plan or antidote to this uniformly depressing set of circumstances, we believe there is a pressing need for accounts of what is happening to teaching that enable teachers to reclaim the voices/discourses/practices of schools. Maxine Greene (1982) calls this the re-creation of a 'public sphere' within which discussions about the lives, aspirations, memories, traditions and trajectories of students and teachers might meaningfully occur.

There is a need to 'critique the canon' (Fine 1991) – that is to say, engage in critical analyses of how power, privilege and status are created, sustained and used to propagate particular versions of schooling. In large measure we envisage this as necessitating a jettisoning of the currently narrow social pathology view of school and students failure, and replacing it with analyses of how educational failure is manufactured by social, economic, institutional and historically structured sets of circumstances. This will require the pursuit of wider analyses of teaching and the construction of more hospitable environments and conditions in which teachers can be assisted to develop 'indigenous' comprehensive theories of their teaching – ones that move beyond an acceptance of blaming themselves as the cause of the problem. This will require a radical departure from the current widespread view that there are generic teaching competencies – if you like, the one-size-fits-all view of teaching, and will require developing forms of agency that situate theories of teaching within the broader social, economic and political forces working to shape that teaching.

It is also important that we are clear about where we position this study. It is an analysis of a policy issue to do with career structure for teachers, teacher appraisal and skills formation within teaching, and we render this

account within a local, national and global set of origins and inter-relationships. While the stories assembled tell much about the hegemonic and the
counter-hegemonic detail of how a particular policy was experienced, lived,
contested and sometimes reconstructed by teachers and the profession more
generally, we believe that it is crucial these accounts be presented and read
not just as localised, but as crucial components of a much bigger picture.

For this reason we position ourselves alongside other critical scholars who
are working to move beyond reproductionist interpretations of education,
schools and teaching to 'reinsert questions of human agency [and the space]
for resistance and counter hegemonic struggle' (Cole and Hill 1996: 5). Like
Apple (1996b) we argue that construals of schooling need to be read from
the vantage point of its 'ideological and economic agenda' for to fail to do
that is not only to ignore the wider forces operating to change the nature of
schools and teachers' work, but to risk falling into the trap of presenting
limited and localised analyses that end up feeding a reactionary post-
modernist discourse. We find Cole and Hill (1996) useful, especially in their
analysis and evaluation of Lather's (1991) claim that there are good and bad
versions of post-modernism – 'post-modernism of reaction' and 'post-
modernism of resistance' – a separation we don't find to be that helpful. We
are more inclined to the view of Beyer and Liston (1992), that:

> while the celebration of multiple voices has its strengths (letting
> everyone have a say, without intimidation) it also has its weaknesses.
> Assuming these voices will sometimes conflict, should we confront their
> status and validity or simply assume that they are equally true (or false),
> equally revealing (or opaque).
>
> (p. 10)

This captures the difficulty we have with research about teachers' work that
fails to give a wider reading of the forces operating to shape it. Such failure
can push us down any number of hopeless cul-de-sacs. The difficulty Cole
and Hill (1996) identify with 'post-modernism of resistance' is that it:

> relates to localised action only . . . [and] its rejection of the enlighten-
> ment project of 'emancipation in a general sense' means that no major
> emancipatory changes in society are possible and it thus plays into the
> hands of those whose interests lie in the maintenance of national and
> global systems of exploitation and oppression.
>
> (p. 10)

Like Hatcher and Troyna (1994) we accept that 'the level of the economic
does not merely provide a context; it actively intervenes in and shapes the
political, the social, the cultural, the ideological' (p. 159).

This book is, therefore, positioned at the intersection between educational policy analysis, and how policy is experienced, interpreted, and redefined by teachers. We realise this is becoming an increasingly volatile and controversial area at the moment, especially as the struggle intensifies over possible explanations of the 'macro–micro problem' in the sociology of education (Ozga 1990; Power 1992; Power 1995; Apple 1996b), which is where we position ourselves. We believe these inter-relationships are of vital importance as attempts are made to explain both the reasons for, and the effects of, wider policy moves relating to teachers' work. We take one illustration, that of the creation of a supposedly new career category for teachers in Australia (Advanced Skills Teachers (ASTs)) and use that to show what happens when teachers are confronted with a contemporary policy issue, what it means to them, how they accommodate to it, how they resist it, and ultimately how (under some circumstances) they reformulate it.

We regard ourselves as making a contribution to the emerging field of 'policy ethnography', in so far as we understand what this term means. We find this an apt label for our work because of the way in which it helps us to distinguish the kind of research we are doing from the already well-established approaches of 'micro-based ethnographies' that tend to focus on limited 'implementation' of policy (see Ball and Bowe 1990). In analysing the development of ASTs as a policy issue, we sought not to examine this as a manifestation of a 'top down' educational reform (even though there were strong elements of that present), nor were we concerned to view it only from the vantage point of what happened when it was implemented (although this was obviously of more than passing interest to us). Rather, our purpose was to try and see what might be possible by viewing it through 'looking both ways' (Herzfeld 1983) – which is to say, what happened when authorities sought to impose a (well-meaning) policy on teachers from which they had been excluded during formulation. We were also interested in the response of teachers as they came to understand what this policy meant for them in the context of their work, and how much they were prepared to tolerate a redefinition of their teaching.

Like Bowe *et al.* (1992) we view policy as more than the 'generation' by one group (usually politicians) and 'implementation' by another (usually teachers and educational bureaucrats). We are less inclined to see these as hermetically sealed 'moments' in some linear process, but rather as a continuous struggle over 'representation' and 'exclusion' of particular viewpoints and set of interests culminating in temporary truces or uneasy settlements (Freeland 1985; Seddon 1990; Sedunary 1996) between contending groups.

Ball and Bowe (1990) come closest to a definition of policy ethnography, when they say:

> For policy ethnography the concern needs to be both with exploring policy making, in terms of the processes of value dispute and material

influence which underlie and invest the formation of policy discourses, as well as portraying and analysing the processes of active interpretation and meaning-making which relate policy texts to practice. In part at least this also involves the identification of resistance, accommodation, subterfuge and conformity within and between arenas of practice. It involves the plotting of clashes and mismatches between contending discourses at work in these arenas, e.g. professionalism vs conformity, autonomy vs constraint, specification vs latitude, the political vs the educational. Policy ethnography should rest on the recognition of a clear distinction between intended and actual policy-in-use, and will attend carefully to processes of mediation and recontextualization. Furthermore it is important to acknowledge that policy intentions may contain ambiguities, contradictions and omissions that provide particular opportunities for parties to the 'implementation' process, what we might term 'space' for manœuvre.

(p. 4)

Like the Educational Reform Act described and analysed by Ball and Bowe (1990) in the UK, in Australia too, there was a 'policy text', constructed largely by federal and state politicians, policy advisers and members of peak teacher unions. The translation of that text into various local 'working documents' for educational bureaucrats, unions and teachers occurred through mediated processes of variegated interpretations of what might be meant by the notion of an AST. But as Ball and Bowe (1990) note, even when there is a detailed piece of legislation on the statute books:

> educational policy is still being generated and implemented both within and around the educational system in ways that have intended and unintended consequences for both education and its surrounding milieu. Analytically and theoretically this requires a process of theorising that treats legislative and policy texts as multifaceted.

(p. 3)

Thus conceived, ethnographic approaches seek to understand and explain the transformative processes at work 'albeit within a broader picture of policy that seeks to grasp the relations between the various dimensions of change' (p. 3). Put in different words, 'policy is a discourse' comprising 'a set of claims about how the world should be and might be' that are 'essentially contested in and between the arenas of formation and implementation' (p. 3).

ADVANCING ON SKILLS FORMATION IN TEACHING

Background to a policy initiative in Australia

The purpose of this chapter is to trace some of the thinking behind a move in Australia of introducing an educational and economic policy designed ostensibly to change the work of teaching by placing an emphasis on the competencies supposedly attaching to the job, while espousing this as a strategic and beneficial career change for teachers. As it has turned out, this became a not particularly well-concealed example of 'saying one thing' while actually 'doing something quite different'. It will be argued here that engaging in this kind of contradiction is not at all inconsistent with the way the state operates when confronted by crisis.

It would be seductive to portray what is happening to teachers' work in terms of a current infatuation with 'competencies' and 'skills approaches' as merely the machinations of governments worldwide manœuvring to reposition teachers' work so they simultaneously become both the 'cause' and the 'solution' to wider problems confronting public education. But, that would be too simplistic a representation – it is far more complex than that.

While we are not inclined to forms of analysis that 'deconstruct' the problem away, it does seem that explanations and possibilities lie in quarters other than simply blaming monolithic capitalism. Like Carlson (1995), we want to argue that:

> a new democratic discourse can only be built by constructing some provisional notions of directionality in social development, and thus some idea of progress. Of course, such an idea of progress cannot be grounded on a linear, monolithic or overly predetermined sense of direction.
>
> (p. 337)

This is not to suggest that answers necessarily reside entirely in 'taking account of divergent local concerns and interests' (Carlson 1995: 338) either, which is where post-modernist interpretations and explanations ultimately lead us. We need to acknowledge that:

> advancing democratic values associated with freedom, equity, and community inherently run into dilemmas and tensions that are not fully resolvable within the context of the situation.
>
> (p. 338)

Perhaps we can find an explanation of this educational policy manœuvre if we look at Stronach and Morris's (1994) notion of 'policy hysteria' as an organising construct for what occurred in respect of the AST process in Australia. This section of the chapter is, therefore, written against a cluster of policy variables that have produced confusion, contradiction, co-option and self-censorship, characterised by:

- shortened cycles of recurrent reforms;
- multiple innovation;
- frequent policy switches, involving inconsistent aims and means;
- tendency for reforms to become more symbolic in nature;
- scapegoating of systems, professionals and client groups;
- shifting meanings within the central vocabulary of reforms;
- innovations suffering from endemic credibility problems;
- erosion of professional discretion by centralising control;
- untested and untestable success claims.

(Stronach and Morris 1994: 6)

Stronach and Morris (1994) argue that it is only possible to understand a specific reform (in this case AST) if it is read against a background of 'recurring waves of reform'; 'multiple innovations' in which one initiative overtakes or overlaps the last, before the effect is known; reforms that are 'symbolic in nature' acting to 'legitimate' political responses rather than 'solve' educational problems; an 'endemic crisis of legitimation' where each successive 'solution' is lost in the persuasiveness of the next one, 'from basic skills to generic skills to subject excellence and 'back to the basics' (p. 7); and, a shifting of the 'educational debate out of professional arenas' and into more '"open" populist debate[s]' (p. 7). All of this, they argue, leads to a 'flux of successive and evanescent reforms designed to construct short-term political support for current policies that address reflections and deflections of the real problems society faces' (p. 8).

The process of highlighting how a particular educational policy has evolved and worked (or not) in practice, namely the introduction of the category of ASTs in Australia, serves to illustrate some of the wider tensions and principles about what happens when systems intervene in social practices like teaching. Such interventions tell us as much, perhaps even more, about the largely undisclosed ideology, discourses and intentions of those who make these incursions, as it does about those whose lives are directly touched through the interventions. Making transparent and unmasking the agenda, at whatever level, is an important and crucial part of any piece of investigation that purports to be research.

From the start, the notion of AST in Australia was (at least in the 'official' rhetoric) predicated on terms of its being a vehicle and a career pathway by which to legitimate and perpetuate a particular view of teaching and learning. Whether done consciously or not, the effect has been to construct a view of teaching as comprising an individual act, capable of dissection into its constituent parts, each of which is linked to a largely unarticulated set of generic 'competencies' or 'skills' of teaching.

But, this supposed shift to a new career structure for classroom teachers has been part of much wider changes to teachers' work. The backdrop against which this turn to 'skills formation' is being written is a much wider and more profound change in the nature of education generally. While it is possible to analyse that process with some considerable theoretical elegance, it is also possible to do some mapping of what is occurring through the accounts of various contemporary commentators. One such account, written by the federal Parliamentary Research Service (McIntosh 1995) as a background paper for Australian federal government parliamentarians, raises the question: 'The Schooling Revolution: Too Much, Too Fast?' The tenor of the document is that change is occurring on so many fronts educationally that teachers are displaying all of the signs of 'reform/change fatigue' (McIntosh 1995: i). This change has been proceeding apace with teachers as major stakeholders feeling that they have not been adequately involved, nor have they been accorded a sense of ownership over what is happening to them educationally. According to McIntosh (1995), one of the major explanations for the current situation resides in the manner in which 'policy development in the last decade [has been so singularly concentrated] on economic imperatives and the need for education to be responsive to the economic' (p. 1). McIntosh (1995) claims that:

> By the mid to late 1980s the emphasis on economic imperatives in the education system was manifesting itself through exhortations to schools to help restructure the economy to become more internationally competitive and improve the skills base of the economy.
>
> (p. 1)

The language was replete with economic rationalist claims about how schools and teachers should engage in 'productivity improvements' and pursue 'efficiency' and 'market outcomes' – in a context of a 'vocational training agenda'. As Milligan et al. (1994) expressed it, these were only a part of the 'linguistic insurgents' being used along with terms like 'skills agenda', 'workplace reforms', and 'restructuring' itself, as everything seemed to be 'up for grabs – structures, practices, ideas and interests' (p. 11). Indeed, the very language being used seemed to be an 'attempt to find ways of describing a rapidly changing educational landscape' (p. 11).

According to McIntosh (1995), as well as being shaped by the language, teachers in Australia were (and are) being shaped by forces coming from four quarters: (1) 'funding volatility' as state governments reduce levels of real funding to education and require that schools make up any shortfalls by doing more for themselves through voluntary levies/fees and outside sponsorship; (2) 'devolution/autonomy' – making those close to teaching and learning increasingly responsible for resource decisions, in an overall context of fiscal cutbacks; (3) a concerted 'vocational push' through moves to a national curriculum requiring that 'schools become more vocationally oriented' (McIntosh 1995: 11) in all kinds of ways; and, finally, (4) a greater concentration on 'technological change' as more and more emphasis is placed on teachers being required to embrace what is reputedly on offer through the 'information superhighway' (p. 11).

Some of the linguistic turns being used officially and their educative counterparts are shown in Table 1.

The turn to generic teaching skills

The turn to generic 'competencies' and 'skills formation' is not without its own quite distinctive material discourses, policies and practices. The question of how teaching is to be represented, in whose terms, and according to what canons, is not an issue that has surfaced regularly in accounts of teachers' work, especially from those of a competencies persuasion.

Absent from such managerialist discourses is any sense of questioning the rightness of the positions they adopt. What is missing is any sense that the language of benchmarking, quality audits, outcomes orientations, competencies and skills formation may be inappropriate lexicon with which to discuss teaching, schooling and learning. Taking Australia as an example, schools, teachers and students are not exactly a minority group, numerically speaking; there are 3 million students, 10,000 schools and 200,000 teachers. To suggest that business and industry be required forcibly to take on the discourses and genres of schooling as a way of describing industrial production is a notion that would be greeted with incredulity. The language of pedagogical caring, collegial collaboration, reflective practice, learning portfolios, resource-based learning, authentic and descriptive assessment, critical language awareness and emancipatory discourse are all ways of describing schools that are indigenous to schools and teaching as distinctive cultural entities. The slightest suggestion that the captains of industry take on such foreign sets of discourses would be greeted with considerable mirth and indeed derision. Yet, that is exactly what it is presumed that schools and teachers are expected to do, as they unquestionably describe teaching and learning in terms that derive directly from business and the military; nothing could be more ludicrous!

One of the major arguments of the past decade has been that schools need to attend better to 'basic skills' (and that teachers are major players in ensuring that this happens) in order to produce workers for industry equipped to deliver enhanced economic competitiveness. By implication, so the causal line of argument goes, we need further to ensure that procedures exist so that teachers are operating in ways that show they possess basic pedagogical and content skills necessary to pull this off. This might appear

Table 1 Mapping the discourses

Official Policy Discourses	Educative Discourses
- systems' policies and priorities	- emancipatory possibilities
- teacher and school effectiveness	- teacher and school identify formation
- partnerships and collegiality	- unforced agreements
- knowledge base for teaching	- teachers' experiential knowledge
- international best practice	- localised and contextual solutions
- public accountability	- teachers' professional judgement
- teacher appraisal	- interrogation of the context of teaching
- learning outcomes	- socially just learning
- competency approaches	- teaching for resistance
- self-managing school	- critical collaborative community
- performance management	- joint teacher theorising
- efficiency	- communicative competence
- benchmarking and standards	- monitoring consistent and compassionate teaching
- classroom management and discipline	- understanding the social complexity of classrooms
- statewide/national skills testing	- student-owned learning portfolios
- parental 'right to know'	- meaningful and continuous dialogue
- literacy	- multifacted forms of communicative competence
- publication of league tables	- inter-personal intellectual growth
- skills formation	- enduring educational relationships
- competitiveness	- solidarity and authentic peer collaboration
- school charters	- democratised school development planning
- restoration of 'the basics'	- revitalised democratic learning
- line management function	- democratised learning relationships
- parental choice	- mutual responsibility
- pre-packaged teacher development	- educationally discursive spaces
- didactic teaching	- dialogic learning
- one-way accountability	- dysfunctional school system
- teacher evaluation	- interrupting the text of teaching
- teacher incompetence	- teacher-as-learner in community
- management by objectives	- creative planning
- confusion	- making sense of complexity
- knowledge base for teaching	- provisionality of ideas

to be compelling thinking, but it is fanciful at several levels. There are too many leaps of faith and not enough substantiated evidence at various points in this supposedly causal chain of linkages. For example, we are increasingly being told that our education systems are failing in their function of preparing students with the requisite skill requirements to operate effectively in industry. The notion that there is somehow a corpus of 'basic skill requirements' and that all that schools need to do is somehow to be better bearers of 'tool kits of skills' (Darrah 1992: 265) – to be transferred to students – breaks down badly upon closer analysis. As Darrah (1992), who has undertaken detailed industrial ethnographies, has argued, workplaces are not anything like stable settings where inputs are systematically and unproblematically transformed into outputs via a technical process. For instance, we know so little about something as fundamental as computational skills actually used in the workplace, that to presume to simulate these in the classroom, and then transfer them to the world of work so as to have some impact, is to go considerably beyond the boundaries of existing knowledge – not least because current descriptions of what really occurs in workplaces are patently 'thin descriptions' that lack the richness, diversity, density and overall complexity of what actually occurs. What we have instead are bland, generic, universal, one-size-fits-all views that are quite misleading; absent are the 'observational studies that incorporate the understandings of the people who actually perform the work' (Darrah 1992: 264). What is presumed, but never actually substantiated, is that there is some kind of 'monolithic' set of generic skills that applies in all contexts. What is clearly missing from the equation about 'basic' and 'generic' skills as it relates to schooling, and by implication, how teachers do their work of conversion, is any fieldwork or thicker descriptions of what occurs in industry: 'Until that process is clarified, it is unlikely that educational reforms predicated on the belief that skills learned in the classroom will be transferred directly to workplaces can produce their desired effects' (Darrah 1992: 265). Continuing to regard the workplace as a 'black box of unknown properties' (p. 265) will not enable us to advance matters significantly even in respect of supposedly important issues like computational skills: 'Although improving classroom performance on computational tasks may be desirable for many reasons, the relationship between task performance in the classroom and at work is not clear' (p. 265).

Likewise, the claim that there is somehow a 'universal, context-free language for describing skills is questionable' (p. 268). Connell (1995) explains the 'human capital' analysis that lies behind the call for a teaching of 'the basics' in these terms:

A clear indication is that employers' opinions of new employees are often expressed in terms of their ability to spell – which is a technical requirement of almost no entry-level job in the economy. This point has acquired, however, a symbolic meaning of diligence, orderliness, and obedience to rules. If employers collectively manage to impose this definition of the capacity to labour on schools, they have won a certain victory in establishing their cultural power over the workplace.

(p. 99)

The language of skills formation

One way of explaining this further is to argue as Janks and Ivanic (1992) do that dominant discourses and perspectives do not occur by accident – they are perpetuated, sustained and maintained in place through powerful groups that have a well-developed capacity to construct their point of view as if it were natural and common sense. Janks and Ivanic's argument is that what we need in such situations is resistant forms of reading – which is to say, 'thinking differently, rejecting the ground rules and the premises upon which [things] are based: actively participating in attempts to change the whole framework on which the ground rules depend' (p. 309). The attempt is to develop an emancipatory discourse that focuses on 'recognising the forces which are leading you to fit in with the status quo and resisting them' (p. 309).

How we choose (or are told) to describe what constitutes 'skills' and 'competencies' in teaching is framed by perspectives held about what is considered to be important. Again from Janks and Ivanic (1992), 'meaning lies not simply in the text but in the social relations in which it is embedded' (p. 307). In other words, if the overarching agenda is one of controlling the work of teaching by measuring what teachers do against standards, then we acquiesce to modes of construing the work that are not only alien but operate through the language in ways that make it ultimately more controllable.

Barrow (1987), arguing from a conservative position, reaches a not dissimilar conclusion when he says that to be drawn to a skills-related view of teaching is to see it as an essentially scientific enterprise:

> Those who conceive of the educational enterprise in terms of skills seem to me to be surreptitiously suggesting, whether consciously or otherwise, that one can develop intellectual, emotional and inter-personal ability in much the same way as one develops muscles. It is a way of keeping alive the view that man is essentially no more than a sophisticated machine and that human interaction is ultimately to be explained in exactly the same way as the interactions of physical matter. I believe that such a view precisely denies what it is to be human.
>
> (p. 195)

Skills in teaching can be construed in terms that variously reflect a capacity to: control children; transmit curriculum; present content in a clear and orderly fashion; inculcate children into ways of accommodating to the world of work; producing future workers who are efficient, effective and competitive; and, generally creating a workforce that is more likely to acquiesce than to challenge the status quo. Furthermore, pursuing these qualities in students can be reinforced by having teachers who are themselves selected, trained, inculcated and rewarded in ways that reinforce these kinds of world views. In many ways, these might be laudatory ideals, in a limited kind of way – indeed, when they are portrayed and celebrated as virtues that are crucial in the 'national interest', they become almost incontestable.

The difficulty with such imperatives is that because they are imported they have quite pronounced limitations built into them, precisely because they present themselves as being so self-righteously correct. Such one-dimensional approaches to competence fall well short of the mark because they obscure and fail to grasp the idea that 'mastery in performance . . . depend[s] upon general comprehension of the work process rather than the accomplishment of specific tasks' (Jackson 1989: 80).

At one level this is an understandable strategy – namely, to produce teachers who work with students in ways productive of a particular perspective or ethos that is consistent with a process of grafting education onto an economy which espouses flexibility, responsiveness and enhanced competencies. As Jackson (1989) so aptly put it:

> The competency syndrome has spread like a socially transmitted disease. It is communicated not only through the persuasive rhetoric of public policy, but also through routine contact with administrative and funding mechanisms . . . [W]ho can be against 'competence'? It is the motherhood slogan of current reform movements in institutions of education and training.
>
> (p. 78)

While it can be argued that the approach adopted in Australia to the issues of skills in teaching is not behaviouristic because it provides the space for a wider interpretation of what it might mean to be a teacher, the emphasis in the way this is interpreted is nevertheless decidedly in the direction of an economic agenda. A flavour of this becomes glaringly apparent in the first page of an article by Bluer (1993) explaining the origins of AST in Australia. Here is a sample of the discourse:

> [to] improve the productivity of the enterprise and increase rewards to the workforce . . .
>   to increase the productivity of the enterprise – the school – by increasing the skills and knowledge levels of the teaching workforce . . .

to increase the effectiveness of the school in terms of learning outcomes . . .

[to show] how [the AST concept] was taken from a professional arena and placed in a strongly 'industrial' context.

. . . This requires an appraisal system of sophistication based on concepts of standards and defined competencies.

(p. 1)

On this one page alone dealing with the rationale of why the AST was introduced into Australia, we find words like 'effectiveness', 'appraisal' and 'productivity' used in ways and with a frequency that leave us in no doubt as to what the real agenda is.

In summary: part of a much larger picture

While there was an open admission by the teacher unions that moves to embrace the notion of the AST were encased within a broader endorsement of the 'structural efficiency principle' designed to deliver 'increases in wages and salaries or improvement in conditions [to teachers]' (Bluer 1993: 2), what seems to be sorely missing is any wider reading of what this might mean in the context of the adoption of such principles by international agencies like the World Bank and the International Monetary Fund (IMF). It is worth briefly reminding ourselves of what structural efficiency means in that wider context, and it does not bode at all well for public agencies like schools. These are matters taken up in more detail in Chapter 5.

Ilon (1994) put it in these terms:

Structural adjustment is, in fact, not a policy – it is a process. The structure being adjusted is the structure of the economy . . . [in ways that] centre around four primary structural shifts: liberalisation, deregulation, privatisation and stabilisation . . . [S]tructural adjustment is usually pursued through self-regulating mechanisms, often moving toward market-determined parameters.

(pp. 95–6)

Ilon's (1994) argument is that structural adjustment is about decreasing the funding available to public education, as real expenditures per pupil are becoming unsustainable in light of 'wealthier segments of society. . . becoming less willing to fund public education . . . as their children are moved towards private schools' (p. 98). This has crucial implications for public schooling – we should not read structural adjustment simply as 'bad policy promulgated by misinformed bureaucrats or high-powered experts promoting a global agenda of domination' (p. 95). According to Ilon (1994) the emergence of global factors are having a profound effect in terms of breaking down notions of 'community', rendering a marked stratification in the nature of differential curriculum offerings in schools and, understandably, producing huge pressures on teachers to sustain quality in a context of sharply declining real resources where there is widespread intensification of teachers' work.

The policy linkages are clear enough and worth bringing together in the Australian context, although the reality may be much the same for other western countries. Basically, they boil down to a belief 'that Australia's economic difficulties were due to its lack of competitiveness on international markets, which, in turn, was directly related to an inadequately skilled labour force . . . [and an acceptance that] the new workforce needed to be skilled generically rather than specifically' (Soucek 1995: 133), and that this applied as much to teachers as to any other segments of the workforce. This took the form of the federal government taking a position on providing national leadership in educational matters (despite this being a constitutional state responsibility in Australia), on the grounds that education had become an important tool of micro-economic reform; education was seen as being pivotal in responding to the wider global imperative. What was interesting about this response, according to Soucek (1995), was that 'the new workforce was to be skilled rather than empowered through achieving intellectual autonomy' (p. 135). In other words, the thrust was to be in the direction of having schools develop 'generic work-relevant skills' (p. 134) rather than through any attempt to produce a society capable of 'critical evaluation of policies and of their impact on a broader society' (p. 136). There was a complete 'absence of critical and creative skills, and a lack of concern for social, moral and psychological development of students' (p. 137). As Soucek (1995) notes, this is an interesting line of argument because, if followed to its conclusion, it means:

> One consequence of this loss of critical sensibility at the national level of policy making could be that the educational initiatives, which originally might have begun as a response to the ailing national economy, will eventually become implicated in a production of a radically new society, described by many as a post-Fordist society.
>
> (p. 137)

Soucek's (1995) point is that this pre-occupation with fitting students to 'work-related skills' has produced a circumstance in educational policy where:

> the concept of work-related competencies appears to be seriously taken on board only in Australia. It would thus appear, notwithstanding that other OECD countries like New Zealand and the United Kingdom have also moved strongly in the direction of restructuring along the lines of

market principles, that 'Australia stands almost alone in postulating neoclassical economics as an exclusive paradigm for public policy making'.

(pp. 140–1)

Australia's singular pre-occupation with the notion of the supposed 'level playing field' (Stewart 1994) has not been embraced with anything like this fervour by its economic competitors such as Japan, the EEC or the USA and the disturbing element is that 'this mode of policy-making . . . is due precisely to the banishment of critical and autonomous voices from policy-making forums' (p. 141).

All of this is by way of saying that policy manœuvres of the kind expressed in the introduction of AST in Australia were predicated on a set of views about what kind of society Australian governments wanted to engineer through teachers and schooling, and it was not by and large one directed at questioning, challenging or producing a more just and compassionate society. In many ways the AST represents a harbinger of an education system that is becoming officially pre-occupied with 'multi-skilling', 'increased competition', 'flexibility', 'responsiveness' and 'market product', while also espousing a concern for 'participation', 'team work' and 'co-operation' – but only as long as these bear on task achievement, and not on challenging the rationale of what is being attempted or its social and economic effects.

Chapter 3

Teaching under (re-) construction

HOW IS TEACHING BEING CONSTRUCTED?

Introduction

In a sense this is a strange question. It could be interpreted in some quarters as suggesting that somehow teaching is being hijacked, or at least manipulated, by forces of evil beyond our control. That, however, would be both too deterministic a view and one that does not rest easily with the lived experiences of many teachers, even though there are some who might readily subscribe to such a view. We are not among them. We are not, therefore, trying to construct the case that teachers are somehow the pawns or cyphers in some sophisticated, distant and orchestrated game. That would be too simplistic, and would deny the active agency of large numbers of teachers in creating meaningful, viable and professionally satisfying lives for themselves and their students.

None of this is to deny, of course, that there are not sweeping, radical and material changes occurring in the pedagogical heartland of our schools, and that it takes expression in more than the isolated grumblings of a few pockets of politically active teachers in staffrooms around the world. The kind of process we have in mind is much more complicated and nuanced than either of these limited interpretations. There are some undeniably profound changes occurring to teaching that have the potential (if they have not already produced the actuality), of altering the purposes, intentions and practices of what passes as teachers' work – but they are occurring with a concerted purpose and within a context that is constructed as eminently sensible, even though we may have substantial difficulty in accepting the efficacy of its basis. A major part of our purpose here is to disclose how the agenda behind the reconstrual of teaching and schooling currently underway is neither innocent nor value neutral – but rather part of a much larger process of structural realignment (in some instances, described as 'structural adjustment') occurring globally – but more about that later.

Let us not be misinterpreted on another score, either. In taking the line that we have, we don't want to be seen to be making a clarion call for some kind of return to a golden era of teaching that never really existed – a kind of yearning for a period when all was well with the pedagogical world, everyone knew their place, and life was settled, predictable, certain and stable. This would be equally misleading. We are not suggesting that teaching return to some older outmoded models.

We want to lay out systematically what we see as the changes occurring to the labour process of teaching and teachers' work, and in the process offer some more expansive and robust (albeit unsettling) explanations and illustrations of what is occurring within and to teaching.

To talk about teaching as being 'constructed' is to use a built-environment metaphor that conjures up images of scaffolding, fabrication, textures, moulding, shaping and fashioning – and, in a sense, this is precisely what we are on about here. The metaphors we live by (Lakoff and Johnson 1980) have an undeniable influence on how we see the world, how we experience it, how we ascertain what is functional and dysfunctional about it, and how, therefore, we proceed to rectify what we perceive to be malfunctioning in it. Using an architectural metaphor within which to encapsulate the argument about what we believe to be happening to teaching conveys the message of busy hands, actively working to create a view of teaching that is proceeding according to some known representation or scheme (in more or less detail). This may be a 'grand scheme', in the sense of some 'master (*sic*) plan', but it may equally convey the image of loosely linked, local, but nevertheless systematic and patterned sequence of changes to teachers' work. Whichever of these happens to be the more accurate (and for the moment we err towards the latter), the interesting questions hover around: whose agenda is represented in this construction; whose views are being silenced; and, whose are being given privileged access? These are questions with social, moral and, dare we say it, 'political' consequences – for whose interests get represented is never far removed from issues of power. Although speaking of the construction of our technological futures, Mike Cooley's (1980) point is just as relevant to the way in which teaching seems to be headed – it can be changed with our active consent and democratic participation, or it can be done by stealth, fiat and the denial of due processes:

The alternatives are stark. Either we will have futures in which human beings are reduced to bee-like behaviour, reacting to the systems and equipment specified for them; or we will have a future in which masses of people, conscious of their skills and abilities in both the political sense, decide that they are going to be the architects of a new form of technological development which will enhance human creativity and mean more freedom of choice and expression rather than less. The truth is, we shall have to make the profound political decision as to whether we intend to act as architects or behave like bees.

(p. 100)

One broad way of regarding the construction of teaching is in terms of the forces requiring that schools service national and transnational economic interests. There is a widespread and deeply ingrained view that recent economic crises have been due in some measure to inadequate forms of schooling, in which teachers need to wear the blame for a failure to inculcate 'basic skills'.

That schools in the current economic climate ought to be considered appendages to industry is far from a novel idea. Almost since organised forms of schooling and education have existed, there has been an expectation, to varying degrees, that schools provide for the labour power needs of industry. Such demands have tended to be somewhat more muted (but they never totally disappear) at certain historical junctures (namely, in buoyant economic times), than in times of economic and social uncertainty, when capitalist economies are undergoing the kind of fundamental restructurings they are experiencing at the moment owing to the emergence of strident newly developing economies in Asia and South America. Periods of economic turmoil, uncertainty and unpredictability have inherent within them demands for at least the outward appearance of certainty. Schools as social institutions are sufficiently familiar to large sections of the population to be convenient institutions required to carry a major portion of the consequences of these kinds of social dislocations. It sounds a reasonable proposition to expect that schools ought to serve the interests of industry and be compliant agents in assisting in the wider restructuring. But, in order to make the argument stick with the kind of veracity necessary for it to have an impact, schools have to be simultaneously blamed for the crisis (that is, be ascribed as the 'cause' of the problem) while also being held out as the path by which restitution might be affected (that is, as the 'solution' to the problem). We have the larger crisis, so we are told, because we have erred by allowing ill-advised egalitarian teaching and learning practices to prevail. Standards in schools have slipped because of inadequate attention to discipline, competencies, rigour, appraisal and testing. Widespread and largely unsubstantiated claims, backed by prestigious commissions of inquiry derived from industry and business, put the view that learning and teaching need to return to modes of the past if we are to have a chance of ever experiencing the hoped-for economic recovery. Schools are exhorted dutifully to deliver literate, numerate, compliant (but not socially critical) skilled workers able to engage in economic restoration. Noticeable in this view of education are perspectives on schooling that largely prevailed in the past − namely, a view of schooling that is about drilling and training. Even worse, this is a kind of cargo cult mentality that says we have risen to earlier forms of economic pre-eminence because of instrumental and utilitarian modes of schooling. The fact that earlier periods of economic ascendancy were almost completely due to the annihilation and colonisation of one part of the world (mainly Afro and Asian) by another (mainly Euro-centric), at the expense and degradation of the former, seems largely to escape attention. To put it another way, mooted changes to education and schooling (and teaching and learning in particular) are being predicated around a set of views that are informed and framed by a set of conditions that are no longer with us, if they ever did have much efficacy as explanations anyway.

To put this yet another way, the 'solutions' that are being arrived at as the way to resolve current perplexities are solutions to do with rigour, relevance, quality, discipline, standards, forms of assessment and competencies that purportedly prevailed during some romanticised golden era when life was good, children listened to their elders, and we all lived prosperously.

This is a style of policy making that is metaphorically akin to driving a car by means of looking in the rear-vision mirror. The fact that reaching back to the perceived comfort and certainties of the past for ways of explaining and resolving present difficulties is totally inadequate as an explanation seems to go largely uncontested by the majority of the community. For those who craft such inaccurate ways of resolving difficulties, what is most astounding and disturbing is that they actually believe in the absolute correctness and rightness of what they offer as solutions in areas like education. Part of the problem here lies with the apparently common-sense nature of much of what passes as schooling – we have all, after all, been students of one sort or another, and the process of teaching did not appear to us to be *that* complicated or mysterious. If we look carefully at the agenda being created for schools by avid reformers outside of schools, what is most uniformly striking about it is its naturalness. There is something appealing about the notion that western capitalism is in trouble because schools are failing to deliver the requisite kind of skilled labour, and what is needed as a consequence are ways of whipping schools and teachers into shape. This ideology is so pervasive and compellingly self-evident as to be almost an unquestionable axiom in western capitalist countries. Arguments abound as to how to proceed to make schools more like industry, with heavy doses of effective, clearly focused, narrowly utilitarian objectives, pursued in a context thoroughly committed to adding value to educational raw material in order to produce the highest quality and most saleable product. It is not whether the argument is *actually* true or not that matters most, but rather the perception that *it might have some credence*, that in the end becomes most compelling – a kind of guilt by apparent association, rather than by a careful and systematic marshalling of the evidence.

The logic of arguments about schools and teaching being 'the problem' breaks down because the 'causation' (bad schools) has not been anywhere near substantiated, nor its corollary, that industrial models of administration, organisation and management are necessarily any better 'solutions' than the modes of operation that they seek so readily to supplant in schools. The unfortunate consequence is that schools are being driven to follow modes of operation that are informed by a largely bankrupt set of ideologies and paradigms from a quarter in which they have proven demonstrably ineffectual (see Smyth 1995a). We only need a cursory glance around the littered landscape of the 1980s to see the rate at which the industrial model of management failed dismally. Rather than a carefully considered approach to 'what's wrong with our schools?' (if anything), what we are tending to experience instead are a set of ideologically driven solutions to as yet only partly (or poorly) articulated or even misconstrued problems – hardly an edifying spectacle for so–called educated and civilised societies.

What we are attempting here then is to summarise, in so far as it is possible to do that for global trends, what is happening to education in advanced capitalist countries. There is inevitably a risk in doing that because of local variations in terms of history and evolution of education, not to mention regional variations in the nature of the way capitalism is being redesigned (see Keegan 1992 for examples of this). However, there is mounting evidence (Smyth 1995b; Smyth 1995c) to suggest some quite remarkable similarities (beyond what could be construed as mere coincidence) in what is happening to educational reform worldwide (Smyth 1993a).

Berliner and Biddle (1995), in their insightful book entitled *The Manufactured Crisis: Myths, Fraud and the Attack on America's Public Schools*, provide a detailed and well-argued case of how the last decade has seen unprecedented attacks on the credibility and veracity of public schools in America. The argument and evidence they provide is of an extensive, persistent and orchestrated campaign of misinformation, deceit, half-truths, misrepresentations, myths and outright lies (p. 4). They label this as collectively amounting to a 'manufactured crisis' about the true nature of contemporary American schooling. To their considerable credit these authors take on the difficult and complex task of presenting the evidence necessary to counter arguments about the supposed crisis in teaching and schooling in the USA. What they present is a carefully considered body of research that, far from showing any crisis of competence in US schools as manufactured by narrow sectional interest groups, reveals instead an agenda that 'diverts attention away from the real problems faced by American education' (p. 4). The real issue is the significant loss of public confidence and dramatically declining public resources for education. Berliner and Biddle (1995) conclude that:

> (1) on the whole, the American school system is in far better shape than the critics would have us believe; (2) where American schools fail, those failures are largely caused by problems that are imposed on those schools, problems that the critics have been only too happy to ignore.
>
> (p. 12)

While it is not possible to cite the extensive body of evidence here, the particular myths that are exploded are:

- Student achievement in American primary schools has recently declined
- The performance of American college students has also fallen recently
- The intellectual abilities and abstract problem-solving skills of America's young people have declined, although – paradoxically – it is also believed that their intelligence and the skills that indicate 'gifted-ness' are fixed and identifiable at an early age
- America's schools have always come up short when compared with schools in other countries, indicating that our educational procedures are deficient and that our educators are feckless . . .
- America spends a lot more money on its schools than other nations do
- Investing in the schools has not brought success – indeed, money is unrelated to school performance
- Recent increases in expenditures for education have been wasted or have gone merely to unneeded raises for teachers and administrators
- The productivity of American workers is deficient, and this reflects the inadequate training they receive in American schools
- America produces far too few scientists, mathematicians, and engineers; as a result, the country is losing its industrial leadership
- Our schools are not staffed by qualified teachers, the textbooks they use promote immorality, and most American parents are dissatisfied with their local schools
- Because they are subject to market forces, private schools are inherently better than public schools.

(pp. 5–6)

The history of these mischievous misconstruals is interesting in itself, but it is not the topic we want to pursue here. We are more interested in why this misperception has been perpetuated, who is working in schools to expose it, how, and what alternatives are being constructed. Suffice to say at this point that Berliner and Biddle (1995) have taken on directly the critics of US education in a most courageous, well-informed and cogent rebuttal of these widespread and largely unfounded criticisms. Their conclusion is most apt:

> recent criticisms of American schools have often been bolstered by impressive claims of evidence that appeared, on first glance, to support arguments about our 'troubled' schools. On closer examination, however, many of these claims have turned out to be garbage . . . People who are sincerely interested in improving American education must be alerted to such chicanery.

(p. 171)

While it is clearly difficult and dangerous to engage in widespread generali-sation about the extent to which such campaigns of public misinformation have been engaged in in other countries, there is evidence that many of the ill-informed ideas (often glamorised with the label of 'reforms') have spread to other parts of the world through the ideology of the New Right. An example of this can be found in 'Something borrowed, something blue? A study of the Thatcher Government's appropriation of American education and training policy' (Finegold *et al.* 1992; 1993).

The reason the American case just cited is so important is that if the level of hysteria generated by the misinformation campaigns of the past decade in that country are in any way representative of what has likely occurred in other countries, and knowing what we do about the extraordinary capacity of American culture to shape global thinking, then recent policies that reflect New Right 'solutions' in other countries could well have all of the same shortcomings outlined by Berliner and Biddle (1995). There seems to be little doubt as to the ideological lineage of calls for educational reform worldwide, despite quite different educational, political and social histories. For example, current moves to 'devolve' school administration are occurring simultaneously in all western countries even though the USA has a history of local school boards, the UK a mediated structure of Local Educational Authorities, and Australia and New Zealand much more centralised systems. All are actively pursuing policies of dismantling and privatising education by means of 'consumer choice', generally disguised behind labels like school-based management, the self-managing school, site-based management and locally managed schools.

The tendency towards technical/rational construals of teaching

The major ideological prism through which it is becoming increasingly fashionable to view teaching is a means–end one; that is to say, one that regards teaching primarily as a conduit or vehicle through which to achieve skills formation and economic agenda. While there is never complete hegemony in representation relating to these matters, only predominant or prevailing tendencies, it is nevertheless the case that at particular historical junctures there are major viewpoints that hold sway and that powerfully shape the language and discursive practices of schooling and teaching. As Dillard and Nehmer (1990) note:

> [the] organisational metaphors being proposed by, and interpreted within, organisation science are ideologically biased. As a result, discourse is being constrained by the rationalisation of the action space through metaphorical representations . . . [C]urrent organisation science metaphors . . . obscure recognition of ideological biases, perpetrating control and repression.
>
> (p. 31)

Sawada and Caley (1985) argue that 'the dominant metaphor for today's education is the Newtonian Machine . . . Newtonian physics holds that the universe is a huge machine and that various parts of the universe can be isolated as though they are self-contained smaller machines' (p. 14). Knowing what we do about the tendency of this particular limited view of physics to promote separation – of people from nature, theory from practice, and experience from science – it is not altogether surprising that when it underpins our views of education, it results in a significant bifurcation. The metaphor of the school and the education system as machine, with its inbuilt tendency towards stable-state equilibrium, has distinct limitations as a representation of reality, as Sawada and Caley (1985) point out:

> The school is a more or less well oiled machine that produces (educates?) children. In this sense, the education system (school) comes complete with production goals (desired end states); objectives (precise interme-diate end states); raw material (children); a physical plant (school building); a 13-stage assembly line (grades K–12); directives for each stage (curriculum guides); processes for each stage (instruction); managers for each stage (teachers); plant supervisors (principals); trouble shooters (consultants, diagnosticians); quality control mechanisms (discipline, rules lock-step progress through stages, conformity); inter-changeability of parts (teacher-proof curriculum, 25 students per processing unit, equality of treatment); uniform criteria for all (stan-dardised testing interpreted on the normal curve); and basic product available in several lines (academic, vocational, business, general). Is this reminiscent of Fords, Apples, and Big Macs?
>
> (pp. 14–15)

Even the briefest of sojourns through the language and the lexicon of teachers' work reveals a panoply of jargon indicative of this mechanistic orientation and an increasing degree of pollution of the atmosphere within which teachers' work is framed and discussed.

Take for example, 'outcomes', 'verifiable statements of performance' and 'performance indicators' which appeared in the early 1980s as the outriders of the new technology of control within education. The outcomes rhetoric has become deeply entrenched in the official discourses of teaching and learning, in the justifications for scientific forms of school and system management, and in the overt and covert mechanisms of harnessing the education 'industry' to the economy. Outcomes rhetoric, as part of a new thesis of economic rationalism and scientific management, has apparently become the discourse of a normal and natural approach to the provision of education, an approach which has largely reduced, marginalised and rendered other discourses irrelevant. At the level of consciousness, outcomes rhetoric is the articulation of a pervasive 'myth' about teaching and learning.

The image of teachers is also revamped by reconfiguring the work of teaching as being about the delivery of knowledge, the testing of learning and the finessing of pedagogical technique. Reality, of course, is that the work of teaching is increasingly routinised and proletarianised as teachers are subjected to the discourses as well as the practices of managerialism – tighter control by outsiders, better forms of accountability, more sophisticated surveillance of outcomes, and greater reliance on measures of competence and performance.

Neave (1988) becomes useful here in his argument about what he terms the role of the 'evaluative state'. He claims that this evaluative role becomes apparent not in the manner in which evaluation is used for routine or system maintenance purposes, but in its exercise over 'strategic change', where education is being used increasingly for the establishment of benchmarks 'against which the performance of particular areas of the national economy may be placed and the allocation of resources undertaken' (Neave 1988: 8). It is in the linkage of these two forms of evaluation that the potency becomes most evident – as Neave (1988) puts it: 'evaluation seeks to elicit how far goals have been met, not by setting the prior conditions but by ascertaining the extent to which overall targets have been reached through the evaluation of "product"' (p. 9). In other words, the focus is not upon the linking of product to objectives through resources, but rather on the 'assumption that targets are more likely to be reached if resource allocation is made subsequent to, and dependent on, the degree to which an establishment has fulfilled specified criteria' (p. 10). Evaluation of this kind, Neave (1988) says, 'works through control of *product*, not through control of *process*' (p. 10). The argument is that this shift away from input has three discernible effects: (1) it shifts the focus away from issues of access, equity and social justice; (2) it enables redefinition of the utility of education in the light of purposes framed in terms of 'national priorities' construed in market terms; and (3) it enables public policy to reach down to the institutional level so as to 'regulate responses' (p. 10). The salient point to be taken from this line of argument is that it is not simply a shift in the focus from process to product, but rather a substantial redefinition of education in terms, not of 'individual demand, but in keeping with the perceived needs of the "market"' (p. 10). While it is neither a product of a single moment, nor a single exclusive ideology, the Evaluative State is becoming perceived as a viable alternative to 'regulation by bureaucratic fiat' (p. 11).

What we have in these circumstances is a discourse that appears to have within it a duality of meaning – 'maintaining central control over the framing of targets' (hence the reliance on centrally devised curriculum, frameworks, guidelines, policies, and the like), 'whilst at the same time giving greater latitude at institutional level to choose which course is best suited to the specific institutional circumstances' (hence the emphasis, at least rhetorically, on devolution, choice, diversity, self-management and autonomy) (Neave 1988: 11). This apparent contradiction is explainable in these terms:

> The Evaluative State is then a rationalisation and wholesale redistribution of functions between centre and periphery such that the centre maintains strategic control through fewer, but more precise, policy levers, contained in overall 'mission statements', the setting of system goals and the operationalising of criteria relating to 'output quality'. Accordingly, these elements form the general framework within which strategic control is managed and to which mid-level co-ordination is entrusted with the task of working out the appropriate means for their attainment.
>
> (Neave 1988: 11)

It is not so much, either, a 'withering away of the state', as a strategic withdrawal 'from the murky plain of overwhelming detail, the better to take refuge in the clear and commanding heights of effective strategic "profiling"' (Neave 1988: 12).

A cautionary caveat

In the kind of analysis we are offering as background to changes in teachers' work, we need to be careful not to portray trends towards vocationalism, marketisation, outcomes-orientation, skills formation, and the like, in ways that allow them to be interpreted in an entirely negative way. Seddon (1994) captured this well in her argument that:

> It is no longer adequate to rail against the terms 'training', 'vocational' or 'instrumental' in a way which treats these traditional categories as symbols to be either rejected or applauded. Rather, the challenge is to get behind the symbols and explore the practices which the changing frames of debate permit.
>
> (p. 64)

In other words, we need to search for 'the possibilities for a progressive politics' (p. 64) of teachers' work generated within the current 'modernisation project' (p. 65) that is producing contemporary educational restructurings. The argument that there are spaces and arenas within which these tendencies can be redefined is both a more optimistic and a more hopeful scenario, as well as one that produces challenges to identify what 'should be retained and protected, and what should be jettisoned' (Seddon 1994: 78). Specifically, the pivotal question becomes:

[How] to create an organisation of work and a relational culture which promotes the development of teachers' powers in ways which allow them both to make in situ judgements about the important developments in education, work and society, and to integrate those developments in a changing practice of work. The aim is to structure teaching in ways which allow teachers to work with effect in changing circumstances.

(p. 78)

As Seddon (1994) has indicated, the kind of tendencies impacting on teachers' work are 'contradictory' and 'contingent' and have to be seen in the wider context of the complex 'modernisation project' underway in western countries like Australia.

The thrust for competencies and skills formation

This is not the place for an exhaustive treatment of the 'competency movement', but some background may be helpful in interpreting what this means for pedagogy, curriculum and assessment issues (Porter *et al.* 1992).

The explanation of the origins of what schools and teachers are currently experiencing as various 'competency approaches' is not easy to nail down. We do know that their current local variants in the UK – 'National Vocational Qualifications' (Hyland 1994) – and the USA – 'Total Quality Management' (Murgatroyd and Morgan 1993) – share the similarity of being responses to the alleged need for economies to reposition themselves in a set of rapidly changing global circumstances, not withstanding Soucek's (1995) point that their 'economic masters [are] now located outside the nation-state' (p. 136). What started out then as an educational initiative aimed at being 'a response to the ailing national economy, will [he argues] eventually become implicated in the production of a radically new society' (p. 137). As Noble (1994) points out in the USA, this tendency is likely to produce 'a veritable frenzy of standardization . . . [based upon] developing national tests, certificates and standards boards' (p. 20). For Noble, 'the proponents of the link between education and the economy aren't merely identifying new skill requirements for a new economy, of course. They are pinning the rap for a bum economy on education and workers' (p. 23). His argument is that it is a sleight of hand: 'The insistent focus on human resources, education and skills is thereby a convenient distraction from economic disasters caused by myopic management with their relentless downsizing in the name of productivity' (p. 24). But, more about that later.

For the moment, suffice to say that the popularity of competency approaches with their emphasis on measurable outcomes appears to be linked to major external threats or crises, at least so far as the US experience is concerned (and borrowed by other countries). Neumann's (1979) analysis of the genesis of competency approaches in education is that they become popular in times of crisis because the emphasis shifts dramatically from 'what you know, to what you can do' (p. 67):

> The experiences of two world wars have . . . left indelible marks on competence-based programs as well as on American education in general. The tendency of these programs to stress mastery learning and to incorporate performance tests as assessment and learning instruments may be seen as a result of wartime education and training experiences. The contingencies of wartime learning did not allow for partial learning. It was important that students learn quickly, but it was absolutely essential that they learn *completely*. And the only truly reliable means of determining whether students had mastered their assignments was the performance test. The final part of every training course had its solo flight, whether it was flying a B-29, repairing a radar unit, or cooking breakfast for five hundred men.
>
> (pp. 67–8)

Speaking of what has become a government pre-occupation to introduce Competency-Based Standards (CBS) into a range of occupational and professional groups in Australia (20 in all, including teaching and teacher education), Walker (1991), who was then the Chair of the Australian Council of Deans of Education, argued that:

> The current interest in CBS is related to an outcomes orientation in educational policy, with a major policy goal being the development of a highly educated and skilled workforce and as a consequence increased productivity in the Australian economy overall.
>
> (p. 1)

The intent was, in his words:

> to increase the effectiveness and efficiency of the workforce, to facilitate the deployment of workers in the productive organisation of their work, and to provide workers with recognition and reward for their skills, with satisfying career paths and effective education and training opportunities.
>
> (p. 1)

Commenting on the extent to which Australia in particular has unproblematically embraced competency approaches to teaching at official levels, Soucek (1995) concludes that 'in education policy, the concept of work-related competencies appears to be seriously taken on board only in Australia' (p. 140). While there may be some debate about the accuracy of his claims, especially in terms of the widespread adoption of competencies elsewhere, Soucek makes this point as part of the wider claim 'that Australia stands almost alone in postulating neo-classical economics as an exclusive paradigm for public policy making' (p. 141).

Once it becomes established that the work-related competencies of learners are what counts (in Australia these are called 'key competencies' – and they bear an uncanny resemblance to the same ones identified by Rumberger (1988) in the USA), then it is a relatively short step both to measure these through student testing, while at the same time exerting direct and indirect pressure on teachers to adjust their pedagogy accordingly. As Ball (1993a) has put it, this amounts to an 'attempt to reconstruct and redefine the meaning and purpose of teaching, both as a vocational practice and mental labour' (p. 106). Furthermore, it raises the spectre that the measurement, hierarchy and regulation accompanying such moves produces a set of circumstances which:

> begins with the testing of students, but raises the possibility of monitoring the performance of teachers and schools and making comparisons between them . . . In all this there is a concern with the quality, character and content of teachers' labour and increasingly direct attempts made to shape the quality, character and content of classroom practice.
>
> (Ball 1993a: 107)

Ball's (1993a) argument is that there is an 'increase in the technical elements of teachers' work . . . and the spaces for professional autonomy and judgement are reduced' (p. 106).

While this may appear as a uniformly depressing account of what may in reality be happening to teachers' work, it needs to be remembered, as Ball notes, that even within policies there are 'discontinuities, compromises, omissions and exceptions [which] are also important' (Ball 1990: 3) as well as 'possibilities for "gaps" and "moments" of progressive and radical insertion' (Bowe et al. 1992: 12). Viewed in this light even apparently dominant discourses like those of competency approaches still have within them 'possibilities and impossibilities, tied to knowledge on the one hand (the analysis of problems and identification of remedies and goals) and practice on the other (specification of methods for achieving goals and implementation)' (p. 13).

Bowe et al. (1992) argue that even within dominant policy discourses there is contestation between 'the arenas of formation and implementation', and in and among the 'ambiguities, contradictions and omissions' there is space for the identification 'resistance, accommodation, subterfuge and conformity' (p. 13).

Lawn (1990) also casts a helpful light when he described the situation in England shortly after the Education Reform Act of 1988. He sketches the backdrop of the post-World War Two shift from 'curriculum responsibility', in which primary and secondary teachers had been pivotal in the democratic reconstruction of schooling, to an emphasis on 'teacher productivity' and the 'new management of teachers' as the post-war consensus collapsed. As he put it:

> Teaching is to be reduced to 'skills', attending planning meetings, supervising others, preparing courses and reviewing the curriculum. It is to be 'managed' to be more 'effective'. In effect the intention is to depoliticise teaching and turn the teacher into an educational worker. Curriculum responsibility now means supervising competencies.
>
> (p. 389)

Lawn (1990) describes a certain consistency and determination within the Thatcher 'political project', whereby the transformation in large measure occurred discursively:

> The language with which schools are to be described is no longer a private educational or curriculum language, made up from its own reference points; it is now the language of the city pages and business news. Enterprise, entrepreneurship, cost-centres, incentive contracts and privatisation are now all educational terms. The language of the previous decade and of the post-war decades has been expunged. Where now is curriculum autonomy, local/central partnership, teacher professionalism and progressive pedagogy?
>
> (p. 388)

Such circumscribed and emasculated views of teaching go close to encasing it in a 'subject knowledge plus teaching skills' (p. 388) approach, whereas the reality is closer to one constructed by teachers as they engage a vast array of social and democratic endeavours: 'Skill is never reducible to technical operations, it always contains within it a social element as an expression of the employer's demand or the employee's control' (Lawn 1990: 389). Curriculum, according to this set of views, becomes nothing more than 'managing the teacher' and marketing the commodities produced by the 'curriculum industry': 'The [curriculum] policy is constructed in-house, the production process contracted out and an ad. agency markets it. Talk of curriculum traditions or communities of discourse seems irrelevant' (Lawn 1990: 390).

Lawn, like many of us, has difficulty with the idea of curriculum as having 'core' and 'peripheral' workers, 'teamwork', 'delegated supervision', 'quality control' and 'entrepreneurial and semi-autonomous profit centres'. He poses the question as to whether an 'oppositional culture' will emerge for 'the many teachers who need arguments to defend the social construction of their skill in their daily curriculum work and so sustain a subversive culture of teaching' (Lawn 1990: 391). He has no answers, but he speculates that the growing shortage of teachers, at least in England and Wales, may hold the prospect of bringing the reforms to a halt, and 'the old idea of partnership may be resurrected' (Lawn 1990: 391).

The image (and that is all it is) being created here is of reforms that amount to a dramatic shift from teachers as 'responsible professionals', trusted with collectively constructing curriculum with others in the direction of educative interests, to teachers as 'competent technicians', working in an industry where the interests have to be formulated elsewhere, most notably in the marketplace and the international economy. The difficulty with this revised image of teachers is that it becomes highly problematic because of the fragmentary and additive way in which it regards and promotes the notion of skill. As Ainley (1993) has noted, and as Polanyi (1969) has pointed out, 'people do not acquire skills just by learning to perform its fragments; they must also discover the knack of co-ordinating them effectively' (p. 12).

What we have argued so far in this chapter is that teaching is being dramatically reframed around a new set of discourses – skills formation, competencies, performance indicators, and the like – in ways that give the outward appearance of being able to respond to the new economic imperatives. But the tendency towards increasingly technical rational construals of teaching are held in place by powerful international forces that are only partially understood. We move now to examine those in more detail.

CRITIQUING THE CANON: GENESIS OF REFORM AND SCHOOL RESTRUCTURING

The international fundamentalist agenda

If we were to search for the beginnings of the forces working to produce the changes currently being experienced in schools around the world – namely, a pre-occupation with outcomes orientations, individualisation, devolution of responsibility, competition, education as a commodity, choice and the market, pursuit of a managerialist ideology, standards, competencies, testing, appraisal and accountability – then we have to go back some years to the end of World War Two. Many of the ideas we are currently experiencing under the ideology of what is fashionably termed the New Right were warehoused in a set of economic conditions incubated in the closing stages of the war. This is not to suggest that some of these ideas did not have a much earlier philosophical legacy, for they clearly did – in many respects going back to ideals of the free market that were prevalent in the nineteenth century. However, it was the special set of circumstances generated by the immanent return to peace-time conditions and the singular event known as the Bretton Woods Conference in New Hampshire in July 1944 that is most important in terms of what has happened since, economically speaking. The knock-on effect has been nothing short of profound, because two institutions were created to facilitate post-war European reconstruction – the World Bank and the International Monetary Fund (IMF). It is remarkable that there is so little public discussion of these influential agencies in the wider public sphere, because they have unquestionably been significant forces shaping global economics and politics in the second half of this century (see Brecher and Costello 1994; Chossudovsky 1997). One thing that is known is that in the fifty years since their inception these two organisations have lent in excess of US$ 312 billion (George and Sabelli 1994: 12) to borrowing countries, mostly in the Third World. We also know that in 1993 the World Bank had a permanent workforce of 7,000, it hired 672 external consultants that year, it had a research budget in excess of US$ 150 million per annum, and its documentation and archives of work undertaken since its inception amount to some 65,000 cubic metres – so large that it recently had to shift from Washington to Pennsylvania because of the exorbitant cost of housing all its records.

It is little short of staggering that such a large and powerful organisation as the World Bank should remain so shrouded in terms of precisely how it works to shape and formulate global ideology, economics and geo-politics. In a short space, we want to try and unravel how the policies and activities of this profoundly influential organisation (and its sister organisation, the IMF) operate to push policies down the line to shape what is happening in schools as public institutions. What is mind-blowing is the extent to which the World Bank is completely unaccountable to anybody, yet it has acquired the capacity to hold so much of the world to ransom through its lending policies and the conditions it attaches to loans. Much of the policy fallout emerging from the activities of the World Bank is hard to 'prove' in terms of its direct effect on education and schooling, given that the World Bank is primarily concerned with development in the Third World. However, the similarity of association between the policies of the Bank and educational policies being actively pursued by governments around the world are so similar as to be uncanny.

The source of greatest concern is how the World Bank has come to wield such enormous political power, despite its proclaiming to be a purely economic institution, while succeeding in George and Sabelli's (1994) words 'in making its own view of development appear to be the norm' (dustcover). According to these commentators, the Bank has an incredibly closed internal culture that is not open to outside ideas, is committed to serving extremely narrow econometric and profit-seeking interests, is totally non-democratic in its mode of operation, and is so unaccountable as to resemble more closely 'the medieval Church or a monolithic political party relying on rigid doctrine, hierarchy and a rejection of dissenting ideas to perpetuate its influence. [Furthermore] its faith in orthodox economics and the capacity of the market to solve development problems is incompatible with its professed goals of helping the poor and protecting the environment' (dust-cover).

To give an indication of why this so apparently secretive organisation was founded and how it is that it continues to exert such an influence, George and Sabelli (1994) put it thus:

> The Bank was conceived for the noblest of reasons; its founders firmly believed it would contribute to human betterment in the postwar world. And indeed, the Bank soon became the largest supplier of infra-structure, providing the underpinnings for industry in the so-called developing countries. Its critics charge, however, that many of its projects also left a wide swathe of physical and social destruction in their wake. Bank projects have been known to dislocate entire communities, displace thousands of people, destroy forests, turn grasslands into deserts, or concentrate land and wealth in the hands of a few rich farmers or entrepreneurs – all in the name of development. Since the 1980s, its 'program' loans designed to encourage widespread policy changes (better known as structural adjustment) have forcibly reoriented entire economies.
>
> (p. 2)

But more than this, it has been the view of reality which the World Bank has been able effectively and arrogantly to impose so extensively that is most strikingly awesome. In other words, it is the Bank's hegemony in defining what is 'correct policy . . . [and] its legitimacy in interpreting the world for others' and 'why it can impose its truth and doctrine on others' (George and Sabelli 1994: 4) that is so breathtaking and so disturbingly arrogant. Possibly the starkest feature is the way in which the Bank operates to deny totally the existence of other alternatives. The force of the Bank's policies lies in the stringent conditions they are able to attach and enforce through their loans, most notably:

> free-market, monetarist economics, free (that is, deregulated) trade, privatisation, reduction of the role of the state and downsizing of the public sector, plus cost/benefit analysis applied to every conceivable object including human life . . . The bottom line of this doctrine, to put it bluntly, is that everything (and everyone) can be assigned a price determined by the market, that everywhere people are, indeed ought to be, motivated by greed and self-interest. They will invariably act upon this self-interest because they are 'out for themselves' and anything goes.
>
> (George and Sabelli 1994: 104 and 107)

The most central and recent aspect of the World Bank's mode of operation has been its principle of 'structural adjustment'. That is to say, the euphemism it uses for imposing what it purports to be 'technical conditions', but which really amount to a stringent package of requirements, inflicted on poorer countries considered to have been profligate. These measures are designed to force economies, considered to have engaged in wanton, reckless, excessive and extravagant behaviour in allowing their public sectors to have become bloated, to come back into line (or become 'adjusted') with those parts of the world (namely, developed countries) that have not been so self-indulgent. Conditions that accompany a government's acceptance of such loans for structural adjustment constitute many of the same policies currently being inflicted upon residents of the so-called developed world (it is hard to know who has influenced who in this merry-go-round world). The following features are rapidly becoming not only the orthodoxy for developing countries, but the trajectories being followed in the developed world, especially as applied to the public sectors in those countries:

- privatisation of government corporations and severe 'downsizing' of public employment and government bureaucracy, exacerbating unemployment tending to affect public service ministries most (health, education, transport, housing, environment et cetera) through drastic budget reductions;
- promotion of exports or raw materials and of export industries to earn foreign exchange; import liberalisation and the elimination of trade barriers or quotas;
- elimination or sharp reduction in subsidies for agriculture, food staples, health care, education, and other areas (generally excluding the military, however);
- restrictive monetary policies and high interest rates to curb inflation;
- a reduction in real wages (especially for low wage earners), which is called 'demand management', also intended to control inflation.

(George and Sabelli 1994: 18–19)

The overall ideology of the World Bank is one that supports the rolling back of the state, deregulation, lowering social spending, cutting the public sector and severely compressing real wages. As George and Sabelli (1994) explain, while the World Bank:

did not invent neo-classical economics, liberalism, [or] free market orthodoxy . . . [it was] however, the first (along with the IMF) to put its doctrine into practice and to convince most of its contemporaries that

the greatest good for the greatest number will necessarily emerge from
its adoption, voluntarily if possible; if not, then under duress.

(p. 72)

All of this is done with the commitment, the assurance, and the self-rein-
forcing culture, codes and rituals typically designed to produce a kind of
divinely inspired religious salvation – it is as if the 'ritual cleansing' (debt
repayment) is only possible if some divinely ordained pathway of natural law
is followed unswervingly. It amounts to the metaphorical equivalent of some
kind of 'neo-conservative, right wing, fundamentalist religious agenda' (p.
96), or in the words of another observer:

> The manner in which the World Bank has presented, promoted and
> defended structural adjustment against its critics closely parallels funda-
> mentalist interpretations of the Bible. The strategies employed by the
> World Bank to guarantee hegemony of its ideology and to deal with
> dissenters also correspond to those of fundamentalism . . . [The Bank]
> not only denies the legitimacy of alternatives, but has actively sought,
> over the past decade, to ensure that all of the options available to devel-
> oping countries have been narrowed to one.
>
> (Mihevc 1992: 4, 12)

The place of the market is abundantly clear in the policies of the World
Bank: 'The laws of the market . . . come to be seen as transcendent, [under-
going] a process of sociological sacralisation. Not only are they given a
higher status, they actually become untouchable, like the laws of nature'
(Santa Ana 1992: 20).

It is an interesting question as to whether the policies of agencies like the
IMF and the World Bank actually work. According to Canadian economist
Michel Chossudovsky (1997), if we take the level of long-term outstanding
debt, then these policies have been a dismal failure:

> The total outstanding long-term debt of developing countries (from
> official and private sources) stood at approximately US $62 billion in
> 1970. It increased sevenfold in the course of the 1970s to reach $481
> billion in 1980. The total debt (including the short-term debt) of devel-
> oping countries stood at more than $2 trillion (1996) a 32-fold increase
> in relation to 1970.
>
> (p. 45)

According to its own analysis of the reasons for its structural adjustment
policies not working, the World Bank responded that this 'represents a
failure to adjust [rather than] a failure of adjustment . . . More Adjustment
– Not Less – Would Help the Poor and the Environment . . . Adjustment is

the necessary first step on the road to sustainable poverty reduction' (p. 17).

Chossudovsky (1997) details the way in which these macro-policies work their way through to education:

> Freezing the number of graduates of the teacher training colleges and increasing the number of pupils per teacher are explicit conditions of World Bank social-sector adjustment loans. The educational budget is curtailed, the number of contact-hours spent by children in school is cut down and a 'double shift system' is installed; one teacher now does the work of two, the remaining teachers are laid off and the resulting savings to the Treasury are funnelled towards the external creditors.
>
> (p. 71)

These 'cost-effective' measures are topped off by giving small loans to enable unemployed teachers 'to set up their own informal "private schools" in rural backyards and urban slums. Under this scheme, the Ministry of Education would nonetheless still be responsible for monitoring "the quality" of teaching' (p. 71).

Intellectual hegemony over educational policy

Connell (1996) recently argued that the influence of international agencies like the World Bank (and their accomplices, like the OECD) is most dramatically felt in areas such as education through what he cryptically described as their 'Tarzan style of policy making':

> A group of hairy-chested individuals swing down from the trees, uttering cries of 'efficiency', 'competition', 'market discipline'; they tip all the huts over, then they swing back into the trees, leaving the villagers to clean up the banana peels.

Connell was referring, of course, to the recent trend worldwide of governments seeking advice from the corporate sector, businessmen and economists as to 'what is wrong with education?' These corporate predators, who draw their ideological sustenance from international agencies like the World Bank, have no difficulty in drawing parallels with what is wrong in the developing world (and the forms of discipline being promulgated there to fix the problem) with what is obviously (in their view) afflicting the public sectors of developed countries. Indeed, they argue, education being one of the largest employers in first world countries has for far too long been treated as a sheltered workshop and is desperately in need of a shot of realism in the form of fiscal austerity and discipline from market forces.

The unfortunate consequence, as Connell (1996) notes, is that these same people are extremely slow to learn about education even when given the opportunity to learn up-close (as they are through being appointed to government Audit Commissions in some countries like Australia and the UK), with the result that they 'overturn a generation of educational debate, negotiation and institution-building'. They seem totally incapable of grasping the possibility that perhaps the market, consumer choice and privatisation may not be the answer to everything, especially in complex processes like education which are in the business of allocating life chances.

While it would be drawing rather a long bow to argue that agencies like the World Bank have actively and directly shaped policy in first world countries in the way they have in the third world, it nevertheless remains the case that these agencies have had a significant influence in shaping the overall policy direction in the first world for more than a decade. They have fostered a policy climate that has been hospitable to competition, social atomisation, economic rationalism, user pays and the depletion of social capital in areas like health, education, welfare and infrastructure – in contexts where 'communities are fragmented and citizens are now politely reminded that they are customers' (Costello 1996: 13). As Costello (1996) put it: 'Government has privatised itself and exchanged civic discourse for managerialism and public transparency for commercial confidentiality. This leaves the market standing alone as the organising principle for society' (p. 13).

The ultimate effect has been that 'competition has become the new public ethic in a society where the common good has been dissolved and replaced by consumer preferences' (Costello 1996: 13). At the level of ideology and discourse, the overwhelming impression is therefore created and sustained that markets are the only game in town.

The kind of 'structural adjustment principles' that underlie the restructuring of education being experienced in Australia and other western countries are clearly being driven by a set of philosophies and ideologies emanating from the World Bank and the IMF.

One of us (Smyth 1993b) has argued thus:

It does not take a lot of sophisticated investigation or analysis to ascertain what these policies have done in the Third World, and what we can expect from them as a consequence in developed countries like Australia. These organisations were 'found guilty' of producing a 'dramatic deterioration of the living standards in the Third World' (West Africa 1988: 1942–3) by the 13-man jury of the Permanent People's Tribunal in West Berlin in September 1988, whose job it was to investigate the effects of the IMF and the World Bank on the disastrous situation in the Third World resulting in over 950 million people living in absolute poverty. This tribunal found that rather than alleviating the problem, these international agencies through their policies have *intensified the problem* such that 'the majority of humankind is worse off now than 10 years ago' (West Africa 1988: 1942). Furthermore, the policies that seem to have produced this situation have been ones of structural adjustment; namely 'cuts in public expenditures, especially in those areas which seem not to be productive, for example social services; cuts in wages; in privatisation . . . [of the public sector]; liberalisation of imports to stimulate competition; devaluation of the currency' (West Africa 1988: 1942–3). In short, while we might need to hedge such connections with a few qualifiers, the overall effect and direction seem clear enough:

There is no doubt that the IMF and the World Bank as international institutions for the regulation of crisis management have failed and that they are therefore responsible for the dramatic deterioration in the living conditions of the peoples in many parts of the world. They serve the interests of the creditors rather than functioning for the benefits of the people of the world.

(West Africa 1988: 1943)

The effect of these policies are a blight on humanity that ought to be roundly and loudly condemned. And it is out of this same ideological ware-house that equally devastating policies are being wrought on education systems around the world aimed at destroying the very notion of state-provided education as we know it (pp. 36–8).

The perceived increasingly 'direct' connection to teaching

From the vantage point of agencies like the World Bank, there is a direct (and overly simplistic) relationship to economic growth. It is a nexus that we all take as something of an axiom of faith, but it is almost impossible to substantiate except at the grossest level. Because there can obviously be so many aspects to education including resources, policy, curriculum, pedagogy, evaluation, student assessment, school organisation, administration, leadership and parent involvement, to mention but a few, the complex interaction of all of these facets makes it impossible to predict with any certainty which mix of them might contribute to economic performance, if any. To suggest that particular teaching strategies might have a discernible impact on economic performance is to stretch the bow beyond what is anywhere near credible. Rather than there being any compelling evidence about what works pedagogically or educationally in terms of 'pay off', we seem to be confronted more by a situation that emerges out of a sense of panic about what might be done to correct intractable worldwide economic deficits – regardless of the more serious social, political and moral deficits confronting societies engaging in restructuring.

Perhaps the analysis is more informative if it is turned around the other way – that is to say, how does broader economic policy operate to shape and inform what passes as educational policy, and in turn influence teaching? We are not looking for definitive answers here, but there can be little doubt that, posed in this way, we are in a climate which is trying to produce directional changes in education. Kelsey (1996) describes the current economic climate as being characterised by: 'market liberalisation and free trade, a narrow monetarist policy, a deregulated labour market, and fiscal restraint' (p. 16). Not only are these trends all underway in western economies, but these broader frame factors are also increasingly coming to surround reforms of teaching in various countries. A good illustration of this is the thrust of reforms to produce 'preferred' individualist remedies – teachers who are self-monitoring, able to explicate clear internal standards, capable of fostering competition and an entrepreneurial spirit in students, and committed to delivering on required systems' learning outcomes – regardless of teachers' own collaborative inclinations (see Hartley 1992).

This 'convergent solution' with its individualist emphasis (Hood 1995: 111) is decidedly at odds with another set of thrusts that has a much greater degree of centralised steering – like national curricula, national and statewide testing, universal schemes of teacher appraisal, and the move towards uniform benchmarks and standards – all of which are, of course, highly susceptible to sabotage by 'egalitarian' tendencies whose commitment is to 'over-ride markets . . . in the hands of local collectivities' (Hood 1995: 108).

If the image policy makers, politicians and economists convey of teaching is of an occupation that should be harnessed more securely to making schools contribute to economic growth, then this is not an image that the teaching profession holds of itself. The view that teaching requires increasing managerialism, tighter specification of outcomes, greater curriculum prescription, more testing of student achievement, enhanced surveillance, making schools more competitive and market-responsive, and making individually accountable places attentive to 'national priorities' is not a view eagerly or widely embraced by teachers themselves. Indeed, teachers put a quite different set of constructions on their work.

Herein lies one of the great paradoxes of teaching – those at a distance from it have quite different construals of the way it is and should be, from those who live and work in teaching. Teachers have a set of images and predispositions about their work that tends to focus around 'interpersonal dimensions' ('relationships with young children and colleagues') and 'personal' aspects ('the intellectual satisfaction of the work' or 'the feeling of being isolated as a classroom teacher') (Warton *et al.* 1992).

Riding over the top of teachers, for that is what it is, and not seeking their understandings of what might feasibly change (if anything) in respect of their work, generates some interesting questions. For example:

- who is legitimately qualified to determine what is admissible as teaching?
- what happens when teachers are troubled by educational policy approaches that would dismember and dismantle their teaching into 'bits and pieces' as if such deconstruction were natural and common sense?
- where do these reductionist policies leave teachers who see relational aspects as being the core work of teaching?
- what happens when teachers are more interested in representing their work in terms of experiential, constructed and localised cultures of teaching, rather than according to outcomes, criteria, standards, performance indicators or other economic rationalist benchmarks?
- what happens when policy is something that is 'experienced in' or 'grounded in' localised definitions of teaching, rather than calibrated against centrally devised national economic imperatives?

In other words, there is a world of difference between proclamations by international agencies who deem to know, and the lived experiences of teachers who are continually reframing the discursive boundaries of their teaching as a normal part of the work. If we are to understand teaching we need to see it in the wider context of the forces that would shape and mould it.

'MORAL PANIC' AS THE BASIS FOR EDUCATIONAL CHANGE

A useful analogy

While there still remains some question as to whether Stanley Cohen (1972) actually coined the term 'moral panic' in his *Folk Devils and Moral Panics*, or whether the term is more rightly attributable to his collaborator Jock Young (1971) a year earlier, there is no doubt that it offers an intriguing way into analysing changes as complex as those that have recently been visited upon schools and teaching. The essence of Cohen's argument, picked up and considerably expanded by Goode and Ben-Yehuda (1994), is that extensive social change often emanates from seeming threats or fears that 'offer striking departures from empirical reality' (p. ix). In other words, even extensive social change can lack a substantial basis or foundation to it and, at best, can be a gross exaggeration in terms of an appropriate social response. Goode and Ben-Yehuda (1994) cite the Scottish poet, journalist and songwriter Charles Mackay, who published a book in 1841 entitled *Memoirs of Extraordinary Popular Delusions* in which he described such phenomena as:

the Crusades, prophecies, astrology, fortune-telling, the witch mania of
Renaissance Europe, belief in haunted houses, popular admiration for
thieves and bandits, political and religious control of hair and beard
styles, and 'tulipomania', or the economic craze that gripped the
Netherlands in the seventeenth century, which entailed buying and
selling tulip bulbs at incredibly high and, supposedly, inflated prices.
Mackay argued that nations, 'like individuals, have their whims and
their peculiarities, their seasons of excitement and recklessness, when
they care not what they do'. Whole communities, he asserted, 'suddenly
fix their minds upon one object, and then go mad in its pursuit;
millions of people become simultaneously impressed with one delusion,
and run after it, until their attention is caught by some new folly more
captivating than the first'.

(p. 2)

These are not grounds, either, for acting in dismissive ways, for to do that
is to miss the point that even apparently erratic, impulsive, sometimes
barbaric social behaviour requires close and further investigation:

They should not be dismissed as unreasonable, irrational or
pathological . . . In short, these fears and concerns are part and parcel of
the human condition, an expression of human frailty. We are all subject
to them; all societies are wracked by them. An investigation of their
bases and dynamics will help illuminate the bases and dynamics of
society generally.

(p. x)

Displacement of the real problem

We will return to this notion of moral panic, in a little more detail, shortly.
But, for the moment, suffice to say that what is happening *to* schools (and
other educational institutions, like universities) amounts to little short of a
moral panic fed by a widespread and mantra-like rehearsal of so-called
economic arguments.

It is given fullest expression in the form of a wholesale displacement of
the indigenous or inherent discourses of schools and a positing in their place
of an alien, synthetic and dependent economic rationalist discourse about
curriculum, pedagogy and classroom practice. What is breathtaking in its
implications is the almost universal silence and lack of concerted collective
action to the intrusion of managerialist discourses into schools – but as
Weber (1996) has noted, 'The less one worries about one's use of language,
the more one is subjected to its effects' (p. 28). It is not that we are
mourning the passing of indigenous educational discourses *per se* (although
no doubt a compelling case could be made for that), but rather we object to

the redefinition and subordination of social and political values to the twin gods of the economy, namely, of producing profits and operating efficiency.

'Notions such as "accountability", "responsibility", "transparency" are all being redefined to assume a direct, fiduciary significance . . . [W]e find a propensity of managerial, administrative and professional discourse to define [schools and educational institutions] in terms of [their] "mission" [narrowly defined in utilitarian terms]' (Weber 1996: 29).

Weber (1996) makes the wider argument that what is purged and lost is the capacity and space for independent thought, judgement, debate and action – in its place is deposited a pervading 'dependence . . . upon the prevailing economic system' (p. 29) where any semblance of having a 'mission' is taken to mean 'being "accountable" to those who pay for [education], whether these be understood to be large corporations, individual taxpayers or even students' (p. 29).

If there is any grieving to be done then it ought to be over the manner in which proud and publicly resourced educational systems in some parts of the world have been dismantled or else made so thoroughly and completely submissive, so quickly, and with so little public resistance and outcry over their loss. We suspect that many people have probably not even noticed their passing. Part of the wider explanation for this indifference and lack of action can be found in the latest ugly buzzword, 'globalisation'. Again, we found that Weber (1996) provides a clear and succinct explanation:

> Globalisation, which refers to the increasing importance of international markets and competition for national economies, designates the progressive intrusion of the economic rationality of a profit-driven system into areas that had hitherto not been entirely subordinated to such constraints . . .
>
> To remain 'competitive' in the global market, the budget deficit of the State must be reduced. And to reduce the budget deficit, there seem for many government policy makers no other way than that of reducing public spending, such as education, health, transport, communications and so on, or by privatising them, which is to say turning them over to corporations whose finality is not that of providing a service but rather of making a profit. The only government 'service' that seems to remain largely, although not always, exempt from such reductionism is the military budget.
>
> (p. 29)

A significant point Weber (1996) makes – and which we take up in detail later – is that, 'In view of the nature of globalisation, it would be a grievous mistake to see the tendency of the economically "developed" countries to reduce State support to education as merely a quantitative and temporary adjustment' (p. 29). In Weber's (1996) view it is the *nature* of the subordination occurring here that is most troubling – a shift from the 'social nexus' to the 'cash nexus' and all that brings with it as the 'dominant medium in which power relations operate' (p. 29). As he says:

> These relations no longer present themselves as primarily 'political' in the traditional sense of the term, which associated 'politics' with the sovereignty of nation States. Instead the political perspectives and options of nation States and their citizens are increasingly subordinated to the exigencies of transnational corporations run by self-interested bureaucracies.
>
> (p. 29)

Genesis of the contemporary panic

The moral panic about the supposed failure of western economic systems and the implication of schools in this has its source in documents like the OECD's *Governance in Transition: Public Sector Management Reforms in OECD Countries* (1995), and earlier variants of it, which provides the environment within which to incubate what it calls a number of 'concerns' which are then picked up and acted upon by policy makers in education (and other social areas) around the world – like the 'impact of globalisation, a perception that public sector performance is inferior to that of the private sector, limits to the growth of the public sector given budgetary constraints, a decline in public confidence in the ability of government to solve economic and social problems and so on' (Mitchell 1996: 18–19).

The answer to the question of why we so readily reach for a technological solution, through what is an economic response, lies deep in the collective psyche, which finds the notion of crisis the best way to deal with it. But as one commentator put it recently in respect of higher education, and the parallel applies equally to schooling: 'Because a crisis of resources preoccupies us . . . there is a serious danger of overlooking a deeper crisis of values' (Reid 1996: iii). We have a history of being so obsessed with having to control the physical world through scientific means that issues in the social and political world are in danger of being treated as mere adjuncts or extensions. Conservative politics feeds these deeply held beliefs, repeatedly repackaging through policy utterances concepts and objectives like the following, which are unproblematically advanced as if they were self-evident truths: 'client-focussed services, best practice, benchmarking, contracting out, corporatisation, and privatisation of many government services' (Mitchell 1996: 17).

Arguments are put simplistically, misleadingly, mischievously and partially so as to construct a crisis that then requires a particular ideologically driven set of policies and solutions to correct it. To take Australia and New Zealand as particular examples of advanced cases of where issues of structural adjustment have been taken on extremely seriously and vigorously over the past 10–15 years, it is clear that in those countries the 'economic rationalist' policies adhere around a number of key notions, summarised as:

- public sector organisations are conceived of as producers that convert inputs into outputs of goods and services;
- the public act as 'consumers' or 'customers' who consume these outputs;
- the efficient delivery of outputs is the principal measure of success, where greater efficiency is produced by reducing the resource cost of producing a given quality of goods and services; and
- competition among providers or producers is the best way of maximising efficiency.

(Hamilton 1996: 29–30)

As Hamilton (1996) notes, the difficulty with this view is that:

It conceives of society as being comprised of individuals whose welfare is derived principally from the consumption of goods and services . . . The primary function of government is thus to facilitate the operation of markets by ensuring that 'market failures' are minimised, either by providing the framework for competition to operate effectively in private markets or, where absolutely essential, by public provision of goods and services that the private market cannot provide, or cannot provide efficiently.

(p. 30)

Viewed in this way, and herein lies its major problem because other views are excluded or denigrated, government becomes:

an institution whose function is to fill the cracks in the system of private markets. Government is seen as the provider of the residual. This view is entirely consistent with the belief that society essentially consists of self-seeking individuals pursuing their interests in private markets, a world in which civil society is, if not otiose then certainly secondary, and in which the public sector always represents a potential threat to individual liberty.

(Hamilton 1996: 31)

The policy process thus becomes one of exhortation by government for organisations to be 'client-focused' so as to 'empower citizens', but as Hamilton (1996) notes, 'These are not services provided collectively by citizens to the citizenry through their elected governments; they are services delivered by corporations to individual customers' (p. 31). Wallace (1993) labels this process as a 'discourse of derision' by which he means the manner in which incomplete views of social reality are constructed to serve particular political interests. He draws from Lawton (1992a) who:

> suggests that ideologies relating to education include beliefs about human nature and society, leading to more specific moral views on the purpose of education and the appropriateness of teaching methods, which link with teachers' preferences about the curriculum and how it is taught.
>
> (Wallace 1993: 325)

Because of the partial nature of these often simplified and distorted representations of why schools exist and what it is that teachers do, this is a ploy that is activated as 'an object of derision' (Wallace 1993: 325) that governments can claim to act upon in order to 'exorcise' the 'canker' (p. 325) – mostly of what is regarded as elements of so-called progressivism that have directly or indirectly led to the current unsatisfactory state of affairs.

These are arguments and issues dealt with in much more detail by writers like Stretton and Orchard (1994) and Kelsey (1995), and because the crisis that is being manufactured goes to the heart of whether government and public administration is being corrupted, these authors should be consulted for the depth they provide to the debate.

The moral crisis constructed around education and the economy (at least in advantaged countries) goes as follows:

- the international restructuring of capitalism that has occurred post-World War Two has resulted in substantial real movements of capital, resources and jobs off-shore to take advantage of lower-cost labour and less stringent regulations of various types;
- this has resulted in the serious depletion and loss of skilled and unskilled jobs in the advantaged world;
- to continue to operate profitably in this deregulated global economy requires that inefficient work practices, industry protection, labour market regulation, high wages and anti-competitive practices all be abandoned and replaced by competitive ('world best') practices;
- to limit job losses further, the advantaged world needs to pursue a path of high-tech-led recovery in which technology is able to out-compete low off-shore labour;
- education is to be the centre-piece of the new technologically led 'skills formation' approach;
- to streamline advantaged economies further, resources should be stripped from public enterprises and activities and used to stimulate private entrepreneurial activity as much as possible;

- the role of schools in all of this is crucial, as they will be required to foster both the new attitudes as well as the high-tech skills – the starting point will be moving education increasingly out of being a public state-run activity, to being a private 'for profit activity';
- teaching in all of this should reflect the new attitudes and values of education as a commodity, and any vestiges of the old 'dependent' culture expunged;
- one of the most effective ways of doing this is to promote a 'consumerist', 'commodified', 'private benefit', 'user pays' view of education, so that it becomes indistinguishable from any other commodity that has a price, and that is bought and sold in the marketplace;
- the final way in which this is to be achieved swiftly and efficiently is through the creation of a 'discourse of commodity production' (Reid 1996: iii) within the administrative/management levels of education and this will percolate throughout through significant 'rewordings' of key activities and relationships.

According to Goode and Ben-Yehuda (1994), for a moral panic to be established certain indicators or conditions need to be evident. For example: a *concern* (a measurable real basis upon which a dominant group feels their behaviour is threatened by the actions of others – for instance, in the form of a 'folk devil' expressed as cheap labour costs off-shore); *hostility* (where the concern can be expressed as some potential harm likely to threaten the values or interests of the dominant group – for instance, a threatened decline in exports with an accompanying plunge in standard of living); *consensus* (where the concern is widespread enough not to fizzle out – for instance the media can continue to massage the story about the evil effects of high-cost local labour and its inefficiencies compared with overseas); *disproportionality* (where there is outright exaggeration and fabrication of the extent of the threat – in the economic case, governments are very skilled at making budget deficits, balance of payments figures and indebtedness appear vastly worse than they actually are); and finally, *volatility* (where the concern can be turned on and off again, as required – the press delights in advanced countries in winding up the level of fear whenever the government decides to issue the latest set of economic statistics or indicators – these can be done at will).

Relevance for teaching

It is not hard to see how this broader construction of the problem has been used to appropriate schools and teaching through the claim that they must be 'failing the system'. This is made the more convincing when the problem is seen to impact most noticeably on the demonstrable inability of large numbers of youth to obtain a foothold in the labour market. Teaching methods and the overall circumstances in which youth are schooled become a convenient scapegoat for a wider economy that has restructured away many employment possibilities previously open to school-leavers.

In some measure at least, the direction of educational change has its origins in the 'policy borrowing' (Finegold *et al.* 1993) as 'like-minded governments are facing similar problems . . . [and the] economic discourse has replaced the earlier focus on equity in educational provision and is now the dominant paradigm for policy discussions in education . . . in the English-speaking world' (Vickers 1994: 25).

The following chapter shows the extent to which there has been policy borrowing, even in a context where there is no compulsion to do so. As Vickers (1994) notes, this has been the medium by which a:

> 'bottom-up' process in which workable ideas were gathered into the national debate has now been replaced by a 'top down' managerialism, whose long-term objective includes the development of a national system for monitoring student achievement . . . Thus, the framework for educational discussion . . . is now dominated by a transnational paradigm in which education is reconstructed as human capital formation and is largely viewed as a strategy for improving national economic competitiveness.
>
> (p. 28)

Vickers (1994) points out that resolving the 'problem', at least in the case of Australia, has been at the expense of creating a significant tension between teaching and administration as the federal government selectively purged and filtered out those aspects of the OECD agenda that were pedagogically oriented in favour of those that emphasised 'the economic function of education [so as to use] this agenda to increase managerial control' (p. 29). Even when given the choice about involvement in 'projects', which is the *modus operandi* of member countries in the OECD, the Australian government 'has participated most actively in those projects that connect education to the economy, and has shown least interest in projects concerned with teaching, curriculum and learning' (Vickers 1994: 36).

These are issues we want to take up in more detail in the following chapter, but suffice for the moment to say that the way the supposed 'problem' and its alleged 'solution' are constructed is not for altogether altruistic reasons: 'Studies have shown that when politicians want to mobilise support for change it is essential they attribute their ideas to some authoritative source' (Vickers 1994: 29).

One aspect of teachers' work that is of growing concern deserves particular attention not only because of the gender composition of teaching as an occupation, but because of the gender-blindness of many of the economic policies just alluded to which impact so severely on schools and teaching.

TEACHING AS GENDERED WORK

Acker (1995a) in a wide-ranging review of gender and teachers' work notes that it has become increasingly common in recent times for the media to engage in another form of moral panic around the increasing feminisation of the teaching force. Claims are made as to the lack of appropriate role models, the difficulty of attracting sufficient males into teaching, and the general de-professionalisation accompanying the gender imbalance. As Acker (1995a) points out, this is an extremely 'slippery' topic, 'potentially enormous', and difficult to pin down because of the multiple directions in which gender intersects with so many aspects of schools and the work of teaching. We would add to these observations that trying to analyse gender, especially by two male researchers, is a potential minefield. Our task is made a little easier than Acker's, but only slightly so, by the fact that we are looking at how the interpretation of the notion of skill operates to frame the gendered nature of teachers' work, and in this we align ourselves with scholars who take a labour process approach to analysing teaching. The overall difficulty, however, with the field of teachers' work is that it is so fragmented, and 'much mainstream research has proceeded without featuring gender, and often without considering its impact' (p. 142), but this is beginning to change, as Acker (1995a) points out in the following lengthy quote:

> The increase in feminist scholarship over the past 20 or so years has led to an alternative body of work that makes gender central, usually by researching the experiences of women teachers. So we now have studies that take up questions such as the nature of the barriers women encounter in seeking career advancement; whether women have distinctive approaches to aspects of teaching such as caring, power, leadership; and how schools as organizations operate gender regimes that deal with sexuality. Most, if not all, concerns of educational researchers about teachers' work can be tackled with gender in mind; for example, oft-identified features of teaching such as individuality and isolation can be looked at in terms of what roles women are (or were) expected to perform inside and outside of teaching. Some of these questions were featured in older, mainstream research, not from a feminist perspective but from one that incorporated commonsense ideas about the difference between the sexes. Thus, teaching might be seen as women's work because women are natural caretakers of children; bureaucratic controls and male management might seem the logical outgrowth of an occupation largely composed of women; and lack of collegiality might be an expected concomitant of women's devotion to family roles assumed to be in competition with commitment to teaching. The gender-sensitive research of the past few decades has swept many of these shibboleths

away, subjecting them to critical scrutiny and revision from a perspective that starts from taking seriously women's standpoints and the social circumstances that circumscribe their actions, as well as investing women with the capacity to be creative social actors devising strategies within the constraints of their situations.

(p. 142)

The point we want to advance from our particular vantage point of examining what is happening to the changing nature of teachers' skills is that there is another kind of moral panic – that which congregates around the claim that teachers have to be reskilled in particular ways so as to shoulder their increasing responsibility for the restoration of sagging international economic competitiveness. But, the difficulty with this common-sense view of skill (and skills formation) as applied to teaching is that it is not a straightforward notion at all – indeed, it represents a kind of fusion of the educational and industrial relations meaning of these terms. Where in educational terms 'skill' has become a human capital concept signifying to employers some kind of 'depersonalised "indicators" of the "outcomes" of learning' (Junor 1988: 135), in industrial relations terms 'skills' signify 'masculine', 'Anglophone' hierarchies of work culture in which the work of women, people of colour and other minorities is largely excluded or marginalised. This is particularly important with regard to teaching where, as Jackson (1991) argues, skills are not purely 'technical', but 'social' and above all 'gendered' relationships. She says, for example, if we start out from this point, then:

the commonsense quality of the concept of skill quickly begins to fade. It ceases to appear as a tangible entity, or a capacity for work that is possessed by some people and not by others and passed along through training. Rather, we see that the concept of skill involves a complex interplay of technical and social forces . . . [and] the interweaving of the technical organization of work with hierarchies of power and privilege between men and women, whites and non-whites, old and young.

(p. 9)

The point being made is that the very definition of skills and what constitutes its presence or absence is largely a political process in which the term itself has been 'emptied of . . . tangible content and imposed upon certain types of work by virtue of the sex and power of the workers who perform it' (Jackson 1991: 12). Discussions about what constitutes skills or skilled work are, therefore, highly charged political debates about how particular groups of workers benefit from the constructed hierarchies of work, while others are disadvantaged (Blackmore 1992).

The artificially constructed boundary between teaching and administration in the work of schools is a good example. As Jackson (1991) has noted, in this regard, 'the character of work in female-dominated occupations is systematically obscured and understated by routine bureaucratic mechanisms for job definition' (p. 19). There is a 'politics of underskilling' operating here in which what is considered important depends upon who is doing the defining and how well that definition has been made to stick as part of the political process (Jackson 1991: 13). Out of class aspects of leadership, organisation and administration of teaching have always been historically valued over and above the fact-to-face work of teaching students – work which happens to be done overwhelmingly by women (Blackmore 1992). It is a fact that women are over-represented in what are regarded as lower-status (which means, lower-paying) jobs, while men are over-represented in supposedly highly skilled managerial aspects of the job (Apple 1986: 56).

A gender analysis of teachers' work (which we are not equipped to do) would involve 'calling attention to the obvious and subtle ways in which cultural beliefs about women and men influence the nature of teachers' work and the perceptions others hold of it' (Acker 1995a: 114). This point is well illustrated in how the nurturing nature of primary and early childhood teaching is often embedded in portrayals of the gender-skewed nature of teaching in those sites (Clark 1990; Biklen 1995; Acker 1995b; Sachs 1997). Another dimension of this occurs when women are allocated gender-specific tasks in school; tasks which emphasise nurturance and de-emphasise those organisational skills that come to have priority for promotion to senior positions in the school (Clark 1990; Sampson 1991).

In quoting Joan Acker, Sandra Acker (1995a) highlights how school workplaces are gendered in 'divisions of labour, behaviour and location; in symbols, images, and language; in conventions of interaction, in consequences for individual identity; and in the underlying logic, rules, and structures of the organisation' (p. 132). The focus on the caring element of teaching, when it is specifically portrayed as a fundamental characteristic of the work of teachers in locations where teachers are mostly women, is a case in point. The discursive construction of teaching as care and as women's work is unhelpful when it decontextualises the care because of the likelihood of the 'essentialist' trap (Acker 1995b). We recognise that the challenge is not to assume that women's experiences can be in any way generalised or subsumed in the development of knowledge based on the experiences of men. In slipping from 'gender and teachers' work' to 'women and teachers' work' there exists a trap that other sociological lenses like ethnicity, class, sexuality, race, age, and so on, are rendered invisible (Acker 1995a). The invisibility of such lenses in the study of teachers' work, other than in profiling statistics, is common.

Assumptions that in more feminist times – or at least at a time when the gendered division of labour in workplaces is better understood – it is easier for women to gain higher status promotions to administrative positions (Sampson 1991), or that women desire upward mobility in the hierarchical structure of schools (Casey 1992; Limerick and Lingard 1995; Blackmore 1996), do not appear to be supported by research data. Studies have shown that women have been unable to use those career strategies relied upon by men and that behaviours and attitudes suited to maximise opportunities in such strategies have not been legitimate ones for women to exhibit (Acker 1995a). By way of an explanation Blackmore (1995) speaks of a 're-masculinisation' even in a context of an increasing feminisation of the teaching force. This takes the form of pronounced tendencies at the policy level towards dominating, hierarchical, managerialist discourses of administration and leadership in schools. This new gendered division of labour produces:

> a tendency for polarisation between the re-masculinisation at the 'hard core' of the financial and policy centre of newly devolved systems, and the feminisation and de-professionalisation of teaching and middle management at the 'soft edges' close to the chalkface.
>
> (p. 49)

Lingard (1995) makes a broadly similar argument in speaking of 'gendered policy making inside the state' (p. 136). According to Lingard (1996) this 're-gendering of educational policy' produces a policy culture reflected in 'the existence of a highly masculinist culture within the power structures of the bureaucracy' (Lingard 1995: 147).

In this chapter we have canvassed some of the wider although generally unacknowledged forces operating to reconstruct teachers' work. We have attempted to show something of the complexity of the genesis of current changes, how they are largely untested, and the ways in which they have material effects as evidenced in and through the gendered nature of teachers' work. Because our analysis has focused on the broader genealogy of educational reforms we have not been able to bring some of the detail into focus; that will be the task of the next chapter in which we will look at themes like vocationalism, quality and enterprise as these provide a window on what is happening to the work of teaching.

Chapter 4

Teachers doing their 'economic' work

AN IDEOLOGY OF PRODUCTION OR THE PRODUCTION OF AN IDEOLOGY?

In this chapter we want to explore the basis for much of the educational reform that has come to surround teachers' work in the past two decades or so. The case has been made from several quarters that since the 1960s there has been growing disaffection and disenchantment worldwide from parents and the wider community with schooling, such that: 'There exists today an "informed scepticism" about educational change that distinguishes the 1980s from the 1960s and has led to the declining appeal of grand principles and all-embracing educational theories' (OECD 1989: 136). The evidential basis for this alleged shift has been made less than clear on most occasions but, notwithstanding, significant changes have proceeded as if the claims had a solid foundation.

The three aspects of recent educational reform that have caught our attention are: (a) an infatuation with issues of relevance of schooling for the world of work, and its expression in the 'new vocationalism'; (b) the emergence of 'enterprise culture' as a convenient rallying point for conservative educational restorationists; and (c) from an earlier period, starting in the early 1980s, 'quality' as a dominant theme for educational policy discourse – one used with considerable force to advance the debate about what education should look like after what commentators on the New Right label the permissive and profligate 1960s and 1970s.

Probably the most pervasive and consistent themes and arguments put in respect of the need for the reform of teaching and education are that it is necessary in order to satisfy the requirements of a rapidly changing world of work. The argument is generally couched in terms of the alleged shift from Fordist to post-Fordist forms of organisation and production, most notably, the move to short production lines, niche marketing, team-work and partnerships, flatter hierarchies, outsourcing, and the construction and management of images and impressions. (For an elaboration of this 'new work order', see Gee *et al.* 1996 and Kumar 1995; and, for

more detailed accounts of how this is worked through in educational
reforms, see Bowe *et al.* 1992; Ball 1994; Gewirtz *et al.* 1995; Hartley
1992; Welch 1996; Smyth 1996a.)

The 'new vocationalism' as an educational response

In respect of teaching, arguments about the so-called 'new work order' boil
down to whether the wider forces of globalisation, international competitiveness and economic production are forcing and requiring the new
marketised, consumerist and vocationalised relationships within schools and
teaching we continually hear about, or whether there are other possible
interpretations. One possibility that deserves consideration and exploration
is that proffered by Moore (1987), who argues that what has become known
as the 'new vocationalism' in schooling may in point of fact be more of a
cover for, and not a direct response to, the economic forces at all – rather it is
an expression of a:

> new 'hidden curriculum' of the possessive individualism of market
> economics [which] reflects political and ideological imperatives, rather
> than the immediate needs of the economy. The 'new vocationalism' is
> seen as an ideology of production regulating education rather than as an
> educational ideology servicing production.
>
> (p. 227)

Some compelling reasons can be advanced for this alternative explanation.
Moore (1987) argues that:

> The term 'new vocationalism' can be taken as a convenient convention
> for glossing over a complex set of interrelated developments ranging
> [in the UK context] from the Technical and Vocational Education
> Initiative (TVEI), the Certificate of Pre-Vocational Education (CPVE),
> the Youth Training Scheme (YTS) and the General Certificate of
> Secondary Education (GCSE), to more specific practices such as
> profiling and wider institutional arrangements such as targeted
> funding, the interventions of the Manpower Services Commission
> (MSC) within the educational system and the National Council for
> Vocational Qualifications (NCVQ).
>
> (p. 228)

Constellations like these are bound together and held in place by:

> a general movement towards an occupationalist integration between the
> education system and the occupational system, mediated by a

behavioural approach to skill training and supported by new institutional arrangements which construct, legitimate and enforce new definitions of knowledge.

(p. 228)

Moore (1987) explains that the 'hidden curriculum' behind notions like the 'new vocationalism' can be captured in what MacPherson (1962, cited in Moore 1987: 231) labelled the 'political theory of possessive individualism'. Put simply, this view holds that individuals are composed of personal capacities made up of bundles of skills, and that they operate in society as 'proprietors of their own capacities' in exchange relationships with each other. The role of government is to provide for the protection of this property and facilitate the orderly conditions under which exchange can occur. In other words, the role of government is restricted to setting up pedagogical processes to enable the creation and delivery of skills modules and to provide for subsequent accreditation. Clearly, within such arrangements, education comprises processes both to promote 'possessive individualism' while also emphasising 'methodological individualism' – what Wellington (1993) calls the 'press for relevance', 'transferable and core skills', skills that prepare for 'rapid technological change', as well as processes that improve 'attitudes to work and industry' – ideas that all sound decidedly old-fashioned, protectionist and outmoded in these new times of the unfettered and free reign of market forces!

Moore (1987) says a 'new hegemonic form' is thus created with which to restructure the educational field – 'its discourses, practices, institutional arrangements and principles of power, control and legitimation' (p. 228). It is not so much that classroom and teaching practices are immediately and directly changed through official proclamations or centrally produced materials and curricula (although that can happen in the case of some individual teachers), but rather that teachers are likely selectively and pragmatically to appropriate what they see as being useful to satisfy 'the specific needs of particular groups of students at given times' (p. 228). In other words, 'There is no simple top-down imposition of any particular approach or policy' (p. 228), but rather a more gradual creation of:

attempts to define the effective characteristics of an ideology which is in the process of acquiring a hegemonic position within the educational field and which, therefore, can both control the agenda of the educational debate and, by becoming the orthodoxy, force liberal and radical opponents into a heterodox position which undermines their credibility and legitimacy

(p. 229)

'Enterprise culture' as the new educational organiser

Another good illustration of the emergence of a new hegemonic form is the concept of 'enterprise culture' which has entered the educational discourse in recent times. This new darling of the educational conservatives in the 1990s has supplanted vocationalism as the glitz word of the 1980s – a new signifier and organiser of all that is considered virtuous and good educationally speaking. As Wellington (1993) notes, this is in part a language game, as the phraseology and the lexicon shift effortlessly from vocationalism to enterprise, with all of the connotations that the latter has about increased emphasis on personal and individual qualities of: initiative, drive, determination, self-monitoring, independence, autonomy, self-reliance, risk-taking, decision making, flexibility and leadership.

Coffield (1990) says there is no consensus about the meaning of enterprise: 'We are not dealing with a tightly defined concept but a farrago of hurrah words' (Wellington 1993: 34). Vocationalism is 'out' because it is considered to place too much emphasis on social and life skills preparation and focus around a collective emphasis, and insufficient on 'competence' as a response to the need for enterprise initiatives, which are on the ascendancy. One of the advantages of a confusing word like 'enterprise' in education is that it is so ambiguous it can be accommodated to all manner of divergent perspectives. As Watts (1993) shows, the political power of a word like enterprise sits comfortably across the spectrum: with governments finding the notion of 'entrepreneurship' acceptable because of the way it conjures up notions of people sustaining activities on their own; with employers who are happy with educating students to 'work in enterprises'; and, with progressives who resonate with the adjectival meaning of 'enterprising skills' (p. 47). Indeed, enterprise is a very potent political word because it can be 'unpacked and used for all sorts of different purposes' (Watts 1993: 48). In Watts' (1993) view: 'there [is] something for everyone in the notion of "enterprise". It . . . provide[s] a rich base for education–business partnerships supported by government, with each putting the frame they prefer . . . around it' (p. 48). It serves to reinforce the power of language, too: 'If you can find words which have that degree of ambiguity, you can form alliances which you wouldn't be able to form otherwise, building upon that ambiguity . . . Ambiguous language can be enormously influential' (Watts 1993: 49).

'Quality' – the longest-lasting educational aerosol word

'Quality' has for some time been a canopy or umbrella term within which officially to house a limited and constrained set of interpretations about the condition of education and schooling, and a basis upon which to warehouse an equally limiting, atomistic and impoverished set of prescriptions as to what ought legitimately to constitute the work of teachers and schooling. From its beginnings in the mid-1980s, quality has been used effectively as a necessary albeit decidedly ambiguous ingredient for a much needed educational restoration. Organisations like the OECD have featured prominently in propagating an international discourse about quality schooling – one that appears natural, common sense, and as having all the right hallmarks of institutional respectability about it. Documents like *The Teacher Today* (OECD 1990), following close on the heels of *Schools and Quality: An International Report* (OECD 1989), make the point repeatedly about the absence of 'quality' from schools, and how teachers need to be reconstructed so as to restore it or acquire more of it. The reason we cryptically describe quality as an aerosol word is that it has infiltrated the educational discourse in precisely the manner of an aerosol deodorant – it is sprayed around! Furthermore, its timely appearance – coinciding as it does with the fiscal retreat by governments around the world from universal and equitable provision of public education so as to allow the market to do its work – has meant that quality has the fragrance of a bouquet word used to cover up the slightly offensive odour surrounding the decay of the public provision of schooling.

A useful but by no means complete way of portraying the way quality has been constructed (and on some occasions contested) as a vehicle for carrying educational discourse, can be gleaned from *Schools and Quality*, and we intend to highlight some of its key themes and elements. We should offer a caveat at the outset – while we do not regard international consortia like the OECD as being the *only* or necessarily the most influential of players in framing educational reform, they have certainly been *one* of the more influential, and while we will never be able to ascertain accurately the full extent of educational policy borrowing from them by governments, we cannot be dismissive of what appears to be their likely widespread effects as policy disseminators and legitimators. Our thesis would be that the OECD has been an important rallying point since the mid-1980s as an international clearinghouse for a number of highly questionable 'solutions' to what is wrong with education – most of which, as it turns out, constitute little more than a slogan system under the umbrella of 'quality'. We will explain this in more detail in a moment.

While much play is made in the Introduction to *Schools and Quality* (OECD 1989) about the importance of not having 'a single, tight definition of "quality"', the need for 'a more detached perspective', a 'restrained aim [so as] to analyse differing interpretations of quality', wanting only to 'inform the debate' rather than 'provid[ing] policy makers with *the* right answers', or crafting 'a standard model or plan that can be implemented in a "top-down" fashion', and the difficulty of 'apply[ing] these goals across

OECD countries', it seems to us that when the report is considered as a whole, this lamenting and handwringing has more to do with the conceptual and practical difficulties of imposing a view than it has to do with any deep-seated pre-disposition not to do it *per se*. The reason we say this is that in the latter sections of the report, once the messy conceptual issues are temporarily laid to rest, the writers get down in remarkably business-like fashion to what looks like a laying out of a quite specific cachet of 'particular policies and practices' (p. 11).

It seems that 'quality' was settled upon by the OECD as an organising construct for what needed to be *done to schools* (our deliberate choice of term) to emphasise the required shift in ideology from a focus on materialist expansion that had characterised the first three post-war decades, to a sharp break with that. Quality was used as a contradistinction to what was regarded (in the veiled terms of the report) as an overdue extension of the worldwide materialist extension of resources to schooling. Reference is made in the report to an earlier OECD document *Compulsory Schooling in a Changing World* (1983), in which the term 'quality' first appeared as a counter to the continuation of 'tangible improvements'.

From the beginning, the emphasis on quality in *Schools and Quality* was, therefore, couched in terms of the need for 'reactions to the era of growth' (p. 15) – where there is only the feeblest of attempts by the writers of the report to disguise their endorsement of the view that as 'OECD economies faltered in the 1970s . . . the simple formula "more education, more prosperity" had been found wanting . . . The link between education and social mobility no longer appeared self-evident' (p. 16). In barely disguised glee, the report goes on to describe the fall in educational expenditures that occurred in OECD countries along with the questions being raised (we are not sure by whom) about 'value for money' and 'how efficient schools were'. From this œuvre, we regard it as a relatively short step to the ideas the OECD sees as the preferred policy options, most notably:

- quality couched in terms of economic imperatives (p. 19);
- qualified support for the re-emergence of 'human capital' views (p. 20);
- the importance of education attending to the 'phenomenon of international competition' (p. 21); and,
- increased pressures on schools for greater accountability (p. 24).

While many of these are carefully hedged and qualified in the report it is hard not to form the opinion that the OECD was not altogether opposed to what it regarded as these self-evident and natural tendencies, and that indeed some of them might not only have been worth while but considerably overdue.

The key themes addressed in the report are conceptually and practically separated and fall into the categories of: curriculum; teachers; school organisation; appraisal, assessment and monitoring; and resources. As with most policy positions, what is explicitly revealed, focused upon and included, is as revealing as the silences and what remains unspoken. In this document there is an overwhelming ideological and conceptual consistency about the frame factors considered necessary for an undeclared and preferable process of remaking teaching – it comes through in the tenor and the tone of the document and in its cultural portrayal of teaching as a subservient technical process. The remedy for the slippage in standards and rigour of teaching lies, it says, in the provision of an entitlement to the 'basics of curriculum for all – a core' (p. 55), in a context where there is greater 'relevance to modern society' (p. 55) through 'work-oriented and practical studies' (p. 61), and with an abiding emphasis on 'clear planning objectives and evaluation procedures' (p. 63). Teachers are to be brought back into line, it says, by 'attracting good recruits' (p. 72), preparing them 'effectively' with the right measure of balance between theory and practice, and by incorporating proper role models through 'lead teachers', 'induction', and ensuring this orientation is held in place with 'competency approaches', appropriate and continuing 'inservice' and 'career structures' (pp. 75–9).

School organisation is construed as a grab bag of items contributing to this overall policy thrust in the form of a focus on 'cycles of schooling and articulation between levels' (p. 86), 'staff/student ratios and class sizes' that are not necessarily at the lower end of the scale (p. 87), higher levels of 'time on-task' (p. 89), extended length of the school day and school year (p. 91), more attention to 'homework' (p. 91) and reduced student 'absenteeism' (p. 91) – all within a context of a 'selected and trained . . . powerful principal' (p. 97), albeit exercising a 'participatory style' of decision making (p. 95) in circumstances where teaching draws on the manifest benefits of enhanced 'information technology' (p. 96). In many respects these are educational softeners for the essence of what the OECD regards as the *sine qua non* of 'evaluation', 'appraisal' and 'assessment' of teaching, learning, curriculum and the school (not withstanding that the pursuit of these brings with it an acknowledged increase in costs). The 'search for efficiency' (p. 115) is not far below the surface here as 'school ethos' (p. 105), 'teacher appraisal' (p. 103), the 'performance of students' (p. 105) and 'the education system as a whole' (p. 122) are monitored through 'central inspectorates' (p. 109), 'national and international' statistical indicators (p. 110) and, if all that does not do the job, then 'parental choice' (p. 106) through marketisation. Resources are considered important, but mainly to 'maintain minimum standards' (p. 119) and to ensure a context of flexible delivery of 'educational aims' (p. 120).

The similarity and the overall tenor of these reforms bear a remarkable resemblance to a set of recommendations for educational reform proposed by the World Bank in its *Priorities and Strategies for Education* (World Bank 1995). Remembering that this organisation is working ostensibly for poor countries assisting them in development activities, it is interesting that many of the same remedies keep appearing. Quoting from Watson's (1996) critique of that review:

> As the Review says, 'Curricula and syllabi should be closely tied to performance standards and measures of outcome' (p. 7). It is also argued that standards would be improved if teachers have a good grasp of their subject, if the school year can be extended, and if the instructional time can be made more flexible . . . and if homework could be set regularly. Above all it is felt that there should be greater institutional autonomy. Head teachers, parents and school governors should be given greater power to run their own institutions because this would involve the local community in ensuring that good standards are achieved. 'School based leadership ensures an effective climate for learning' (p. 8).
>
> (pp. 47–8)

It is hard not to reach the conclusion that this veritable cornucopia of educationally conservative elements of what is considered to constitute educational 'quality' are not somehow the vestiges of a now defunct corpus of 'teacher and school effectiveness' literature discredited and discarded some time ago (see Angus 1993; Proudford and Baker 1995). Like its sibling 'excellence', quality makes about as much sense to teachers as the Latin mottoes once emblazoned on school letterheads and school uniforms. Both are hurrah words that are used simultaneously as buzzwords and as criteria for success – herein lies their problem.

So far in this chapter we have argued that much of the ideology or restructuring that has affected teachers, at least in English-speaking countries, has been incubated in and through international organisations. The indirect effect has been the promotion of certain concepts which, while they seem fairly innocuous, bring with them some unfortunate baggage, mostly of an educationally conservative persuasion.

In the next part of this chapter we provide a way of 'reading' how dominant discourses of teaching are constructed through the language employed.

DEVELOPING A 'READING POSITION' ON TEACHING

Oppositional and resistant reading

When we speak of a 'reading position' (Hodge and Kress 1993: 180) we are referring to the act of adopting a declared political position with respect to how we regard teaching. This is not to say that we intend adopting some overt partisan political position, but rather to argue the importance of taking a considered, resistant and strategic stance in which the intent is to open up debate and discussion about the multiple pedagogical perspectives that inform and shape teaching. We believe it is important to attempt to break out of the official forms of totalising language and discourse currently operating to frame teaching as alluded to in the earlier part of this chapter, and to find instead new and more energising discourses, images and forms of signification. The way we produce social and psychological realities are sometimes referred to as 'discursive practices' (Bizzell 1992; Harre and Gillett 1994). Davies and Harre (1990) put it that:

> a discourse is to be understood as an institutionalised use of language and language-like sign systems. Institutionalisation can occur at the disciplinary, the political, the cultural and the small group level. There can also be discourses that develop around a specific topic . . . Discourses can compete with each other or they can create distinct and incompatible versions of reality. To know anything is to know it in terms of one or more discourses.
>
> (p. 45)

How we position ourselves reflects something about a range of aspects to which we attach value, as well as telling us about what we consider to be important:

> Once having taken up a position as one's own, a person inevitably sees the world from the vantage point of that position and in terms of the particular images, metaphors, story lines and concepts which are made relevant within the particular discursive practice in which they are positioned.
>
> (Davies and Harre 1990: 46)

What we are reacting against and resisting here are the impoverished forms of 'tunnel vision' and the 'failure of political imagination' (Walter 1996) that have currently come to paralyse what passes as 'official' discourses about education and teaching – the kind of ideas behind code words like 'quality', 'enterprise' and 'excellence'. Trying to move away from the dominant economistic, reductionist and exclusively resourced-based views currently holding sway in educational discussion means that we need to be much more tuned into the voices and forms of knowing that are pushed to the margins – that means, the least advantaged in our schools, including the voices of students, parents and teachers.

The oppositional and resistant reading (Kress 1985; Janks 1991) which we wish to bring to an understanding of the work of teaching emerges out of a critical approach to language awareness (Fairclough 1992a) – one that regards readers (as well as actors in particular social contexts) as being vulnerable and open to manipulation unless they understand how language constructs and locates individuals and groups in certain ways. The reason 'dominant' and 'dominated' discourses are important, Fairclough (1992b) argues, is that certain views get to be represented, sustained and maintained, while others are relegated to the category of being subservient, unworthy, unimportant or irrelevant. Furthermore, while some views are naturalised and labelled as common sense, others are considered dangerous or deviant. As Fairclough (1992b) puts it: 'The stake is more than "mere words"; it is controlling the contours of the political world, it is legitimising policy, and it is sustaining power relations' (p. 90).

To take an example; if the language in which teaching is spoken about is predominantly that of productivity improvement, value added, cost-efficiency and effectiveness, measurement of achievement, learning outcomes, flexible delivery, markets, and the like, then it should not be too surprising if this lexicon gradually begins to have the appearance of being credible, natural, logical and a common-sense way of talking about what is important in teaching. What gets excluded or rendered inaudible are the indigenous discourses teachers use to represent their work. Again from Fairclough (1992b):

> if a discourse type so dominates an institution that dominated types are more or less entirely suppressed or contained, then it will cease to be seen as arbitrary (in the sense of being one among several possible ways of 'seeing' things) and will come to be seen as *natural*, and legitimate because it is simply *the* way of conducting oneself.
>
> (p. 91)

When dominant viewpoints do not completely encase or obliterate, they exist in relations of 'opposition' to a dominant one: 'The linguist Michael Halliday calls one type of oppositional discourse the anti-language. Anti-languages are set up and used as conscious alternatives to the dominant or established discourse types (Fairclough 1992b: 91).

While a reading position is crucial to us as researchers in order to have a way of situating the violence being wreaked on teachers through so-called reform processes, it is equally important to us as well having regard to the fact that we are not ideologically innocent, either. In the kind of research we do into teachers' work we consider ourselves to be involved in a form of critical literacy that is something akin to 'reading and writing against the grain of academic discourse' (Kramer-Dahl 1995). In other words, we are constantly struggling with maintaining an awareness that we are confronted with a contradiction. The kind of up-close inquiry we engage in with teachers can simultaneously contribute to being 'a form of regulation and exploitation and a potential mode of resistance, celebration and solidarity' (Batsleer *et al.* 1985: 9–10). It is only if we continue to struggle with what Threadgold (1988) calls 'critical examination of our discursive positioning'

(p. 329) that we are able to see how our own agenda as researchers contradicts and is implicated in reproducing stereo-typical representations of their work.

While it was an agonising process of travelling this far in coming to grips with our own positionality as researchers *vis-à-vis* teachers and learning, this paled by significance to the task of trying to find where to start the dialogue about the counter discourse of teaching. In the end, it seemed that Richard Pring (1996) provided the breakthrough we needed. He conceptualised dominant or hegemonic discourse as being concerned with 'defending standards' through the by now familiar 'site-based management with conditions for quality assurance, centralisation of control, . . . diminishing unit of resource, and quasi-market conditions with the attendant language of "performance indicators", "efficiency gains", etc.' (p. 139). Pring (1996) likens the counter-hegemonic to the 'affirmation of an ideal' – a moral framework for discussion and inquiry and from within which all students can receive an education according to age, ability and aptitude. There is a major contradiction here – research about matters committed to defending standards is 'perceived by those who endure them as an intrusion into a distinctively educational world, and perceived by those who promote them as the protection of educational standards [and, therefore] as proper' (p. 139). This impasse can only ever be resolved, Pring (1996) says, if research attempts to understand 'how children learn and behave and how teachers plan and teach and how schools reconcile the many demands upon them' (p. 139). These are important research questions, and much research may not be addressing them: 'That is why educational researchers must, by and large, be in close touch with educational practice' (p. 139).

Any informed discussion about teaching has to begin with an acknowledgement of the inherent complexity of the work. Pring (1996) again:

> Teaching is, as we all know, a very complex activity – made even more so by the social and institutional framework within which it takes place. Those who are not aware of that complexity and of the subtle ways in which interactions between teacher and learner, and between teacher and teacher take place, will try to impose tidy and simple categories to provide a framework . . . which is manageable. But in doing so they will say something which will seem irrelevant to the world teachers inhabit.
>
> (pp. 139–40)

A starting point might be with what Kupferberg (1996) characterises as 'the rather disordered and unstructured everyday reality of teaching' (p. 227) – which is not meant to be insulting to teachers, but acknowledges that 'teachers spend their days in a social reality where the need to improvise and to be highly alert to unexpected events is [high]' (p. 229). This situation in which 'reflection-in-action' counts more than 'technical rationality' (Schon 1983) generates a confrontation. As Kremer-Hayon (1994) says of teachers' knowledge:

technical rationality depends on the agreement of clear ends and means, which cannot work in confusing and ambiguous situations, where conflicting paradigms and pluralistic views are accepted as inherently characteristic . . . [P]rofessional practice has unpredictable elements which cannot be dealt with by systematic pre-planning.

(pp. 54–5)

This is quite different to 'reflection-in-action' which is a real world activity based upon 'using knowledge, of thinking about something while doing it . . . and is characterised by spontaneous and intuitive behaviour' (Kremer-Hayon 1994: 54–5). This need to craft teaching knowledge on-the-job and through experience is related to an understanding of the nature of students, why they are in classrooms and the

very real problem of maintaining some kind of discipline among inherently unruly pupils who come to school for the many various reasons, most of which have little to do with the motive of learning as such.

(Kupferberg 1996: 229–230)

[P]upils attend classes because they have to, not because they want to. Gradually individuals find reasons other than fear of reprisals for going to school, for instance, companionship, intellectual curiosity, boredom at home, etc. However, this does not turn the act of attending classes into a voluntary activity. It remains a duty, as does most social behaviour.

(Kupferberg 1996: 244)

The other important framing reality in teaching is that what counts in a classroom is more like a 'conversation' than it is like a carefully structured or scripted 'performance' (as in the case of a university lecture). While there are certainly routines followed in classrooms, there is less structured order (than in lecture halls). Therefore:

Emotional tensions are more pronounced and are only marginally related to the subject matter. The teacher's authority is constantly tested in the classroom and the teacher feels a need to address the class in a diffuse as well as a selective way.

(Kupferberg 1996: 244)

Teaching as 'readerly' or 'writerly' text

One way of approaching teaching is to think about it from a literary perspective as a kind of metaphorical 'text' – in the sense of a script or a document to be both written and read. It is in a continual process of being constructed, as well as understood, challenged and unveiled. Moore (1996), drawing upon Eagleton (1983), argues that some written texts, such as legal documents, 'are more "hardened" than others, and present as if they were timeless, neutral, beyond challenge and ultimately "intimidating"' (p. 204).

Bowe *et al.* (1992) in their *Reforming Education and Changing Schools: Case Studies in Policy Sociology* raise questions about the amenability of texts, especially those written *for* and *on behalf* of others. They draw on Roland Barthes' useful conceptual starting point about the extent to which text gives the reader a role or a function, or whether the reader is rendered idle and redundant. The question really comes down to whether a text is, in Roland Barthes' (1975) terms, 'readerly' or 'writerly'. Readerly text is one in which 'there is a minimum of opportunity for creative interpretation by the reader'. 'Writerly' texts, on the other hand, 'self-consciously invite the reader to "join in", to co-operate and co-author' (Bowe *et al.* 1992: 11). In their words:

> 'Making sense' of new texts leads people into a process of trying to 'translate' and make familiar the language and the attendant embedded logics. In this process they place what they know against the new. Readerly texts, however, presuppose and depend upon presumptions of innocence, upon the belief that the reader will have little to offer by way of an alternative.
>
> (p. 11)

It is an interesting question, therefore, as to the extent to which the view of teaching currently being constructed through various educational reforms worldwide actually provides the opportunity for hearing voices, without closing down the spaces or the frontier for discussion. Trying to steer a path between the following sets of tensions, therefore, appears as a formidable challenge:

- trying to manage the work of teaching, without appearing to be impositional or top-down;
- producing a direction for education policy that connects it to wider trends in globalisation, while giving the appearance that this is a natural or inevitable trend;
- providing spaces from within which teachers can be constructed as participatory carriers of the prevailing ideology without, however, giving them so much space that they can develop a coherent undermining ideology.

In the next three sections of this chapter we examine the topics of 'skills', 'markets' and 'management' using notions of oppositional and resistant reading. We shall be trying to argue for a more 'writerly' and inclusive text for teaching, rather than one that is authoritatively prescriptive and definitive.

DISCURSIVE PEDAGOGICAL SKILL CONSTRUCTION IN TEACHING

Hodge (1993) uses an interesting but not especially elegant term to describe the most important way teachers enact their work – he calls it 'teacherese' (p. 118). It refers to the preponderance of dialogue in the language-rich nature of teaching. Examining the linguistic nature of what teachers do tells us much about what they regard as important, as well as how they explicitly and implicitly construct and frame their work. The reason linguistic forms are so important in teaching is that they are the means through which teachers foster 'creativity' and handle expressions of 'resistance' from students, both of which constitute primary energy sources within classrooms. According to Hodge (1993) teacherese is not an especially natural form:

> No one speaks pure teacherese outside the classroom. All pupils are exposed to it and they can understand it passively from the outside, but it is very different to the active grasp that they must acquire when they become teachers themselves. The conscious effort that is required has its dangers. Like anyone learning a new language new teachers tend to over-correct, speaking teacherese better (more rigorously) than experienced teachers, though failing to see some of the subtleties and variations that are a part of the language in its fuller form . . .
>
> There are two basic strategies for teacher-talk. One is deductive, a top-down, hypotactic approach, which starts from explicit, well-ordered descriptions of clear intentions (what to teach and how to teach it). It puts these into practice and then evaluates the results. The other approach is inductive, a bottom-up, paratactic approach. It scans teaching practice as a complex text, looking for regularities and anomalies. The generalisations it comes up with are paratactic. They may never be fully integrated with one another into a single theory of good teaching, but they connect more directly with experience.
>
> (p. 118)

Dialogue is, therefore, the exchange teachers use to keep the mobilisation of creativity in balance, so that the fine line between students acting creatively and impulsively for difference does not become so negative and oppositional that resistance to authority gets in the way of learning (Hodge 1993: 61). Teachers are thus continually acting in ways in which they harness the utterances of students so they become 'balanced and thoughtful responses' (p. 65) of a kind appropriate for open classroom discussion. That skill in teaching is to a large extent verbal and linguistic is given added poignancy by the way control and discipline are exercised in teaching, as Hodge (1993) indicates:

> When you stand in front of your first class for the first time and see rows of eyes looking back at you, you know without question that teaching is a form of struggle in which the numerical advantage is undoubtedly with the enemy. At such a time, neophyte teachers commonly wish they had learned more about 'discipline' and ways of maintaining control, and less about theories of curriculum. In their later career they will often have days when they reflect ruefully on the meagre instruments of control that lie to hand, and the hell that follows when control has gone. Yet the exercise of power has its cost, and the time and effort taken up in its maintenance are a distraction from teaching and learning . . . Different styles of teaching involve different attitudes to power and different levels of investment in its exercise, but for no one can it be the only virtue. The relationship between teacher and pupil necessarily involves an asymmetry of knowledge and power, but that asymmetry takes many forms and has to be negotiated in different ways.
>
> (p. 24)

AST: indications of policy disjuncture

As a way of providing an *entrée* into teachers' voices about their work, we would like to turn our commentary to the framework of the policy agenda we listened to, and which is the subject of detailed analysis from teachers in Chapter 7 – the AST. We find it more useful to give some broad brush-strokes before hearing the teachers' voices, because of the way in which this analysis brings out the macro issues discussed so far in this chapter.

A way into the policy disjuncture of an initiative that was supposed to elevate teachers' self-worth, but ended up being subverted to other ends, is to pose the question: what view of skill was behind the AST process?

Teaching is never innocent – it always includes some things, while excluding or denying others; celebrates some perspectives and actions while discouraging and denying others; co-opts, favours and promotes some ways of working with students, while punishing, ignoring or silencing other views of teaching. What constitutes legitimate teaching, therefore, depends on who is doing the defining, and their perception of the valued social end or purpose to which the teaching is directed. If the attempt is to contain, control or shape teaching to promote national economic imperatives, then teaching will become a tool of micro-economic reform and will look quite different than if teaching was a genuine attempt to formulate schooling as a more relevant curriculum response to the complex lives of contemporary youth. Teaching will look different again, if the primary interest is that of parents who want their children to succeed vocationally, or employers who want a literate, numerate and compliant workforce. These multiple and conflicting interpretations of teaching have to struggle to co-exist with each other and arrive at uneasy forms of settlement at particular historical moments. Which set of views gets to have preference over others is invariably a hotly contested political question, even though the real agenda may be obscured and not always overtly obvious.

In the case of the attempt to construct a view of what constituted 'advanced teaching skills' in Australian schools in the early 1990s, there were a number of competing interests and discourses: the official or policy aspirations; the lived realities of how the official aspirations were lived out at the level of the process of selecting the teachers; and, the accommodation, contestation and resistance displayed by teachers as they acted to give voice to their own local or indigenous definitions of skilful teaching. It was clear that these various constructions were not always heading in the same direction, nor were they one and the same thing.

The major point of departure was at the level of the paradigmatic view of teaching – official views endorsed a 'competencies' approach of displaying attributes, traits and behaviours consistent with a series of pre-formulated criteria; at the level of teachers, there was a regret that the impositional approach was not more nuanced and consistent with teachers' preferred ways that tended to favour storied and narrative styles of portrayal. Teachers often put this in terms of what they saw as skills that endorsed 'bureaucratically preferred ways'. Teachers became angry when these were ranked higher than what teachers themselves regarded as being most important. Some teachers claimed that when criteria of competent teaching were developed external to and at a distance from teaching, rather than being the consequence of any process that was up-close or internal to the understandings of what it meant to be a good teacher, then considerable damage was done. Accumulated wisdom acquired through many years of successful classroom teaching was denigrated because it did not necessarily or readily equate with the skill requirements embodied in the criteria: 'experience', 'commitment', 'status' and 'self-esteem' did not necessarily equal skilled teaching as measured through the application of criteria.

Accommodated and subjugated knowledges of teaching

The paradigmatic preference for what amounted to technicist ways of regarding teaching also manifested itself in other ways – for example, the strong emphasis in the AST selection process on evidence and what appeared to be a quasi-judicial process of an adversarial type, in which teachers were required to account for their skills in written form, supported by evidence from in-class observation, at interview, and in response to questioning by a panel. The verification of claims about personal teaching against the standards embodied in the AST criteria produced levels of tension and frustration that many teachers found difficult to live with.

At another level, teachers found the requirement of having to meet specified criteria as 'limiting the boundaries of admissible evidence'. They argued repeatedly that the process of 'narrowing down' teaching (some drew the parallel with 'dumbing down') to meet criteria produced a situation in which large and important aspects of teaching are made deliberately 'invisible'.

For some teachers this whole approach smacked too much of having to jump through criterial hoops, displaying just the right amount of policy gloss in terms of familiarity with the latest government ideology, in order to receive a meagre reward. Teachers regarded this as akin to using school sites as conduits for the latest educational ideology, where being rewarded with an acknowledgement of AST amounted to being a carrier of this new ideology. Being successful, paradoxically, meant moving spiritually and linguistically away from the classroom, at least in terms of being able to converse freely in the jargon in order to demonstrate convincingly the ability to mouth the rhetoric. For teachers who were successful, this amounted to a form of policy assimilation of the new skills discourse of competencies. It was as if skill in teaching was somehow being used as a kind of ideological manoeuvre with which to produce policy conformity. This tended to take the form of the requirement to demonstrate knowledge of systems policy, and was further exacerbated as the 'gaze' of self-regulation was driven back into routine aspects of teaching. This led, teachers said, to a kind of self-imposed performance accountability of desirable visible teaching traits, which was ultimately corrupting. We would not want to deny, however, that there *can* also be a positive side to systemic policy concerns, for example, the way in which teachers enact policies of social justice in their classroom practices (see, for example: Queensland Department of Education 1996), but this was not, however, an issue that teachers spoke of in the AST study.

Teachers spoke frequently of the guilt they experienced in electing to undergo the process of being selected as an AST – to satisfy the requirements of putting together the very detailed written proposal (often taking weeks or months to prepare), they had to forego the dedicated attention they normally gave to their daily teaching duties – especially out-of-hours activities like evening and weekend marking of student assignment work. In order to become recognised as an AST it seemed they had to be prepared to become temporarily negligent.

The playing of 'language games' through the written application and the subsequent interview was seen as having the effect of devaluing the essence of the work of teaching – the relational aspects of classroom teaching did not appear to many teachers to be highly regarded – it was a case of being able to show that they were somehow competent classroom managers. Teachers experienced this separation of 'performance against criteria' from the wider lived totality of their self-worth as teachers as a kind of artificially constructed exposition of a 'performance facade'.

The presentation of evidence about their teaching to a panel and the associated interview process caused a lot of grief among teachers – one teacher described it as an 'ordeal by representation'. There was a widely held view that some teachers were better at the 'interview game' than others and that the combative nature of the process unnecessarily put many in the situation where fear of failure led to 'nervous omission, rather than complete and meaningful disclosure' of what they knew about teaching. The view was put that the kind of skill necessary was one that was about 'talking your way around the criteria' and 'impressing outsiders', rather than any genuine attempt to get at core understandings about real issues of teaching in complex contemporary circumstances.

There was almost universal condemnation of the situation of discomfort experienced by most teachers in having to engage with 'necessary forms of self-promotion' in order to manufacture and manage impression and performance during the selection process.

Fundamental questions were raised by teachers too about the value to the school and its wider community of a 'personal classification of skill'. For many teachers, teaching is no longer the isolated and insulated activity it used to be, and therefore, to reward individual teachers with an individual classification flies directly in the face of the collaborative reality of the way these teachers experience their work. This point was picked up repeatedly by teachers in the way they talked about the extraordinarily high levels of collegial support they received while enduring the selection process. Many made it clear that without the very tangible assistance of colleagues they would not have been able to proceed. This raises serious questions about why individual rewards are persisted with when schools themselves refuse to treat teachers as if they were islands. The competitive model is not only outdated – it may actually be highly counter-productive to schools.

With the allocation of rewards being such a public process, and so significantly related to the life of schools, this had its drawbacks too. For example, not only was there 'shame, humiliation, anger and loss of confidence at failure', but after years of positive peer and community affirmation, good teaching could be quickly shattered through a failure at criterial assessment – a situation exacerbated by a total absence of any official procedure for 'after-the-process' support for individuals who failed to meet up to arbitrarily set and administered standards of good teaching. The inextricable embeddedness of self-worth in teaching meant that failure produced huge emotional and social disjuncture.

Any teachers agreeing to putting themselves forward for selection as ASTs were placing themselves in a situation of considerable personal and professional vulnerability – the 'hidden costs' of being an applicant were not insignificant in a context where the fissure of misunderstanding over the meaning of competence was always a palpable reality. The literalistic discourse of skills continually rubbed abrasively against the oral tradition of teaching, a circumstance that was bound to produce a context of incongruence between 'professional' and 'criterial' notions of assessment. In brief, there was a deep and irresolvable confusion and tension throughout between the *alleged* 'celebration' of good teaching and its *actual* 'evaluation'.

The form of 'contrived colleagiality' (Hargreaves 1994: 80) that was manufactured through having a colleague on the selection panel did not wash with most teachers; they were quick to see this shallow contrivance for what it was – an attempt to disguise traditional bureaucratic forms of evaluation. Well-meaning colleagues were often regarded as lacking credibility, from the vantage point of teachers who were more interested in the benefits derived from being part of a genuine learning community – exchanging ideas, trailing new teaching approaches and generally supporting one another.

While the overt and demonstrable aspects of being selected as an AST were often spoken about in less than edifying terms by teachers, there were also references to the not so easily seen aspects. Although teachers did not use the term, there was a feeling of complicity of peers in 'horizontal violence', as colleagues became implicated into forms of pseudo-ownership of the process through involvement on school-based selection panels.

Teachers' resistant discourses and readings of the AST

One theme that consistently emerged from the interviews was the oral, storied and discursive tradition of teaching as a site of resistance. The issues of what was admissible and inadmissible as evidence of advanced teaching skills, what was masked, opaque and therefore beyond dispute as criteria, were by no means settled in the eyes of teachers. They were troubled by the approach of dismantling their teaching into 'bits and pieces' as if such deconstruction were natural, common sense and inevitable; they resisted this in the ways they presented accounts that emphasised teaching in its totality. The relational aspect of teaching, which teachers insisted was at the core of their work, failed to feature prominently in the official criteria. While teachers were certainly keen to receive symbolic recognition of the significance of their work, they were unprepared to accept this without challenging the medium of representation especially if this was at the expense of artificiality. Contestation and politicisation were seen as the most effective antidotes to literal, detached and shallow renditions that failed to judge teaching in the milieu of its connected context. For example, requests throughout the AST process to provide evidence of how criteria were invisible carriers of systems policy, and how these were 'applied' in teaching, were responded to by teachers with instances of policy as being 'experienced in' or 'grounded in' and actively redefined through a shared experiential construction of a localised culture of teaching. In other words, teachers were continually engaging in reframing the discursive boundaries of their teaching in situations where sharing insights about their teaching was a normal part of a wider community-building process.

It seemed that in many respects the AST process was about producing a 'marketised' and 'managed' set of relationships in teaching. We turn our attention to these twin elements now, drawing our examples from New Zealand, the UK and the USA.

MARKETISED RELATIONSHIPS IN SCHOOLS

The argument

Given the intention of governments to have schools managed like businesses, it is clear that the mechanism by which teachers are to be controlled is through techniques of business management. The consequence as Ball (1988) notes is that 'The task of schooling is increasingly subject to the logics of industrial production and market competition' (p. 292). Hatcher (1994) argues that 'market relationships are becoming the organising principle of the school system' (p. 42). As evidence of this he cites the experience from Britain of introducing new management regimes from the private sector incorporating:

> certain structural changes including devolved organisation, expanded role definitions for line managers, new forms of control systems and new forms of production system. Accompanying these structural changes there appear to have been certain 'cultural' changes such as new management styles designed to give renewed emphasis to customer orientation, innovation, enterprise and competitive edge.
>
> (p. 42)

According to Hatcher (1994) even the recent attempts of policy sociology to alter this have been less than successful because of a focus on the 'top' end of the 'top down' approach: 'Ordinary teachers are afforded the potential of an active oppositional role in their theoretical analysis, but they are largely absent from the empirical research' (p. 44).

The crucial linkage that is missing from the attempt to translate the new management regime from business to schools is the vastly different culture of schools (see Westoby 1988 for a full treatment), and furthermore, the 'new management regimes in the private sector takes [sic] place in a context in which the work process is directly governed by market relationships' (Hatcher 1994: 45).

The topic of markets in schooling is of interest to us here primarily in the way it casts light on how teachers' work is shaped pedagogically. We do not offer an exhaustive treatment of the notion of markets in education, but refer instead to others who have treated the topic in detail such as Bowe *et al.* (1992), Keep (1992), Kenway *et al.* (1993; 1994), Gewirtz *et al.* (1995) and Marginson (1995; 1997).

The idea that markets should be the primary organising and motivating feature of schooling has been central to educational reforms in the UK, New Zealand, Australia and the USA for a decade or more. The argument in which teachers are constructed as 'providers', principals as 'managers', parents as 'employers', and students as 'consumers', is overly simplistic, but it goes something like this: poor school performance lies at the root of national economic under-performance; teachers have for too long had a monopoly over the content and direction of educational decisions; they have occupied a position of 'producer capture' and engaged in 'feather bedding' as a way of protecting their own self-interests; what is required to rectify this is the introduction of market-led reforms in which schools and teachers are required to compete against each other; what will happen as a consequence is that schools and teachers will either lift their game and become more effi-cient, or go out of business as parents exercise their choice of schools; 'if protectionism is lifted and competition encouraged, products will sink or swim depending on their ability to compete' (Sullivan 1994: 4).

While the key theoretical assumptions may be clear enough, namely that 'self-management will ensure that schools are able to match their services directly to student need and that market forces will ensure that "standards" are raised as schools compete for students and seek to stabilise or maximise their income' (Ball and Bowe 1992: 58), what is far from clear is how this reaches down into the work of teaching to make teachers more efficient and effective; the 'black box' of the classroom has been studiously ignored in all of this theorising about market relationships in schools.

The New Zealand case does provide some not so encouraging pointers.

New Zealand and the effect of markets on teachers' work

While the marketised argument sounds convincing on the surface, we are only beginning to arrive at a position when we can judge some of the effects of these policies on the work of teachers, and it is considerably at variance with the theory. Sullivan's (1992; 1994) New Zealand study of marketised reforms on teachers' professional ideologies is especially noteworthy because of its consistent finding that the reforms undermined the 'high-trust colle-gial' (p. 9) basis of teachers' 'implicit contracts' (p. 13) – that is to say, the high levels of 'goodwill' upon which competent teaching depended, with teachers actually working hours very much longer than their 'explicit contracts' (specific roles in classroom teaching), in order to maintain public confidence in schools. As Sullivan (1994) said:

> This means that they were willing to do everything that employees in a 9 to 5 job would do, but also spend many extra hours at school and home preparing stimulating and new materials for their pupils, counselling children and families, taking children on camps where teachers would in effect be on duty 24 hours a day, developing children's creative skills by organising musical performances during lunch hours and after school, as well as developing athletic team skills by taking after-school sports teams.
>
> (p. 13)

In contrast to this high-trust/implicit contractual view of teaching, the creation of a 'low-trust (and hierarchical) atmosphere' (p. 13) in which teachers are excluded from wider decisions and discussions about their work, blamed for the so-called crisis, treated as part of a structure that denies the importance of social and collective responsibility in preference to an emphasis on possessive individualism as the motivating force, all leads to the production of narrow forms of accountability and the erosion of a wider sense of 'community–teacher partnerships' (p. 7):

> In this context, where people are concerned less with social responsibility than with their own power, status, and wealth, the main purpose of social institutions will be to control any excesses and to make certain that production is market led, that people produce to the needs of consumers. Individuals in this context are mistrusted and controlled.
>
> (p. 7)

There are some broad indicators we can obtain of what marketised approaches mean within schools. Sullivan (1994) points to several ways in which teachers in New Zealand indicated the marketised model impacted on their work:

- Accountability became construed more as a series of 'managerial checks' (p. 10) on individual teachers, rather than a school-wide focus for the support of teachers through professional development. To that extent, accountability became a way of controlling teachers rather than being 'framed in relation to the building of a positive relationship between teachers as a group and the school's community' (p. 9).
- Management practices in schools started out from the presumption (without any supporting evidence) that 'schools are not performing

well . . . and principals [and] the community can demand improvement' (p. 10). There was not only a lack of trust in the professional competence of teachers, but a 'bureaucratisation of goodwill' (p. 12) as teachers became 'overburdened by extra tasks . . . [and] accompanying paperwork . . . having to keep and maintain extensive records on children' (p. 12):

the problem of accountability is made worse in a free market situation by the tokenism of such record-keeping and by the commensurate demands 'to sell their school'. One teacher [said] that her school now prepares a special parents' evening . . . [as] a marketing exercise to convince parents that they were getting value for money so they would continue to send their children to this school rather than choose another.

(p. 13)

- There was a marked change in principal–teacher relations as principals were required to operate less like educational leaders and professional colleagues, and more like managers and chief executives, with the emphasis in schools shifting from 'organisational consensus to management by hierarchy' (p. 14). This kind of arrangement disempowered teachers 'by taking away their contribution to the consensus [as well as having the effect of isolating] the principal from the support required for the effective running of the school . . . Thus the principal/teacher relationship becomes one of manager/worker' (p. 15). Principals were required to separate themselves from their teachers in becoming accountable to their Board of Trustees.
- An Educational Review Office designed to keep teachers in line replaced an inspectorate that had previously existed to enact an adjudicating role from outside of schools acting as a check and balance on the power of principals. Accountability shifted from being focused at the school level, to focusing on the deficits of individual teachers, with the principal being the responsible officer.
- Models of business management were used in schools in everything from 'student selection' processes to raising funds to hire extra teachers.
- There was a strong sense of teacher 'betrayal' of professional competence, as mutually supportive 'creative working partnerships' between teachers, the community and Education Department were jettisoned in favour of low-trust, hierarchical, self-seeking, consumerist behaviour. Teachers regarded this an 'inappropriate subversion of basic principles' (p. 14).
- The complete irony in all of this is that supposedly free-market policies are not free at all in the way they operate with regard to teachers' work – they are very 'administered' (Strain 1995). As Sullivan (1994) put it:

Although the free market espouses deregulation and competition, the imposition of a market model onto school management and especially onto the role of the principal in fact imposes regulation and control. It restricts options and reduces the ability of the principal to work collaboratively with teachers and pupils, and in the low-trust climate the teachers are less likely to work within their implicit contracts.

(p. 16)

Gordon (1992) labels what has happened to teachers in New Zealand as a 'repositioning' – that is to say, 'changes in the institutional, ideological and industrial relations of teachers resulting from the reform process' (p. 23) . . . from 'professional' to 'proletarian' (p. 40). The nature of this repositioning in its effect on teachers' work is such that:

The role of teachers is to teach. They should have no involvement in policy processes. Instead of collaborative management and staff development, they are to be subject to the discipline of strict industrial relations and surprise inspections . . . The old professional settlement of teachers, in which they were involved in every aspect of the system from teaching to national policy-making, and were concerned to develop the system as a whole, is over . . . Further, they are to compete with each other and with other schools.

(p. 34)

Expressed in terms of this 'discourse of the market' and a 'quasi-privatised environment', there is:

the need for firm contracts between 'principal' and 'agent', the separation of policy from operations (so those making policy will not have a vested interest in the outcomes of their deliberations) and a series of mechanisms that will ensure the state does not unduly grow due to bureaucratic and provider capture.

(p. 29)

The most disturbing aspect to Gordon's (1995) research is that the effects of these consumerist policies of 'choice' have nothing to do with *educational* value of schooling or what teachers do pedagogically:

the major finding of school choice research is that the mechanisms by which education markets operate owe little or nothing to education that goes on in schools, and most or all to the social and economic processes that surround these markets.

(p. 1)

A number of studies of school choice have been carried out in New Zealand, and collectively demonstrate that, far from overall improvement, competition is causing a polarisation between schools on the basis of geographical factors and the perceived social class and ethnic composition of the school.

(p. 5)

The reasons for parental choice, which is supposed to produce enhanced levels of efficiency in schools by requiring teachers to provide better educational services, relate more to 'social aspiration' than 'academic achievement', says Gordon (1995). A number of strategies are followed that aim at enhancing image:

> The first is attempts to pitch their message to parents of a higher social status than the average population of the school, especially in mixed neighbourhoods. The aim is to persuade these parents not to bypass the school in favour of other institutions . . . The second is an emphasis on social order within the school. School uniforms which look good and are worn correctly provides [sic] a mobile form of advertising . . . [And] there has been a big increase in the numbers of children excluded from schools in both New Zealand and England, which reflects increasing pressure on schools to demonstrate good behaviour amongst their student body. The third strategy may be characterised as providing 'novelty' . . . set up a technology speciality [or other areas] such as drama, music, cultural studies.

(pp. 10–11)

The tragedy is that to date there has 'not been a single piece of research that demonstrates even one market that is working as neo-liberal governments have predicted' (p. 16).

The paradox is that this marketisation of schooling is supposed to occur at precisely the same time schools are even more tightly managed institutions. So, how do we interpret this, and what does it mean for teaching?

MANAGEMENT FOR ALL SEASONS: MANAGING TEACHING THROUGH MARKET CONSENT

Structural changes to teachers' work

Questions about how teachers in schools are (or should be) managed are never far off the public agenda. The persistence of this desire to control teachers seems to be caught up with the wider desire to apportion blame for the economic demise while, at the same time, attempting to proffer solutions as to what should be done to fix the situation. We do not intend to rehearse any more the scapegoating of teachers that has occurred worldwide with such vehemence (see Lingard *et al.* 1993; Hargreaves 1994; Berliner and Biddle 1995; Woods *et al.* 1997). But, appreciating the effects of the hostility of this attack on teachers becomes important in understanding the most recent attempts (at least in England and in New Zealand, and increasingly in Australia) to control teachers through market-driven forms of educational policy. It is only when we take account of the importance of teachers' work culture and the centrality to teachers of concepts like co-operation, work ethic, commitment to children's learning, and the intrinsic worth of teaching itself (Smyth 1992), that we can come to see the reluctance of teachers to embrace and deliver on the market agenda 'and thus it is that management comes to assume such significance' (Nicholls 1995: 3). Nicholls (1995) explores how in 'hitherto market-insulated primary schools' (p. 1) in the UK the 'rhetorical and ideological force of marketisation, together with the shifts in management–workforce relations that it fosters' (p. 3), produce a set of circumstances in which 'it is in this sphere of management–workforce relations that the market rhetoric does its "real" work' (p. 3). He claims that the steering of the educational market in the UK has come about largely through devolution of responsibility and function as schools have been provided with funds according to 'success', and where success is defined in terms of attracting students and funding (Ball 1993a: 109). The logic of the constructed educational market is such that schools are encouraged 'to seek potentially successful pupils, while other pupils, with low market value or expensive needs, are not targeted' (Nicholls 1995: 4). Importantly:

> the steered education market is characterised by differentiation and stratification, though the rhetoric is that of choice, diversity, responsiveness and flexibility. This rhetoric is also abundant in the description of the emergent forms of teaching labour force, and similarly conceals stratification and segmentation, as well as the market's tendency to reinforce inequality.
>
> (p. 4)

The way this came about in England was through the 'occupational re-structuring' of the teaching force – through (a) direct regulation of pay and promotion for teachers, and (b) the deregulation and devolution of financial control to schools allowing them greater flexibility in employing teachers. The first of these worked through the abolition of teachers' negotiating rights, the fixing of pay scales, and giving principals the power to 'reward for good performance as measured against indicators' (Nicholls 1995: 5). The second occurred through governing councils being able to appoint teachers according to budget, the rise of ancillary and auxiliary teachers, and the 'virtual disappearance of financial support for inservice training [which] means that teachers fund their own professional development' (p. 5). All of this operates in England to produce an increasingly differentiated and segmented teaching force, where previously it had exhibited 'all of the characteristics of unalienated, integrated labour' (Nicholls 1995: 6).

The 'same' but 'different' situations of teachers in the UK and USA

Lawn (1995: 347) makes the point that restructuring of teaching in the USA and the UK have what appear to be similarities in that they both have pursued the touchstones of 'decentralisation of school management' and the 'development of quasi-markets in education' – but these surface similarities belie more substantive differences. While this is not the place to go into elaborate comparative analyses of reforms in the respective countries (see Weiler 1989; Hess 1992; Lawton 1992b; Nias et al. 1992; Murphy and Hallinger 1993), Lawn (1995) says that while some of the same language is used in relation to the reforms in both countries – collaboration, collegiality, responsibilities beyond the classroom, a professional view of teaching, delivery of national curriculum, greater involvement in school-wide policy – there are quite different sets of forces operating in the two countries. In the USA the thrust has come from attempts to move teaching beyond allegedly inefficient educational bureaucracy, trying to garner teacher involvement and empowerment from a situation in which teachers had historically been treated punitively and in teacher-proofing ways – in a phrase, the attempt was to promote more 'teacher professionalism'. In the UK, while the touchstones were the same, the history and the circumstances were quite different; teacher exclusion from the reform process; a shift away from existing partnerships between teachers and government; a greater emphasis on privatisation; more individual responsibility; greater centralisation and regulation (Lawn 1995). In summary, while the rhetoric of 'collegiality and collaboration' have been used on both sides of the Atlantic to frame teacher reforms, in the UK it was being driven out of a push to create a market ideology for education, while in the USA it was an attempt to ameliorate the worst effects of bureaucratic forms of management (Lawn 1995: 349). It has to be said that the reforms in the USA, beyond the appearances of enhanced professionalism for teachers, were fundamentally also about introducing market forces through 'consumer' choice.

The effect on teachers in both places has been similar – 'a differentiated, flexible workforce in teaching'. In the UK the emphasis has been upon 'pay flexibility' – freeing-up teachers from centralised salary and promotions structures, giving school governors the power to set pay scales, and through 'workforce pliability' (Lawn 1995: 355) involving skilled, semi-skilled and unskilled teachers with differing tasks, modes of training and entry, and varying supervisory responsibilities. As Lawn (1995) put it: 'New kinds of teachers and classroom assistants are appearing in England who have the potential to act . . . as low-skilled workers alongside the new core workers, the multi-skilled teachers' (p. 358). 'The idea of a professional standard of work can be seen to be moving from a collective responsibility to an individual's performance and from a definition created by the teacher (or, more accurately, teachers) to that created by management' (p. 352).

Managing teaching through the 'new management discourses'

Nicholls (1995) studied twelve primary schools in the UK and focused on their responses to marketisation, particularly parental choice, competition between schools, and the significance of image management. His research is of particular significance (and will be examined in detail) for the light it casts on how marketisation works through the construction of new management relationships in schools. Nicholls (1995) found that 'despite the absence of classically defined markets, there is evidence that primary school managers feel obliged to act as though they were competitive business managers . . . and felt they must hold down costs' (p. 10).

The integration of the ideology of the market and managerial sets of relationships, and their effect on teachers through the way teams of senior managers acted in the schools Nicholls studied, can be summarised thus:

> Pressure on schools to be accountable to clients and to attract clients through performance levels increases the monitoring and surveillance functions of these teams. Because schools must attract to survive, the pressure on such teams to eradicate problems and establish smooth production is correspondingly greater. Deviations from, or variations on, school policy seem less likely to be tolerated. The status of the class teacher is threatened by the quasi-managerial function of post-holders and the growth of supervisory functions implicit in collegiality. Indeed the connections and relationships between the growth of supervisory functions in teaching, which may 'extend' professionalism of a particular kind to some, and the deskilling of other educational workers, especially women and part-timers, connects to current debates about the changing nature of the workforce in Western 'post-industrialist' societies and in particular to the emergence of core and flexible workers.
>
> (p. 10)

Furthermore, this was given particular expression in the primary schools studied:

> there is evidence of considerable development in the practice of primary schools in terms of important areas of activity, including 'client' awareness, market research, image and impression management, unofficial

selection, and the development of a visible 'mission' or ethos encapsulated in the school development plan.

(p. 11)

Nicholls (1995) argues that there are strong surface similarities between some of the features of primary-school work cultures – collegiality, flat management structures, flexible work arrangements, teamwork, and the like – and the precepts of Human Resource Management (HRM) that 'may assist in the manufacturing of consent' (p. 17). He warns, however, of making too much of this apparent connection on the grounds that to do that would be to misunderstand the nature of the new forms of management. The marketisation ideology operates through two mechanisms: (a) the notion of the 'flexible firm' (or organisation), and, (b) the discourses of HRM and Total Quality Management (TQM). We have already seen how flexibility works in the UK through the creation of internal labour markets in schools based on fragmentation of the work of teaching, functional flexibility for schools, the breakdown of a 'homogenous labour force' (p. 7), and constructing new jobs for some requiring additional skills and tasks. What is produced is a 'threat of visible job substitution' (p. 7) in a circumstance where: 'workers live with the shadow of their use-value firmly attached to remind all other workers of the disciplining operation of the labour market' (p. 7).

Workplace discipline 'which had traditionally been embodied in the form of management, supervision and bureaucracy is translated from an organisational contrivance to a seemingly external imperative derived from the very nature of the economic system which lies beyond the firm' (p. 7).

Some understanding of how the dual discourses of TQM and HRM have seeped into schools, particularly in the UK, but also extensively in other countries, is important (for an elaboration, see Smyth 1991; Smyth 1995d). Nicholls (1995) encapsulated the essence of TQM when he says that it 'raises the level of measurable quality in outputs by introducing the previously external relationships between customer and producer into the workplace through the employment relationship' (p. 7). It is a particularly smart arrangement because of the way it 'draws the principles of the market directly into the shop floor with the discipline of the "customer's gaze" installing an ever-watchful eye on the workforce' (p. 8). Through its emphasis on teamwork and measurable targets TQM, therefore, establishes a new pattern of relationships among workers where 'colleagues remain attentive to their tasks and aware of each other's level of contribution to the productive effort' (p. 8). HRM operates out of a broadly similar crucible emphasising a cachet that underscores the importance of 'individual employee identity' and 'evaluation on the basis of individual performance' (p. 8), where the stress on 'competitive individualism' and the extirpation of third party intervention resonate nicely with 'the language of the marketplace' as embodied in notions like 'teamwork', 'enterprise culture' and 'cohesive workforce' (that avoids solidarity) (p. 8). There are tensions here in HRM, but they are over-ridden by an 'enabling' and 'empowering' commitment of management to 'integrated', 'co-ordinated' and 'target-driven activity' within a 'flat/flexible' organisational structure of clearly articulated 'shared purposes' (Nicholls 1995: 8–9).

In this chapter we have looked at some of the more proximate sources of educational policy options via international agencies like the OECD, and discussed the way in which they framed a particular kind of discourse about the nature of schools. In contradistinction, we explained the importance of developing an oppositional reading to these positions and gave some preliminary insights into what transpired in the AST initiative in Australia – framed by a consideration of the changed marketised and managed relationships increasingly coming to characterise teaching in other places as well. What remains to be done in the next chapter is to examine in more detail how the new structural dimensions being introduced into teaching actually operate.

Chapter 5

Managing the 'preferred' teacher

GOOD TEACHER/BAD TEACHER: MANAGING 'DOCILE BODIES'

Developing a position

It would be tempting from the vantage point being sketched out so far to adopt the imagery of Foucault's (1977) 'docile bodies' as an explanatory framework for analysing modes of educational policy and reform. While this line of analysis has a certain amount of appeal, there are also some decided limitations. We are more than a little troubled by the notion that teachers might be conceived of as inert or inactive – but we will proceed with the notion of docility for a moment.

Dwyer (1995) claims that Foucault's perspective derives credibility from the emphasis it places upon 'the operation of power within custodial institutions' (p. 468) in places like schools through themes of 'discipline', 'surveillance', 'normalisation' and 'examinations' (Dwyer 1995: 468). While critiques of educational policy from this quarter 'raise an important issue about the way policy is being used to enforce a particular agenda' (Dwyer 1995: 468), there still remains some question as to 'whether there is a conceptual basis beneath the imagery which might substantiate the recourse to Foucault' (Dwyer 1995: 468), or whether such analyses are too limiting because of their denial of 'human agency' and 'counter discourses'. Dwyer (1995) argues that the mantra of the competencies movement, with the appeal of its 'training agenda' to a more flexible set of aptitudes/capacities to enable students to meet alleged demands in the workplace, has the potential to cast teachers increasingly in the mould of equipping students with the individual forms of knowledge and requisites to accommodate to these circumstances. According to Dwyer (1995):

> There is now a ferment of activity particularly in the technical education and training sector to develop tightly-organised modules and courses that have quite detailed performance criteria written into them . . . The

accumulated effect of this pre-occupation with specific programs is to construct a compliant body of practitioners competing against each other for the training dollar, and a processed group of graduates who measure up to behavioural objectives . . . Thus, in Foucault's terms these graduates are the new 'docile bodies' of a new social order who have 'agency' only to the extent that they adopt the prescribed agenda, follow the rituals and co-operate in putting the new policy prescriptions into place.

(p. 472)

Dwyer (1995) draws on the example cited by Robinson (1993) who found that the teachers she worked with in the training sector 'accepted unquestioningly the subordination of educational practice to overarching economic goals' (p. 472). In Robinson's (1993) words:

The teachers in my study were able to repeat the catechism – 'the lack of a skilled workforce is the major reason for our current economic problems, Competency Based Training will create a skilled workforce' and in meshing of prophesy and promised pleasure our problems will be solved.

(p. 139)

Now, while this notion of teacher-as-technician has considerable contemporary currency in certain quarters, in order to pursue this line further we need to make a detour. Nicholas Rose (1988) in a paper entitled 'Calculable minds and manageable individuals' provides a historical analysis of how the emergence of the psychological sciences in the mid-nineteenth century was a response to a need for ways of governing increasing areas of social and economic life 'in order to achieve desired objectives; security for wealth and property; continuity, efficiency and profitability of production; public tranquillity, moral virtue and personal responsibility' (p. 183). In words that have an uncanny contemporary ring about them, educationally speaking, there was a growing belief:

in the necessity and possibility of the management of particular aspects of social and economic existence using more or less formalised means of calculation between means and ends: what should be done, in what ways, in order to achieve this or that desirable result.

(p. 183)

There was not only an attempt to:

calculate and manage financial flows, raw materials, the co-ordination stages of production, and such like, but also . . . the 'psycho-physical' apparatus of human individuals, in the belief that achieving objectives depended upon the organisation of the capacities and attributes of those individuals.

(p. 183)

Rose (1988) argued that this required two things:

First, a new vocabulary [with which to represent] . . . the domain to be governed, its limits, characteristics, key aspects or processes, objectives, and so forth, and of linking these together in some more or less system-atic manner . . . [But] before one can seek to manage an economy, it is first necessary to conceptualise a set of processes which is amenable to management.

(p. 184)

Put more directly, this meant: 'For a domain to be governable, one not only needs the terms in which to speak and think about it, one also needs to be able to assess its condition . . . [which is to say, put it] . . . in a calculable form' (Rose 1988: 184).

It was through the institutions embodied in these 'calculative practices' that focused on observing, recording and codifying habits, propensities and the registration of differences, that the 'psychological sciences [came] to play a key role in providing the vocabulary, the information, and the regulatory techniques for the government of individuals' (Rose 1988: 185). Furthermore, individualising humans in this way through 'classifying them, calibrating their capacities and conduct, inscribing and recording their attributes and deficiencies, managing and utilising their individuality and variability . . . [worked to] . . . establish a regime of visibility in which the observed is distributed within a single plane of sight' (Rose 1988: 187). Attending to the regulation of detail also enabled institutions to establish 'a grid of codeability of personal attributes' (Rose 1988: 187):

The development of institutions and techniques which required the co-ordination of large numbers of persons in an economic manner and sought to eliminate certain habits, propensities, and morals and to inculcate others, thus made visible the difference between those who did or did not, could or could not, would or would not learn the lessons of the institution. These institutions acted as observing and recording machines, machines for the registration of human differences.

(Rose 1988: 188)

Identities were 'inscribed' through new systems for:

documenting and recording information concerning inmates – files, records, and case histories. This routine notation and accumulation of the personal details and histories of large numbers of persons identifies each individual with a dossier consisting of the facts of his or her life and character accorded pertinence by the institution and its objectives. The individual here enters the field of knowledge not through any abstract leap of the philosophical imagination, but through the mundane operation of bureaucratic documentation.

(Rose 1988: 189)

Given that the study and appraisal of teaching and the way teachers have been historically trained owe so much to the discipline of psychology (sociology and anthropology are very recent phenomena), and what we now know to be the legacy of psychology to the inscription of individuals for reasons of controlling them, it is not surprising to find so much emphasis being placed, then as now, on the pathology of individual teaching and learning styles. It was the rendering of live three-dimensional people into two-dimensional representations through observation and measurement, more than anything else, that produced the means by which variation was to be reined in. Rose (1988) gives an example:

> The first contribution of psychology to the project of individualisation was the psychological test of intelligence. The psychological test was a means of visualizing, disciplining, and inscribing difference which did not rely upon the surface of the body as the diagnostic intermediary between conduct and the psyche . . . A group of children suddenly became apparent who, whilst looking normal to the untrained eye, could not learn the lessons of the school. They accumulated in the lowest classes, a financial burden on the authorities, a source of concern to those who regarded the school as a vital apparatus of moralisation, and an affront to those who considered education to be the right of all citizens. Children would parade before the doctor who would seek to find marks of pathology; stigmata, misproportioned limbs, unbalanced nerves and muscles. But it proved difficult to align the gaze of the doctor with the requirements of the institution. Difference no longer marked itself unmistakably on the body's surface. It would have to be made legible.

(p. 191)

Rose (1988) explains that once human variability was able to be marked out by a normal distribution curve, the 'simple act of comparison of the respective amount of a particular quality or attribute possessed by two members of a group enabled the mathematisation of difference' (p. 191). In other words, it was through this process of making something 'legible' that individual difference could be 'inscribed' (that is to say, imprinted or the quality marked on the surface) so that it could be understood in a way not hitherto possible, but that also made it controllable and manageable in reality. Rose (1988) summarises these as procedures of 'visualisation and inscription of difference' (p. 192), and it was through this mechanism that childhood was 'first made *visible*, in relation to the normalisation of behavioural space within the clinic, then *inscribable* through the refinement of procedures for documenting individuality, then *assessable* through the construction of scales, charts and observation schedules' (p. 193).

While some of this may appear at first blush to be a little opaque (even a tad fanciful for some), it can be rendered more accessible if we think about it in the following terms. The images of teachers and the language with which teaching is increasingly being spoken about are not far removed from those that would have it closely aligned to the economy and the international marketplace, and it is not a huge step from here to suggesting that teachers be judged 'good' or 'bad' according to their measured contribution to narrowly defined economic goals. Thus construed, teachers become technicians interpreting and implementing agenda formulated and decided at a distance from schools, classrooms and learning. For others, the kind of reading we have given here may seem a little too pessimistic and deterministic in that it appears to stamp out teachers in a certain way, with too little scope for agency, resistance and counter-hegemonic struggle. We do not believe this to be the case, and distance ourselves from such unhelpful interpretations, largely because we believe that there is still considerable scope indeed, even from within such an apparently oppressive regime, for optimistic and resistant possibilities for teachers, and we turn to those in a moment (see Smyth 1996b).

Regulation of time, space and the management of self in teaching

Bruce King (1995) has provided three useful conduits through which to begin to trace the processes by which teachers are disciplined: (a) division of space; (b) regulation of time; and (c) surveillance of teachers' work. Each of these, he says, constitute internalising mechanisms by which teachers can be rendered 'self-regulating individuals' capable of reforming the profession itself and 'shaping their identities, control[ling] their work, and induc[ing] them to conform' (p. 15). King's point about how teachers are disciplined and regulated is an important one: 'As Foucault (1977) suggests, discipline is not accomplished through explicit force but is continually constructed through the participation of individuals in self-regulation' (p. 18).

At the same time, teaching is the kind of activity in which it would not be difficult to create a contemporary picture of overbearing external control and surveillance. This would be easy and convenient because as schooling becomes more closely aligned with servicing the needs of the international economy, what transpires in schooling is increasingly coming under the gaze and purview of those charged with formulating public policy. But, such an analysis while useful up to a point would be limiting because it overlooks the manner in which teaching is itself a technology of discipline and has sedimented within it a number of significant self-controlling devices. Paradoxically, teaching is both a technology of discipline in the way it orchestrates and manages the lives of students, while at the same time itself being the object of disciplinary control by policy makers through the way the work of teaching is organised.

Teaching is a technology of discipline in the sense that consent of all involved – students and teachers – is continually in the process of being managed and renegotiated; that much has been clear since the 'birth of the schoolroom' as Jones and Williamson (1979) have called it. As a labour process teaching is also an occupation that has historically been the subject of extensive, continual and changing forms of disciplinary authority, and what we are witnessing around the world at the moment as various attempts to 'reform' teaching are symptomatic of attempts to cast an even wider net. Yet, even though teaching may give some outward appearances of being an isolated, insulated and rather solitary activity, reality is that it occurs in a highly regulated and controlled space (King 1995: 23). As King (1995) notes, the essence of disciplinary technology through teaching, at least as it applies to students, occurs through the 'partitioning of students by individual and separate desks . . . [and] the division of the school itself into discrete classrooms' (p. 23). This partitioning of space is also an important means by which the architecture of the school operates to control teachers through regulating their 'intermixing' and 'collaboration' (King 1995).

The timetable and its effect on breaking up knowledge into discrete bite-sized chunks not only pre-dispose teaching (and learning) to a kind of transmission technology – from teachers to students – but they also provide a way of batch-processing students in groups through sequences of time (30- to 50-minute lessons), with palpable effects on students as well as teachers in terms of regulating how curriculum is delivered, in what quantities, according to what ordering, to whom, and with what intensity. Obviously the embroidery of this differs from primary to secondary schools, but the basic pattern is still the same – time is indeed a convenient frame within which the disciplinary mechanism of the 'temporal elaboration of the act' (King 1995: 19) of teaching occurs. Instructions, directions, restraints, even bodies and gestures, can be controlled through progressively elaborated school, state and national stipulations about how time is to be spent in schools, and teachers internalise this through content and material to be 'covered' (p. 19). This kind of regulation also carries over into regulating the bodies and gestures of students as well as teachers. King (1995) gives examples:

the teacher is constantly monitoring the gestures of students, from how they sit when writing, to how they line up to go to the lunchroom, to where they look when taking a test. Teachers too are subject to this mechanism of discipline . . . [T]hey must restrict their dress to within accepted boundaries . . . [and] teachers' manuals that accompany curriculum tests regulate the gesture as well . . . Typically, teachers' gestures for initial class sessions with students are prescribed for them. At the beginning of each school year, they are to make sure all textbooks are numbered and a record is kept of what book goes to what student; to present students their academic standards and expectations for behaviour in class; to inform students of their grading procedures and homework policies. They are reminded by administrators that policies established at the outset are superior to those developed as situations arise. Notions of efficiency and utility increasingly discipline teachers' gestures as they become part of the discourses of improving a specific type of student learning.

(p. 20)

Apparently high levels of autonomy in teaching, for example when the class-room door is closed, therefore, disguise the true extent of how power works on teachers and teaching. Schools and classrooms are places that very effec-tively locate students and teachers in time and space through various methods of surveillance. For example: 'the principal – the authority, the patriarch – can walk in or invade over the PA system at any time' (King 1995: 23), and while teachers monitor what students do on a continual basis, the reverse is also a powerful influence over teachers' work:

From early on in their school experience, students develop perspectives and expectations for what school is supposed to be all about. The disci-plined routine is accepted by students and this acceptance is understood by the teacher . . . [L]ittle wonder that the style of pedagogy, student behaviour management techniques, lesson design and other aspects of teachers' activities all have a high degree of consistency throughout the educational system.

(King 1995: 23)

If extended, this also leads to the conclusion that, with such powerful internal mechanisms of control operating within teachers' work, 'formal techniques of observation of teachers are rarely employed' (King 1995: 23), for they are unnecessary in such a tightly controlled process of self-policing. Even with classrooms being such apparently isolated workplaces, hierar-chical observation of teaching occurs in potent but less direct ways: 'Through the submission of teachers' lesson plans and tests to the principal, and the various forms of documentation of student attendance, behaviour and performance, teachers' work is continually under surveillance' (King 1995: 22).

We certainly do not wish to create the impression of teaching being an occupation manacled with all manner of oppressive structures and procedures of control – that would be far from an accurate portrayal. However, it would be just as inaccurate to posit a view of teaching as being largely autonomous and self-managing – which is the image and language being created and used by the current wave of educational reformers. The reality on this score is a far cry from what might seem to be the case. Rather, what we are trying to do is present as complete a picture as we can of the culture of teaching that shows not only the nuanced nature of the work, but how the nature of teaching itself has implicit within it a number of significant shaping influences. Within this, as King (1995) correctly points out, 'there is always room for refusal, resistance, and alternative practices' (p. 17). Another way of putting this is in terms of a 'pedagogy of liberation' (Shor and Freire 1987) or teaching for 'an oppositional world' (hooks 1989: 49). Embedded within the common, routine, mundane and everyday life and practices of teaching there are points of potential affirmation for the status quo, as well as points of possible resistance and reconstruction that operate as significant 'sites of struggle' (King 1995: 27) over how teaching is ultimately to be represented regardless of official policy or edict.

While King's (1995) notion of regulation of time, space and management may not appear to suggest anything dramatic has changed in respect of the control of teachers' work, there are some salient points that can be made about these recent regulatory modes within these domains. For example, while we can still see the external apparatus of teacher appraisal as a prominent controlling mechanism, there are also a number of new 'nasties' on the block. We are beginning to witness and experience a range of self-regulatory devices, such as the notion of professionalism, school development planning, marketised forms of management, performance and outcomes-based indicators, competencies and skills formation, basic skills testing, to mention a few – all of which bring with them compelling common-sense forms of justification, but which also have significant aspects of internalised control as well. Hartley (1997) summed this up in terms of Foucault's notion of governmentality: 'Commands no longer come from outside; they also come from within' (p. 150). The decided merit from a managerial point of view in these modes is that once there is widespread acceptance of them, then they have ways of exerting their own forms of control simply by virtue of the way they carry people along with them. The accompanying ideologies and agenda mean that teachers' work is constricted and constrained both in terms of how they conceptualise as well as enact their teaching. This *does* represent a major and significant shift in the way teachers' work has been controlled compared to the past.

Getting 'real' about teaching: a view from inside the work of teaching

While there is always debate, and usually undisclosed ideologies as to what teaching should look like, it is sometimes easier to see the productive possibilities by starting out with the more impoverished views. Haberman (1991) argues for a move away from a 'pedagogy of poverty' – the view that teaching constitutes a series of basic traditional core functions, such as 'giving information, asking questions, giving directions, monitoring seat work, assigning homework, settling disputes, punishing non-compliance, giving grades' (p. 291).

Haberman (1991) argues that pedagogy of poverty does not work because:

> The classroom atmosphere created by constant teacher direction and student compliance seethes with passive resentment that sometimes bubbles up into overt resistance. Teachers burn out because of the emotional and physical energy that they must expend to maintain their authority every hour of the day.
>
> (p. 291)

Good teaching, on the other hand, says Haberman (1991), has quite a different genre that is much clearer about what it is that is being managed – namely, learning, life chances and the opportunity to challenge entrenched and oppressive views. In Haberman's (1991) terms:

- whenever students are involved with issues they regard as vital concerns, good teaching is going on;
- whenever students are involved with explanations of human difference, good teaching is going on;
- whenever students are being helped to see major concepts, big ideas and general principles and are not merely engaged in the pursuit of isolated facts, good teaching is going on;
- whenever students are involved in planning what they will be doing, it is likely that good teaching is going on;
- whenever students are involved with applying ideals such as fairness, equity or justice to their world, it is likely that good teaching is occurring;
- whenever students are actively involved, it is likely good teaching is going on;
- whenever students are directly involved in real-life experience, it is likely that good teaching is going on;
- whenever students are actively involved in heterogeneous groups, it is likely that good teaching is going on;

- whenever students are asked to think about an idea in a way that questions common sense or a widely accepted assumption which relates new ideas to ones learned previously, or which applies an idea to the problems of living, then there is a chance that good teaching is going on;
- whenever students are involved in redoing, polishing or perfecting their work, it is likely that good teaching is going on;
- whenever teachers involve students with the technology of information access, good teaching is going on;
- whenever students are involved in reflecting on their own lives and how they have come to believe and feel as they do, good teaching is going on.

(pp. 293–4)

ORGANISING THE ICONS OF THE 'PREFERRED' TEACHER

The 'new public administration'

Stuart Hall (1980) has used the term 'preferred meaning' as a shorthand way of describing the way language acts to 'anchor' some meanings in preference to others. More recently, Gillett (1996) has used the term 'preferred principal' as a way of describing the principal who is prepared to acquiesce to the educational reforms that would convert schools into businesses. Over the past decade or so it has become commonplace to frame discussions about educational reform in language, idioms and within frameworks of administration and management. The supposed logic is that if we can get the language, structures, organisation and administration of schooling right, then the right kind of pedagogical practices and desired forms of learning will flow from that.

Because education is largely a public sector activity it would be relatively easy, at least in theory, to make a connection between what is happening in public administration, and how this acts to shape the work of teachers and schools. Indeed, there is a significant body of literature emerging, known as the 'new public administration' (Stewart and Ranson 1988; Aucoin 1990; Alford 1993; Hood 1995; Pollitt 1996; Yeatman 1996), in which its proponents argue that there is a new set of internationalised ideas for the management of public sector organisations labelled in some quarters a 'post bureaucratic paradigm' (Barzelay 1992). These ideas have formed mainly around notions of marketisation, commodification, competition, privatisation, and generally making public sector providers responsive to their consumers.

While the evidence on the emergence of a new set of organising icons for public administration is extensive, and in many respects compelling, on the other hand, there are those who dispute what this pervasiveness means. Hood (1995) says that: 'It is easy to be carried away by grand claims of historical inevitability and global convergence on some new epoch-making paradigm' (p. 105). The new 'managerial catchwords' may have become so extensive as to constitute a 'new global vocabulary' (Hood 1995: 105), but such similar tendencies occurring in different parts of the world can often be 'for quite different reasons, reflecting different political agenda . . . [and] when we go below the superficial level of common global management "seminarspeak", very different concrete things seem to have been happening' (Hood 1995: 106). There may well be a bias for a preferred mode of management in public administration – one that is decidedly consumerist with a strong tendency towards 'government by the market' (Self 1993). In Hood's (1995) words:

> Powerful international organizations such as the OECD and the World Bank are by their *raison d'être* committed to a view of international convergence on some single 'best practice' model which it is their institutional role to foster, in helping the 'laggards' to catch up with the vanguard. And within the domestic context, managers, politicians and bureaucrats facing criticism often try to build up bipartisan support for reshaping organisations in their preferred direction by arguing that what they are doing reflects 'international best practice'.
>
> (Hood 1995: 108)

Even within the context of such apparently powerful, compelling and built-in sets of 'biases towards exaggeration of similarity, . . . it is important to weigh such claims carefully' (Hood 1995: 108).

The obvious question here, and that is prominent to the argument being pursued in this book, is: to what extent do changes occurring in the sphere of public sector management impact on the administration of education, and in turn, how much influence does this have in shaping the nature of what passes as teaching and learning? This is bound to be a controversial question, one on which there are likely to be a range of divergent viewpoints. We cannot claim to have the definitive answer on this, nor access to an indisputable pile of evidence. However, we do believe that this is one of the most important questions confronting contemporary education, and this book is committed to worrying about that question.

What we need to address is the direction in which the tide is flowing, not just the prevalence of the 'same management buzzwords [which] tend to be widely diffused', and try to get to the important question of 'whether what is happening underneath is also uniform' (Hood 1995: 109). Put another way, the question is whether the broader changes to public management and the administration of schools is so significant and extensive as to constitute a fundamental repositioning and reconfiguring of the work of teaching.

On several counts, we would argue that evidence is emerging that two things are occurring simultaneously: at the level of management above teachers, there is certainly a sharp break with the past, with the increasing intrusion of managerially oriented literature, albeit still a 'babel of tongues' (Hood 1995: 106); but teachers in classrooms remain cynical about its relevance to the ways schools are organised and in the absence of compelling evidence we would have to say that teachers still appear to remain largely insulated from excessive direct managerial interference. While at one level this institutionalised managerialist 'education-speak' appears to be an all-embracing technology with a certain aura of authority about it that is difficult to dismiss (or repel), at the level of classrooms, teaching and learning, it appears to have relatively little leverage (for reasons we will explain in more detail shortly). This is not to suggest that the attempt to 'reinvent' schools through management discourses have been completely benign, but rather that its potency has been markedly diminished because of the fundamental incompatibility of many of its elements and the reality that power resides very much at a rhetorical level in 'the ability to convey different messages to different audiences simultaneously' (Hood 1995: 107).

A discourse unlikely to succeed

Our own preference is for the line of reasoning pursued by Spann (1981) that 'tendency and counter-tendency are present simultaneously' (p. 14) in attempts to change teaching through managerial discourses. One of the reasons we suspect that managerialist reforms will ultimately have so little real effect in the long-term in schools and classrooms is that they are prone to be faddish and relatively short-lived, even in this era when repeated reforms continue to emerge from the same neo-conservative crucible. In the long run it may be their lack of stability and their incoherence that lead to their eventual demise or, at least, to a severe limitation in terms of a pervasive effect at the classroom level. A good illustration of this is the thrust of reforms to produce 'preferred' individualist remedies – teachers who are self-monitoring, able to explicate clear internal standards, capable of fostering competition and an entrepreneurial spirit in students, and committed to delivering on required systems' learning outcomes. This 'convergent solution' with its individualist emphasis (Hood 1995: 111) is likely to be decidedly at odds with attempts that have a much greater degree of centralised steering – like, national curricula, national and statewide testing, schemes of teacher appraisal, and the move towards uniform benchmarks and standards – all of which are highly susceptible to sabotage by 'egalitarian' tendencies whose commitment is to 'over-ride markets . . . in the hands of local collectivities' (Hood 1995: 108). Grace (1997) highlights this contradiction in speaking about the moves in the UK to transform schooling culture without proper attention to the collaborative and professional aspects, and the attempt further to spot-weld individualist cultures onto schools:

> While the majority of head teachers have welcomed the greater freedom for manœuvre involved in local management of schools, they have wished to operate that freedom in a responsible relation with reformed local democracy in education and not as individual cultural entrepreneurs in the market place.
>
> (p. 4)

It would be to misrepresent what has occurred, Grace says, to see what has happened in England as some kind of move by the majority of schools, their headteachers and their communities, to free-standing schools operating at the individual site level in response to market democracy of consumer choice. A more likely interpretation is of a representation of 'headteacher resistance to market democracy as professional conservatism, vested interest and "fear of freedom". On the other hand it is possible to interpret it as informed professional judgement about the limitations of market values when applied to schooling' (p. 5). If the image policy makers, politicians and economists convey of teaching is of an occupation that should be harnessed to making schools contribute more to economic growth, then this is not an image that the teaching profession holds of itself. The view that teaching requires increasing managerialism, tighter specification of outcomes, greater curriculum prescription, more testing of student achievement, enhanced surveillance, and making schools more competitive, market responsive and individually attentive to 'national priorities', is not a view eagerly or widely embraced by teachers themselves. Indeed, teachers put a quite different set of constructions on their work. This is one of the great paradoxes of teaching – those at a distance from it have quite different construals of the way it is and should be, from those who live and work in teaching. Teachers have a set of images and pre-dispositions about their work that tends to focus around 'interpersonal dimensions' ('relationships with young children and colleagues') and 'personal' aspects ('the intellectual satisfaction of the work' or 'the feeling of being isolated as a classroom teacher') (see Warton et al. 1992).

These are important issues that need to be taken up in putting teachers' voices back into the public construal of the work of teaching. It is possible, of course, to view teaching from the perspective of the management discourses that have come to claim such a dominant position when teaching surfaces in public and official discussion. But, on the other hand, quite a different picture is likely to emerge if we take a reading position from the stance of teachers' stories, narratives and teachers' own indigenous theories about their teaching – an issue we shall turn our attention to shortly. Meanwhile, what follows will begin to point in the direction of a discourse that is less disrespectful of teachers.

DEFORMING EDUCATIONAL REFORM

The search for a less disrespectful discourse

We would like to take Donald Macedo's (1994) notion of educational reforms that deform (p. 142) as a way into discussing how these have been used as an organiser for the 'preferred' teacher.

By any standards, the past decade or so of educational reforms has produced a set of circumstances that has at best been very cosmetic. They have been a dismal failure because of the limited agenda and opportunity they have provided for genuinely expansive educational debate. As Macedo (1994) put it: 'Educationally, the decade of the 1980s can be best characterised by an overdose of educational reform pollution controlled mostly by a conservative discourse that celebrates a language of management, competition, testing, choice and free enterprise' (p. 137). Macedo's (1994) argument is that the myth of what has been propagated under the guise of educational reform has really been a form of 'management and free enterprise [that] do[es] not necessarily translate into human freedom' (p. 137). There has been a palpable dearth of 'pedagogical spaces' (Macedo 1994: 137) in which to debate the 'illusion of individual freedom' and forms of educational reform that deny any connection with issues of human misery, poverty, oppression and hopeless inequality in society generally. As long as educational reforms like 'choice' of schools are allowed to masquerade as if they are progressive innovations, then they will continue to fly in the face of the reality that 'not all of us have the same privileged position from which we can exercise our right to choose' (Macedo 1994: 138). These are, however, a far cry from the kinds of transformations necessary to move schools out of the circuit of reproducing demonstrably unequal life chances. For Macedo (1994):

> The term 'reform' in the conjunction with education produces a positive effect to the extent that, without threatening the core values of the system or the people who run it, the term announces changes in a system that has been determined to not be working effectively. In this sense reform produces a positive effect in that it tranquillises people who consciously recognise that some cosmetic changes must occur while they adhere to those same values and mechanisms that created the need for reform in the first place.
>
> (p. 139)

[In other words] reform is being carried out by those players who have been and are part of the problem they are trying to solve.

(p. 140)

The effect has been a kind of 'deficit-orientation model' based on the myth that 'schools are very much independent of society and dislodged from the political reality that shaped them historically' (Macedo 1994: 140). As long as the notion of 'quality of community life' is allowed to remain unconnected to the 'quality of public schooling' then we will continue to rehearse feeble-minded and impoverished educational reforms like these that miss their mark. Hargreaves (1994) described the way this has worked its way through to teachers:

In England and Wales, policy makers tend to treat teachers rather like naughty children; in need of firm guidelines, strict requirements, and a few short, sharp evaluative shocks to keep them up to the mark. In the United States, the tendency is to treat teachers more like recovering alcoholics; subjecting them to step-by-step programs of effective instruction, conflict management or professional growth in ways which make them overtly dependent on pseudo-scientific expertise developed and imposed by others.

(p. xiv)

It is not simply that measures like these are 'disrespectful' or that they 'fail to show regard for teachers' professionalism' (p. xiv), but that they competely miss the mark by mythologising the view that schools can be fixed up if teachers are fixed up. What goes unexamined is the wider set of social circumstances in which unequitable and unjust structures militate strongly against many children accessing education as presented to them. Cookson (1994) put it in these terms: 'School reform policies that are not driven by a sense of educational and social justice are bound to fail. Excellence and equity are not meaningful alternatives, because without equity there can be no excellence' (p. xi).

Macedo (1994) claims that unless educational reformers tackle head-on the social and economic structures that produce poverty, encasing and characterising the lives of increasing numbers of children (especially those in inner urban areas), then the latter will be denied access to education (or at least to forms of education) that are meaningful to them – this will constitute the ultimate 'pedagogical entrapment' (p. 167). Most educational policy reforms are predicated on what might be called the 'politics of engorgement', as already emaciated public education is further stripped of resources in the unabated transfer of funds to already advantaged private education. This produces a potentially ugly scenario:

by shifting more public moneys away from already decrepit schools to private and middle- and upper-class public schools, reformers are sentencing lower-class students to a de facto boot-camp minimum security detention center parading under the veil of urban public education.

(Macedo 1994: 167)

Giroux (1993) endorses this argument saying that what is missing from the language of educational and social reform is a 'primacy of the ethical, social and civic in public life' (p. 128). Issues of 'equity', 'social justice' and 'liberatory education' are subjugated to 'individualism', 'privatization' and 'competition'.

The kind of image being constructed of the teacher through these educational reforms is one that portrays the teacher as being calculable, flexible, accountable, entrepreneurial, manageable and, above all, marketable.

Emerging cameo of the preferred teacher

Within the kind of educational reform context described here, teaching is increasingly being constructed as work in which there needs to be maximum opportunity for a flexible response to customer needs and where the teacher is hired and dispensed with as demand and fashion dictate. This ethos of schools as marketplaces also means a differentiated mix of teachers, some of whom are fully qualified, others who are cheaper to employ for short periods of time and who can rapidly be moved around within auxiliary and support roles to help satisfy growing niche markets. Coupled with this is a mindset in which the teacher is required to act as a kind of pedagogical entrepreneur continually having regard to selling the best points of the school, promoting image and impression, and generally seeking to maximise the school's market share by ensuring that it ranks high in competitive league tables. A crucial element of this educational commodity approach to teachers' work is the attention to calculable and measurable aspects of the work, especially educational outputs, for without that kind of information the capacity of the school to promote itself successfully will be severely circumscribed. There will be a need for teachers to be team members within the corporate culture of the school always mindful that anything they may do will impact in some way on the schools' outside image. However, team membership which will sometimes be glorified with terms like 'collegiality', 'partnerships' and 'collaboration' will reside very much at the operational and implementation level, for to incorporate strategic decision making might be to threaten the wider mission of the school. Interactions with students will occur within an overall framework of 'valued added' in which students are 'stakeholders', continually deserving of receiving educational value for money. Teaching will be increasingly managerial in nature, both as teachers are managed and themselves manage others – there will be clear line management arrangements with each layer providing appropriate performance indicator information to the level above about the performance of individual students against objectives, and the success of the teachers themselves in meeting school targets and performance outcomes. The remuneration of both the teacher and the school will be based on attaining these agreed performance targets. This sketch may not be that inaccurate, for as one teacher in the UK put it:

> I think we can predict what schools will look like by the end of the century. A much increased private sector, government specials, . . . and at the bottom, an under-resourced state sector. You won't be able to tell the difference between supermarkets and schools. Middle-class areas will have Marks and Spencers types of schools, and corner-shop types for the inner-city. Marketing, targeting and performance indicators will be the language of education. Heads getting together boasting about the quality of their sponsors. We'll have cigarettes and beer advertised in the school and we'll be told that it improves the pupils' discussion skills, to prepare them to make real choices in the real world. This lies behind all the policy changes now taking place. They're not as benign as they look. It would have seemed like fantasy ten years ago. Now, you are regarded as a liberal reactionary if you oppose the brave new world.
>
> (Macan Ghaill 1991: 299)

INTERNATIONAL PERSPECTIVES: DOES ANYONE ELSE HAVE THE ANSWER?

Policies of the kind being canvassed in and around the AST in Australia have been tried in other guises in places like the USA, albeit using different language like 'merit pay' and 'career ladder' schemes. Bacharach *et al.* (1990) define merit pay as being where special payments or increments are made to some teachers 'based in part on some form of evaluation of their performance . . . [that usually results in] discourag[ing] cooperation and sharing of job knowledge among teachers, by forcing them to compete with each other' (p. 134). Career ladders 'typically create hierarchies among teachers and provide for promotion from one level to the next [usually based on] some reduction in the amount of classroom teaching as the teacher advances up the ladder' (p. 135).

Ingvarson and Chadbourne (1996) capture what was being attempted in Australia from the early 1990s, for an international audience, when they said:

> In principle, the AST classification represented a shift from a career ladder model to a career development model for teacher compensation, as described by Bacharach, Conley and Shedd (1990). In Lawler's (1990) terms, it was to be a pay system based on professional knowledge and

skill, not on the position occupied in an administrative hierarchy. In Australian terms, it was a venture into the unknown – a shift from the traditional model of 'merit' (competitive) selection for advertised positions to 'criterion' based assessment of current performance. The aim of the AST reform was to reward teachers for demonstrable improvements in the quality of their practice and to provide additional opportunities for them to take up leadership roles in relation to curriculum and staff development. Such an offer, it was hoped, would keep good teachers in the classroom, provide all teachers with an incentive to continue their professional development, and attract higher calibre recruits to the profession.

In a sense Australia attempted to implement a version of the career development model on a massive scale . . . as there were over 100,000 teachers who were eligible to apply.

(p. 3)

In drawing out the Australian example, Ingvarson and Chadbourne (1996) note that while there have been numerous attempts in the USA to reform teachers' work through pay systems and changes to promotional prospects, 'reviews of research in their implementation (Murnane and Cohen 1986; Rosenholtz 1986) indicate that few are well received by teachers or benefit student learning' (p. 3).

The USA has had a chequered history in this regard. As recently as the mid-1980s Murnane and Cohen (1986) note that while merit pay and career ladders are often touted as 'solutions', 'more than 99 percent of public school teachers in the United States work in districts that employ uniform salary scales' (p. 2). They trace the intellectual history of US merit pay schemes back to 1918 and conclude that while these schemes have promised much, 'most attempts to implement merit pay for public school teachers over the past seventy-five years have failed' (p. 1). The major shortcomings, according to Murnane and Cohen (1986), lie in 'the goal of merit pay's advocates to put the power of money into the evaluation process as a way to improve teachers' performance. That goal is misguided' (pp. 16–17). Malen and Hart (1987) concur that 'one of the most visible and controversial aspects of school reform' (p. 9), career ladders, are 'not likely to produce substantial changes in teacher work roles, responsibilities and reward structures', and that 'vanishing rather than sustaining effects are likely to prevail' (p. 22).

At the core seems to lie the fact that while attempts to motivate teachers through performance-related pay arrangements (merit pay) or career ladders based upon 'positions of responsibility, such as department chairs, year level, curriculum and staff development coordination . . . [on the way] toward senior administrative jobs' (Ingvarson and Chadbourne 1996: 4) rely upon extrinsic forms of motivation, these options are not considered attractive by teachers who continue to regard as most important, work that occurs within a flat hierarchical structure. Firestone and Pennell (1993) note that attempts to advance teacher commitment in the USA through policies of differential incentives hold the seeds of their own demise:

> the competitive aspects of such policies often undermine teacher commitment. These aspects include selection mechanisms that pit individual against individual (and to a lesser extent individuals against a fixed standard) as well as incentives that increase the stakes in winning. Increased competition raises serious concerns about fairness that undermines the intrinsic rewards of teaching and reduces the limited support for collaboration among teachers and the modest learning opportunities that already exist in schools.
>
> (p. 517)

Firestone and Pennell (1993) go on to point out that while there is an upswing of popular support in the USA for policies that aim to move teachers through competition, individual selection criteria and external differentiated incentives, these are precisely the policies that undermine teacher commitment and explain why 'school incentive programs have not caught on as an improvement policy' (p. 518). The alternative, they say, lies much more in strategies that encourage collaboration and learning opportunities for teachers.

Speaking again from a US background, Mohrman et al. (1996) and Conley and Odden (1995) claim to have found a way to 'spur systemic thinking about the role of compensation [in teaching] by offering a concrete proposal that includes skill- and competency-based pay' (p. 51) drawing upon parallels from business and industry based on creating 'high involvement' management strategies (p. 53). It would seem that the untested idealised blocks of 'depth skills', 'breadth skills' and 'vertical or management skills' of Mohrman et al. (1996), congregating around 'provisional', 'novice', 'teacher' and 'expert' categories, bear many underling resemblances to the failed AST processes in Australia. By advocating skill-based forms of pay for teachers derived from the private industrial sector, it would seem that proponents like Malen and Hart (1987), Firestone (1994) and Mohrman et al. (1996) have selectively and systematically closed their ears and their eyes to the overwhelming evidence from an extensive history to the contrary in their own country that these processes simply don't work for teachers (see, for example, Johnson 1984; Nickerson 1984; Brandt 1990; Arnstine and McDowell 1993). Rosenholtz (1986) argues that:

> Not only is merit pay ineffective as a means of inducing greater collaboration among teachers and involving them in the development of school

programs, it also produces behaviors that become part of the same problems that reforms are intended to solve.

(p. 527)

As to career ladders, Rosenholtz (1986) says that 'only if they are executed with the precision of a drum roll [do they hold the prospect of] improv[ing] the working conditions of a school' (p. 527) and even then only if there is significant, authentic and widespread restructuring of the way the school organises itself. For example: 'Principals would have to treat teachers as competent professionals . . . Leadership would have to come from many people within a school, and professional conversation would increase' (p. 527).

Speaking of the recently ill-fated experiment with AST in Australia, many aspects of which bear close relationship to merit pay and career ladders, Dinham and Scott (1997) conclude from a study of 900 government primary-school principals and teachers that:

> Despite high expectations that attended the introduction of the AST position, serious problems have been experienced. Difficulties have occurred in filling the position in schools, and ASTs have reacted negatively to the increase in the number and range of their responsibilities.

(p. 37)

The category of 'lead teacher' was recommended in the Carnegie Report (Carnegie Forum 1986) and came into effect in many US states in the early 1990s. The intent was to 'restructure the teaching force, and introduce a new category of Lead Teachers with the proven ability to provide active leadership in the redesign of schools and in helping their colleagues to uphold high standards of learning and teaching' (p. 55). Speaking of the unfulfilled promise of the lead teacher initiative in Pennsylvania (and it was representative of what happened in many other parts of the USA), Ceroni (1995) concluded:

> It is plagued by similar problems associated with plans such as merit pay, career ladders, differentiated staffing, and mentorship programs. Like these programs, the lead teacher initiative . . . tended to create competition, jealousy, and suspicion among teachers, contributing to a pervasive sense of low morale. By introducing status differences among teachers, it often thwarted the development of collegial relationships.

(p. 224)

Competition also served to increase isolation and inhibit communication among teachers. Additionally, it reinforced the notion that classroom teaching is less than fully professional since most of the teacher leader responsibilities were quasi-administrative.

As a classroom teacher Ceroni's (1995) bitter disappointment both personally and professionally was painfully evident when she said:

> What has been most difficult to accept and confront is not that the Lead Teacher Initiative failed to fulfill the promise I had hoped it would, but that it was never intended to do so. The rhetoric of promoting the professionalization of teaching is a rhetoric I now interpret as masking a move to exploit teachers and indirectly gain control over the work they do.
>
> (p. 228)

In other parts of the world, such as the UK and New Zealand, the restructuring of teachers' work has proceeded apace, but it has not taken on quite the face of horizontal violence that has become apparent in Australia and the USA – at least for the moment! The educational climate in the UK and New Zealand is no less chilly, and there is a strong pre-disposition to reform teaching in ways damaging to the work (see O'Neill 1997 for developments in this area in New Zealand). In the UK it is clear that teachers' lives are being radically redefined according to a model of professionalism derivative of the principles of the 'new public administration' with an unswerving focus on competitiveness, efficiency, effectiveness and forms of 'policy steering' (Hoggett 1996: 20). This pronounced trend towards 'teaching in the managerial state', as Mahony and Hextall (1997a) term it, was well in place before New Labor came into office, and had a number of distinctive features:

> greater centralised control of a National Curriculum (and perhaps, teaching methods); devolution of financial management to schools and a weakening of Local Educational Authorities (LEA) powers; the introduction of competitive quasi-market policies exerting pressure on schools via published league tables of exam performance and inspection reports; open enrolment to deliver parental 'choice'; and, the reintroduction of differentiated schools.
>
> (p. 5)

Evidence that an extensive wide-ranging reconstruction of the teacher in the UK is underway can be gleaned from the activities of the Teacher Training Agency (TTA) (Mahony and Hextall 1997b) which Mahony and Hextall (1997a) argue has created 'a whirlwind of initiatives which have impinged upon every stage of teacher education and professional development' (p. 3). It seems that a new set of arrangements are poised to descend upon UK teachers in the form of continuing professional development, appraisal systems and, most importantly, a National Professional Qualification (NPQ) framework that will produce a pronounced staged career development plan from newly qualified teachers (NQTs), to expert teachers (mooted in some quarters likely to be called 'Advanced Skills Teachers'), to subject leaders and to school leaders (Mahony and Hextall 1997a: 7). There can be little doubt that these calculated manœuvres are designed to exacerbate a dismal scene, in which schools are already very hierarchically organised, and where closer surveillance will produce even greater levels of specification over what occurs in schools. It seems that the intent is to specify:

> how the occupants of these [new] positions relate to others within the school . . . [It] is predicated upon a particular version of 'leadership' . . . which delegitimates the negotiating space accessible for other, competing styles of leadership . . . Underpinning these moves are mechanistic and technicist assumptions . . . For the bulk of teachers, their roles will become increasingly defined as technician-professionals, working to directives established elsewhere.
>
> (p. 8)

The end result appears to be designed to create a teaching workforce where there is 'a neat and tidy model of career progression from point of entry through to subject and school leadership and to invest this model with very tight specifications of required "knowledge, understanding, skills and abilities" ' (Mahony and Hextall 1997a: 11).

Ball (1997) argues that a range of other attempts to control teachers in the UK through enhanced 'disciplinary technologies of surveillance', such as Total Quality Management (TQM), School Development Planning, and Ofsted (Office for Standards in Education) inspections, are not only unhelpful but are fundamentally flawed because 'schools cannot be represented adequately within research (or evaluation) by simple stories or single essentialising tags; "good/bad", "successful/failing" – they are inherently paradoxical institutions' (p. 317). Ball (1997) encapsulates the complexity in these terms:

> Schools are complex, contradictory, sometimes incoherent organisations, like many others. They are assembled over time to form a bricolage of memories, commitments, routines, bright ideas and policy effects. They are changed, influenced and interfered with regularly and increasingly. They drift, decay and regenerate.
>
> (pp. 317–18)

His argument is that it is not possible to render schools and the work that teachers do down to a 'set of simple performatives and representations' (p. 318) and, furthermore, that attempts to do so will produce 'bad effects' in terms of: 'the intensification of teachers' work (often on administrative tasks unrelated to teaching/learning processes, a reduction in teacher collegiality, and the production of fabricated and manufactured representations of "the school")' (p. 318). Ball (1997) sees devices like TQM, School Development Planning and inspections as 'relay devices' or forms of 'cultural engineering' for the 'imprinting of core values, for the transmission and interpretation of external priorities' linking 'government mentalities and policies' with 'everyday organisational realities' in schools so as to produce 'calculative compliance' (p. 327). The attempt is to change teachers through dramatically reconfiguring the culture of the school.

In mapping the relationship between school restructuring at the macro level and the practices of teachers in classrooms, Gewirtz (1997) tells a very similar story about teachers in the UK. She puts it in terms of the effect of the 'post-welfarist educational policy complex' – a shorthand way of referring to the installation of 'new management regimes' in schools that have the following features: 'a growing preoccupation with balancing the budget' (p. 221); 'a growing preoccupation with target-setting and performance monitoring in order to improve league table performance' (p. 222); and 'a narrowing definition of performance with what can be quantified and a particular emphasis on exam results' (p. 222). The effect of these new management regimes becomes particularly apparent in terms of the intensification of teachers' work, with a number of effects: 'the emotional consequences' of the 'manic grind', of the 'frenetic pace of work', and the feeling of being 'squeezed dry' (p. 224); the 'consequences for the social relations within the school' are profound as the sense of sociability breaks down, as people are required to compete increasingly against one another; and 'pedagogical consequences' are created through a narrowing of the focus, more utilitarian approaches, heightened forms of surveillance within the school and the 'general decline in the vitality and creativity of teaching', amounting to an overall shift from 'progressive' to 'traditional' pedagogies (p. 224).

In making such international comparisons (and we could have made many more), we do need to be extremely careful as Maguire and Ball (1994) note, because while the 'problems' confronting education in the UK and the USA appear similar, the 'solutions' have only a 'superficial resemblance' (p. 5). Teachers in the UK have been accused of involvement in 'producer capture' (operating on the basis of their own self-interests), of not being able to be trusted and, as a consequence, being largely excluded from the reform process. Their counterparts in the USA, on the other hand (and without over-romanticising the situation), have in the latter stages of school restructuring been provided with more opportunity (even within a strongly oriented testing regime) for innovation and risk-taking:

[In] the UK reforms seem aimed at closing down the possibilities of both institutional and local democratic control of education. Schools are to be controlled in the interplay of central powers, the decisions of unelected quangos and competitive individualistic choice-making. In effect, schooling is no longer being articulated as a public service but rather as a state-regulated private good . . . [But] in the USA reforms could well be described as demonstrating at least some 'correspondence' with the characteristics of post-Fordist organisational forms and production processes . . . innovation . . . informal and networked social relations and flat or lateral hierarchies.

(Maguire and Ball 1994: 14)

'LOW-TRUST' POLICIES FOR TEACHERS

It is always easier in respect of complex social activities like teaching to have sharper vision in hindsight. One such aspect is the crucial importance of regarding teaching as having a 'public dimension', which is to say, 'the promotion of a collective as opposed to the individual' life of teaching (Bottery and Wright 1996). Thinking of teaching as going beyond the private confines of a classroom opens up a second crucial dimension of the work of teaching, labelled by Bottery and Wright (1996) as 'the ecological context of teaching', which is to say, locating the practice 'within wider political and social issues [which] deepens the teaching profession's understanding of itself' (p. 82).

Much of the atomisation of teaching currently proceeding under the auspices of marketised approaches have been aided and abetted by a historical predilection of teaching regarding itself primarily as a solitary activity, with only minimal opportunity or requirement for joint or collective dimensions. Bottery and Wright (1996) claim that market rhetoric and consumerist ideology have been able to take hold in schools because 'the teaching profession spends too little time thinking about issues which ask fundamental questions about the purposes of an education system − and therefore of a teaching profession − within a particular kind of society' (p. 83). A wider defence of teacher professionalism, these commentators argue, is 'only possible when teachers are aware of the public context of their teaching, and of the historical, political and sociological reasons for the current nature of practice' (p. 83).

It is possible to conceive of teaching in at least three broad ways (clearly there are more, but we will take these as being useful starting points for discussion): (a) as a technical activity; (b) as a craft, artisan or guild activity; and (c) as a moral, intellectual and political pursuit. Now, while teaching rarely falls neatly into any of these categories, they nevertheless represent orienting tendencies within which to talk about teaching.

The case of *teaching as a technical activity* takes the stance that, in teaching, problems present themselves and require the teacher to search 'through his

or her bank of expertise and select the appropriate solution and apply it'
(Bottery and Wright 1996: 84). Schemes of behaviour management lend
themselves to this kind of treatment, in which pre-formulated responses and
rules have to be matched up with displayed student infractions. This is a
fairly sterile view of teaching that relegates it to the realm of being a
wooden and mechanical activity. There is little opportunity for being inven-
tive or for much in the way of deviation from some pre-invented script,
either to take advantage of idiosyncratic situations or to shape the situation
by the force of one's own personality or charisma.

Teaching as a craft or artisan activity conveys the feeling of teachers operating from a tradition where there is a profound understanding of the
materials being worked with (human, physical, emotional, intellectual and
psychic) and the responsiveness of contexts being worked in. There is much
focusing and reframing along the way, as ideas about what works are shaped
and reconfigured in the light of lived experience about teaching. In Donald
Schon's (1983) terms, there is a process of 'reflection-in-action', a kind of
artistic framing and reframing of problems – a 'reflective conversation with
the materials of the situation' (p. 31). Teaching has many of the attributes of
a process of making sense of an 'uncertain craft' (McDonald 1992), of struggling with 'tensions, contradictions and uncertainties' to present images that
illuminate complexities, of expanding the scope for adding to personal
repertoires and inventories of teaching strategies, and of providing ways of
giving authentic voice to the way teachers 'read' situations (McDonald
1992: ix). This is a valuable and crucial perspective and one that advances
considerably beyond the inflexible technical process of drawing from a bank
of expertise. However, it does still have quite severe shortcomings, most
notably in that there is still a certain amount of closure built into it because
it is unwittingly 'generated by, and supportive of, a particular position of
power' (Bottery and Wright 1996: 84). It does not have a way yet of moving
outside of itself or its own frame of reference, its own self-regulatory norms,
or its own 'occupational closure' to 'participate influentially in debates about
its role within . . . society' (Bottery and Wright 1996: 85). In other words, it
is not yet open to 'macrosocial issues' of professional power. For example, a
craft-like view of teaching would have difficulties with the idea of a national
curriculum, but its difficulties would stem from an uncomfortableness with
the inevitability of proclamations of universal knowledge, rather than from
any profound understanding that national curricula are deeply implicated in
selecting some forms of knowledge while actively excluding others.
Curriculum struggle for these teachers would be limited to invisible difficulties experienced with particular groups of students in classrooms.

Teaching as a moral, intellectual and political activity would start from a
different set of premises than the other two. Here there would be an active
process of engaging with and deciding *'what the issue or problem is,* by reference partly to [a] wider context' (Bottery and Wright 1996: 86). The teacher

here operates in much the same way as a social critic might work – asking questions about how things came to be the way they are, what forces sustain and maintain them, whose interests are served and denied, and what changes can feasibly and prudently be made. There is a sense in which there is an 'awareness of the need for others' help in the framing of problems' (Bottery and Wright 1996: 86), not just to get a wider lens on the issue, but as a way of constructing and organising the constituencies, coalitions and alliances necessary to create and carry forward alternative social change. These are teachers who have an ability to see their students not as 'consumers' but as 'citizens' working with them to create a fairer, more just and equitable society for all. These teachers could rightly regard themselves as 'public sector professionals' (Bottery and Wright 1996: 89), not only able to conceive of their private role as teachers within classrooms, but able to see that there is a crucial wider public aspect to teaching as well in 'the promotion of collective life as opposed to the prosecution of individual interests' (Bottery and Wright 1996: 87).

To take the national curriculum example used earlier. Teachers operating from an understanding of the public dimension of their work would be engaged in debates about why a national curriculum was necessary, whose values get to be priorities within it, and what kind of society is created as a consequence. Teachers of this persuasion tend, in the words of Edward Said (1994), not to be 'a functionary nor an employee completely given up to the policy goals of a government or a large corporation, or even a guild of like-minded professionals. In such situations the temptations to turn off one's moral sense, or to think entirely within the speciality, or curtail scepticism in favour of conformity, are far too great to be trusted' (p. 64).

Such teachers might, for example, engage with the following kind of questions:

- is competition the best way of running an education system?
- what is the appropriate balance between public and private provision in education?
- are internal markets the same as ordinary markets?
- are other professions facing similar market-led changes?
- are pupils and parents merely customers, or something more and different?
- does the use of industrial analogies affect the way teachers think and speak? Is this helpful or unhelpful?
- how can we obviate any excesses of a market situation?

(Bottery and Wright 1996: 87)

Not only is there an understanding here of the impact of teachers' work on the wider social context, but also a sense of how that wider context impacts on the practices of teaching. Teaching thus construed moves beyond individualistic, low-trust, market-oriented approaches to education, because it is able to argue from the basis of its being a public good 'where a society acknowledges the need for provision of a service for all, even for those who cannot afford it, because its provision is seen as essential for the wellbeing of that society as a whole' (Bottery and Wright 1996: 88). Bottery and Wright (1996) claim that teachers of this type not only display an understanding of their public role, but they also show an appreciation of the 'ecology of teaching' and how that teaching is related to the wider social and political framework within which it occurs. These are what might be termed 'high-trust' approaches in that they acknowledge teachers as having an expansive view of the nature of their work. These teachers would, for instance, experience considerable difficulty and dissonance with one-off, quick-fix, episodic styles of short-course inservice education for themselves, because of the way they would experience this as de-professionalising them as teachers, denying them the opportunity to situate and locate their learning in the broader social, political and cultural context of the work of teaching.

In this chapter we have canvassed the notion of the 'preferred teacher' – a shorthand way of alluding to the kind of educational worker employers prefer, and which is exemplified in the contemporary reforms of teaching. The argument put was that the prevailing orientation and discourses were in the direction of creating a teacher who was prepared to work in an acquiescing fashion within the managerialised, marketised, performance-based cultures being created for schools. While these might be the aspirations of governments, they are certainly not those of large numbers of teachers (Shor 1996). Far from acting in docile and subservient ways, teachers have continued in large numbers to construct increasingly collaborative ways of collectively articulating a culture of teaching within/across classrooms, and through professional associations and unions, that give them and their students increasing power and voice over their teaching and learning.

As we shall see in the following chapter, moving beyond 'low-trust' approaches to teaching is possible where there is a recognition of the importance of redrawing the discursive boundaries of teaching in ways that permit and keep alive alternative discourses of the work.

Chapter 6

Interrupting the dominant view

KEEPING ALIVE ALTERNATIVE DISCOURSES ABOUT TEACHING

Redrawing boundaries

Indicative of the way growing numbers of teachers around the world feel at the moment about what is happening to their work, a teacher in England put it like this:

> I sometimes feel that I have fallen asleep for five years and just woken up to a radically altered situation at school. Everything has changed for the worst. At the same time we are told that everything has improved; careers, teaching style, resources and opportunities for the kids. Everyday a new initiative to maintain the illusion. Of course it's just rhetoric but it's becoming more difficult to distinguish the myth from the reality. And this is destroying our work, destroying teaching
>
> (Macan Ghaill 1992: 177)

The rapidity, pervasiveness and thorough-going nature of these changes make it very difficult accurately and comprehensively to trace, let alone grasp, the full extent of their impact. As early as the mid-1980s, Ozga (1988) cited a number of the early policy initiatives reshaping teaching in England as being 'changes in the contractual relationship between teachers and employers; [the abolition of] teachers' negotiation rights; [loss of] control of curriculum and examinations; and changes in the pay and promotion in teaching' (p. ix), and that was *only* in the mid-1980s!

As Mac an Ghaill (1992) summarised it:

> Until the early 1980s, a teacher's occupational identity, educational philosophy and pedagogic practice could be traced to its roots within the public elementary school cultural traditions. More recently this hegemonic framework which defined the occupational parameters

within which teachers worked, providing a consensus for a highly differentiated group (Lacey 1977), has been fractured, leaving many teachers
with a feeling of anomie . . . [This] suggests that teachers' occupational
culture is in crisis, with the emergence of intensely differentiated and
polarised bifurcated teaching ideologies.

(p. 178)

Clearly, there has been some dramatic redrawing of the boundaries around
teaching in recent times. From a situation a few years ago where teaching
was seen by and large to be in the hands of educational professionals, we
have now moved in most parts of the world to a set of ideologies, policies,
practices and discourses where consumerist, contractualist, managerialist
and marketised values and beliefs are what supposedly counts most in
shaping teaching. The teacher as an educational 'producer' is no longer in
charge – the 'customer' (however defined) is supposedly in the driving seat.
We have moved from a situation of alleged 'producer capture' to one of
'consumer sovereignty'.

These changes being experienced to teachers' work are not simply of an
order of magnitude that constitutes the passing away of a bunch of worn-
out, old-fashioned, out-moded views about how teaching and learning
should occur. The way in which existing pedagogical and educational values
surrounding schooling are being systematically purged represents something
far more fundamental than that. It is not clear that the changes currently
being inflicted upon schools actually amount to a paradigm shift – but they
certainly represent the replacement of a set of discourses about the educational and social utility of schooling, to ones that are driven by narrow
vocationalist, managerial and economistic agenda. What we have is a set of
views about how schooling *ought to be* (for that is all it is). These views are
undebated, untested, have no empirical basis to them, are without foundation in terms of an established nexus with known forms of teaching and
learning, and hold no hope for the creation of more socially just, tolerant,
compassionate or egalitarian societies. There are big question marks as to
whether they even have the capacity to make us more efficient, effective or
internationally competitive.

There is little point in simply noting and bemoaning the passing in
sombre tones of a set of cherished pedagogical values and practices, and their
replacement by vulgar alternatives; a more apt response is in terms of doing
something about it, and this is far from an easy task. We believe the starting
point has to be with what Agger (1990) calls the 'decline of discourse' and
the need to reinvigorate the idea of a 'public space' within which what
passes as teaching is able to be debated and discussed in the context of a
wider community-building process. To put this more concretely, we believe
there needs to be an opening-up of the spheres and spaces within which
teachers can become more active theorists of their own and one another's

teaching. In this book we are arguing for forms of 'theory building' about teaching that are not of the 'high theory' type, but rather forms of theory that genuinely contribute to the formulation of a 'solution' and not those that become implicated as a part of the 'problem'.

Our starting point is, therefore, to argue for a rediscovery, a reclaiming and a reassertion of the primacy of the discourses of teaching and learning in schools. In what has to be the most remarkable aspect to the so-called educational reform around the world, there is a uniformly and strikingly consistent emphasis on the restructuring of management, organisation, administration and control of schools – none of it having anything to do with the essence or substance of teaching and learning. In our view, this amounts to a defacement, disfigurement and grotesque distortion of the ways we traditionally talk about the work of teaching. We are witnessing a move away from regarding teaching as being primarily about educational matters, concerned with equality, social justice and the improvement of children's life chances, to seeing it in terms of its own limited internal forms of efficiency, effectiveness and accountability.

Before considering the alternatives, we need a window on where we are currently heading. Most parts of the world have unproblematically embraced a competencies approach: in the vocational area, the UK has had the National Council for Vocational Qualifications with its competency and outcomes approaches to curriculum design (Barnett 1994), and more recently the 'profiling' process for beginning teacher competencies (Moore 1996); the USA is at an advanced stage of producing its National Standards for the Teaching Profession through the National Board for Professional Teaching Standards (King 1994); and Australia has recently announced a national review of teacher education to produce skills inventories of national teacher education standards for intending teachers in university programmes. This hardly represents a resounding vote of confidence from governments around the world on the abilities of teacher educators or the professional integrity and judgements of classroom teachers. But then again, perhaps it also tells us much about the 'state we're in' (Hutton 1995) and the capacity for the current batch of governments to go to any lengths in scapegoating. It is indicative of a total 'failure of political imagination' (Walter 1996) that we could end up with such a case of terminal tunnel vision, where 'solutions' as intellectually bereft as 'casino capitalism', 'market forces' and a constant harping about 'international competitiveness' are the best that are available.

'Competencies' as a dominant discourse

We intend examining in some detail a specific illustrative example of what's wrong with the competencies approach as *the* singular educational discourse. It comes from the implementation of guidelines of CATE (the Council for the Accreditation of Teacher Education) in the UK, profiling competencies for teacher education institutions; the instance occurred at Goldsmiths College, University of London. Moore (1996) reported a study of how beginning teachers perceived competencies profiles as a help or hindrance to good classroom practice. The overall finding was that competencies frameworks 'tend to constrain the modes and parameters within which to think about . . . practice . . . [while at the same time producing] a pathologisation of the individual practitioner' (p. 200). Beginning teachers in the study not only found the statements of competencies to be a 'daunting document' (Moore 1996: 203), experienced considerable difficulty with it as a 'universal blueprint' for teaching and the manner in which it excluded consideration of the 'idiosyncratic, contingent elements of classroom practice' (Moore 1996: 201–2), but they encountered significant 'inventorial difficulties' (Moore 1996: 204) in the way competencies presented themselves as 'fundamentally fixed and unchallengeable' appearing 'as products of the collective, disinterested wisdom of "other people"' (Moore 1996: 204). In other words, the teachers had difficulty reconciling the perception of the 'closed' language of the written competencies with their own much more 'open' verbal and unrecorded discourse in which they lived, experienced and experimented with teaching. They found lists of competencies to be 'intimidating' because of the appearance they gave of being 'pre-fixed', 'handed down to you even before you can start making your own discoveries in practice' (Moore 1996: 204), in the words of one teacher.

Because the requirements of a good teacher were seen as having been externally fixed with given skills and areas of understanding and knowledge prescribed, there was no sense of the teacher's prime function being to 'interrogate' practice, participate 'in a range of discourses' about teaching, or generally embark on a process of 'discussion, debate and reflection about good practice' (Moore 1996: 205). Despite being urged by teacher educators to regard the competencies otherwise, for beginning teachers these options had an 'inventorial' appearance and presented as being foreclosed and not open to debate and discussion. In the words of one teacher, there was the feeling that 'there just isn't anything left to be said' (Moore 1996: 205). The effect was not one of encountering possible candidates about teaching upon which to engage in considered and constructive reflection, but rather of instructions to be followed so that 'all will be well' (Moore 1996: 206). The negative side of this was significant indeed when things began to go wrong in the classroom: 'In this situation, far from being useful, the competencies list became a rod with which the [teacher] beats her own back' (Moore 1996: 206). This leads, Moore (1996) says, to a 'pathologisation of the individual' which takes the following form, as put by one teacher: 'These are the things I'm told I have to do. I'm doing them, but things are still going wrong. Therefore I can't be doing them properly' (p. 206).

In other words, lists of competencies pre-dispose teachers to engaging in unwarranted forms of self-flagellation, at the same time as denying them the invitation to experiment with and playfully appropriate aspects of their teaching, 'absorb[ing], interrogate[ing] and elaborat[ing] through interactive, interpretative processes' (Moore 1996: 206).

The other major problem Moore (1996) encountered with the singular framing discourse of competencies was the way in which they served to 'mask appearances' – in other words, how they worked to cover up 'inevitable, unresolvable antagonisms or contradictions' (Moore 1996: 207) in complex social contexts like teaching. This produced, Moore says, a 'fissure' between the practitioner and the practising context such that, when things don't work out, the antagonisms of the context are papered over or masked, with the individual resorting to explanations of the problem with reference to the list of competencies, or else attributing it to personal failure – both at the expense of 'reflecting on the systems within which one is practising' (Moore 1996: 208). In other words, when things go wrong a cover-up occurs and the system gets off because it is regarded as being free of major problems.

The greatest danger in the competencies discourse lies in its capacity to represent itself as authoritative, and not merely as one among many possible discourses about teaching. For Moore (1996): 'The real difficulty emerges when the competencies discourse replaces other discourses by becoming the dominant discourse' (p. 209). The tragedy is that we wind up 'masking those very fissures in our educational and social systems that we may want our [teachers] to be critically aware of' (p. 210).

The process of discourse displacement

What is happening to teaching is happening around the world to a range of other public sector workers. There is a 'displacement of discourses' (Smyth 1996c) occurring as local and indigenous ways of talking about the work are replaced by generic, global and universal discourses. Amanda Sinclair (1996) from the Graduate School of Management at Melbourne University speaks of the need in these circumstances for forms of leadership to 'rediscover a lost discourse' of public administration. She puts this in terms readily recognisable by educational workers:

> In the remaking of public sector management, the linking of social ideals and institutional purposes with personal values and aspirations has become largely undiscussed and undiscussable. One of the legacies of the new hegemony of generic management models in administration is a language and discourse which casts public sector management as a technical activity rather than a social commitment or moral practice.
>
> (p. 229)

There are resonances here in the way we are increasingly being urged by educational policy makers to think and act in schools. It is worth pursuing Sinclair's arguments here for a moment because of what she has to say about what is happening to public administration and the way it operates as a canopy for activities like teaching in schools. The language and ideology of 'service-oriented and customer-driven administration' is alive in education as in most other public sector agencies, but as Sinclair (1996) argues, this new 'post-bureaucratic' public management is just as mechanistic as the model it purports to replace, and the discourse through which it is expressed is as 'bereft of the moral concepts and social purposes of administration as scientific management' (p. 231). The new discourse characterising the management of activities like education 'places a broader understanding of purposes outside the legitimate concerns [of educators]. Debate of the "what" and the "why" of administration has been superseded by a fixation on the "how" ' (p. 229), says Sinclair. What is not being pursued are the broader moral questions of 'what is it all for?' As Sinclair (1996) says:

> If the best that she or he [the manager] can come up with is: 'meeting my targets', 'a business focus', or even 'excellent customer service', this offers slender spiritual nourishment. Living on a diet of such thin work purposes provides individuals with little joy or satisfaction in achievement.
>
> (p. 243)

It is an intriguing question then, as to how we have come to be in this situation. Sinclair (1996) suggests that, in part at least, we need to look to the language we have allowed to give meaning to what we do in organisations like schools, and how it is we permit it to hold sway. She says:

> Language is not an inert vehicle through which ideas are expressed but an active sponsor of certain 'regimes of truth' (Hollway 1989: 39). Discourses are combinations of words and phrases which, taken together, organise into our sphere of attention certain values, concepts and ideas. Discourses thus create meaning or 'truths' for those speaking, listening and reading. Examining discourses illuminates the process by which language is a willing conspirator with our paradigm in determining what we know and of what we can remain ignorant.
>
> (p. 231)

Discourses map 'the historical and social contexts within which social decisions and policies are made and institutions created, sustained and transformed' (Harmon and Mayer 1986: 322).

How people locate themselves in relation to discourses also reflects the socially sanctioned dominance of certain ideologies and subjugation of others. Because discourses vary in their authority (Gavey 1989: 464) at one particular time one discourse, such as managerialism or a market approach, seems 'natural' while another, say, a morally justified commitment to the public interest, struggles to find expression in the way experience is described.

(p. 232)

Putting this another way, language reconstructs what we do through 'censoring understandings' (Sinclair 1996: 232), or as Hood and Jackson (1991) put it: 'supersession of one ruling . . . doctrine by another occurs through a rhetorical process not by the marshalling of incontrovertible evidence' (p. xi).

How dominant discourses work and how they might be contested so as to establish a 'rediscovered discourse of purpose' as Sinclair (1996) terms it, to be replaced by more emancipatory possibilities, is the job of the next section.

A 'rediscovered discourse of purpose'

The case for a rediscovering of the discourses of teaching can be made on at least four grounds:

1   Innovative, dynamic and vibrant schools have an expansive rather than an impoverished, utilitarian or economistic view of their own social value and purposes. Such schools have 'imaginative spaces' that correspond to 'democratic public spaces'. Teachers in these schools have been able to develop ways of working in which they connect with the lives of their students, rather than becoming caught up with mindless bureaucratic incursions and measurement of performance against standards. They have very effective ways of collaboratively analysing and articulating what kind of schools they are and what they stand for, and continually operate in ways that involve the wider community in ownership of their vision. Teaching has transcended the isolation of cellular egg-crate ways of organising classrooms, and teachers share, debate and trial new ideas with one another through joint planning and classroom processes. There are no private granaries of knowledge in these schools – what is known to some is accessible to all. Above all these schools have a passion for social justice and democratic decision making in all aspects of what they do. Changes occur, but they are not dramatic or ill-considered – they come only as a consequence of extensive discussion and at a pace everyone feels comfortable with.

2   We know from the enlightened quarters of the business sector that a 'singular discourse does not capture or mobilise the diversity of aspirations employees seek in their work' (Sinclair 1996: 234). Schools are

multi-faceted, multi-vocal, multi-cultural sites that survive and thrive on multiplicity and diversity; their survival depends on vigorous discussion, debate and argument about their moral and social purposes. At the moment, by and large that is not happening – a particular 'preferred' template of what schools should be like is being imposed from outside without any public debate. Rather than be encased with a singular, narrow and largely meaningless discourse that has the effect of amputating, homogenising and obliterating indigenous discourses about teaching, learning and schooling, we need processes that foster difference and diversity. We need to 'unmask the diversity that already exists within our own public sector organisations [schools] and [highlight] the dangers of a simplistic embrace of a discourse of an elite' (Sinclair 1996: 236).

3   Schools are being controlled and co-ordinated in new and different ways, and teachers need to find ways of reinserting and reinscribing the educational and the pedagogical back into the debate about those new modes of control. We are in a 'new age' of accountability relationships, and teachers have to develop responses to the demands for these that are more amenable and indigenous to schools and the work of teaching. This means being more articulate about the norms that govern the work of teaching, so as to avoid having alien forms of control inappropriately inserted into teaching.

4   People who occupy leadership positions in our schools and school systems (increasingly described as 'managers' and 'CEOs' (Chief Executive Officers)) need to be thoroughly imbued with an educative rationale for their jobs – the managerial needs to be there, but only in order to address the wider social and moral purposes for which schools exist. Put another way, we need more emphasis on 'purpose' and less on 'strategy'. From teachers' perspectives (and those who work with teachers) this means capturing the vitality and the complexity of life in schools through the authentic, personal and institutional discourses of narratives and life-like portrayals. This involves more than simply celebrating teachers' work – it requires recognising where these 'personal discourses' (which are often tentative, colloquial and ordinary sounding) stand in relation to the intrusive, muscular, authoritative, managerialist discourses that appear so reassuring and that get conveniently 'wheeled out' in situations of evaluation, review and accountability (Sinclair 1996: 238). The question to be answered is: when (if at all) and under what set of circumstances are these *synthetic discourses* going to be allowed to hold sway over the *authentic (or indigenous) discourses* of schools, teaching and learning?

Like Sinclair (1996) we are arguing for 'an alternative discourse of purpose' (p. 241) as an antidote to 'inert goals and lifeless performance indicators [which] activate little commitment apart from contract delivery and keeping the auditor at bay. The emotional emptiness of efficiency propels a mechanical and often fearful managerial performance' (p. 241).

We consider the new synthetic discourses of schooling to be emotionally, socially and educationally bankrupt. Failure to craft a counter discourse will mean that teachers will remain 'slaves to . . . the administrative fashion trade of pop management' (Hood and Jackson 1991: 24).

Breaking the hold of synthetic discourses

How we manage our schools and the teaching and learning that go on within them must, therefore, be informed by the broader question of how lives are to be lived out in schools, and whether these are to be driven by notions of *courage*, *compassion*, *trust* and *character*. Such a rediscovered discourse:

> would then be a dynamic and debated institutional philosophy about why [a school] operates, what distinctive values it brings, where it is located in its environment, and what it is aiming for. Rather than a set of values frozen in a mission statement, the discourse would be the outcome of many conversations.
>
> (Sinclair 1996: 243–4)

As long as the language and ideology that are allowed to hold sway around teaching are managerialist and marketised, then we will continue to have patterns of domination and subordination being reproduced. As Janks and Ivanic (1992) point out, when we change the language practices, it becomes possible to break the circuits of domination. How power operates through asymmetrical relations is as important to understand in schools as in society generally. Janks and Ivanic (1992) argue that 'subject positions' are constructed for and by us:

> In any asymmetrical relation of power there is a top dog and a person or persons below, the underdog. How people get to be on top in a society has to do with what that society values. It may be age or maleness or class or cleverness or a white skin. It is easier for those who have power to maintain it, if they can persuade everyone in the society that there is nothing unnatural about these arrangements. Things are this way because that is the way they are meant to be. We all know, because of the society we live in, that doctors know more about their patients' illness than the patients themselves do. We all know that teachers know what their students need. We all know that parents know better than their teenagers. Knowing these things we consent to the power that society accords to those with expertise and greater age and experience. And in using these examples we have not even attempted to address the problem of the continuing consent given to racist, sexist and class-based values in society. The more these values are seen as uncontestable givens,

the less coercion is needed to maintain them. They work as the prevailing 'common sense' of a society, through what Gramsci (1971) calls 'hegemony'.

(p. 306)

How we become subjugated by language is important, notwithstanding that 'it is easy to resist accepting the preferred meaning if one is positioned differently to start with. From that different position the reader is able to offer opposing content, other language and alternative emphases' (Janks and Ivanic 1992: 307). But, if we are in agreement with the text a critical or resistant reading becomes much more difficult. Janks and Ivanic (1992) explain that we become 'interpellated' (or unconsciously inserted into the construction of the texts we live out) in a variety of ways. For example:

We do not need to be 'named' as patient when we enter the doctor's consulting rooms. A range of social practices, of which language is but one, construct this position for us. These practices include such things as patients having to wait, the keeping of files on patients to which they have no access, as well as the language of traditional doctor–patient interviews.

(p. 308)

In much the same manner, when schools are framed by discourses and practices of management and administration, it follows that teachers unconsciously 'read' themselves into positions of subordinated followers required unquestioningly to acquiesce and implement edicts, priorities and practices developed at a distance from schools and classrooms. This process is 'naturalised' through the construction of teachers as civil servants required to be silently accountable by virtue of their being paid out of the public purse. When confronted by requirements to 'implement' a national curriculum, statewide/national testing, competency approaches to teaching, performance management schemes, or the like, teachers are often inclined to position themselves as having to accommodate and accept preferred meanings and adopt the 'subject position' (p. 309). There is a clear distinction to be made here between 'opposition' and 'resistance':

'Opposition' means thinking which goes against the existing ground rules, negating them, valuing their opposite. This is opposition which stays within the existing framework. 'Resistance' means thinking differently, rejecting the ground rules and the premises on which they are based: actively participating in attempts to change the whole framework on which the ground rules depend. Emancipatory discourse is to do with opposition and resistance: recognising the forces which are leading you to fit in with the status quo and resisting them.

(p. 309)

So far in this chapter we have actively pursued the argument that in teaching there needs to be a multiplicity of voices, not just the one dominant one of managerialism that is coming to frame what occurs in schools. We are disturbed by the apparent move to expunge so readily teachers' voices through a reform process that denies their viewpoints. In the next part of this chapter we bring to a culmination the arguments for teachers' missing voices.

THE MISSING VOICES OF TEACHERS

In trying to make sense of the possible linkages between the cacophony of 'preferred discourses' of educational policy and the discordant, dissenting, resisting but barely audible voices of teachers, it is hard not to be left with the impression that teachers worldwide have been pushed to the margins when it comes to being consulted about changes to education. That teachers in the USA have been largely excluded from discussions is well summed up by Cohn and Kottkamp (1993) in the title of their book *Teachers: The Missing Voice in Education*. Cohn and Kottkamp's observations of the exclusion of teachers in their part of the world resonate with experiences in almost all other countries. The consistency with which teachers have been omitted from a significant say in moves to reframe both the specifics as well as the broader context within which teaching occurs would have to be one of the most remarkable aspects of contemporary educational policy. While at one level we can understand the reasoning behind wanting to keep a large, self-interested and potentially powerful group like teachers at arm's length, in other ways we find the strategy hard to accept, mainly because you need to understand something about the nature of the work of teaching, in order to appreciate why the educational reform agenda is fundamentally flawed. In one way or another, most recent educational reforms have implicit within them an accountability agenda – which is to say that teachers can be changed by making them more compliant.

Teaching is a highly 'relational' activity – which is another way of saying that one of the primary reasons teachers come into this line of work is because of the opportunities it presents them with to connect with and help shape and form the lives of others – students, colleagues and members of the wider community. Teachers repeatedly tell of getting their most important satisfaction in teaching from the opportunities to participate closely in formulating the circumstances which help to improve students' life chances. The single most important reward repeatedly reported by teachers is the knowledge that they have contributed to student learning, growth or development, either in the short or longer term (Cohn and Kottkamp 1993: 63). One teacher put it in these terms:

A good day is when I can actually teach and get my lesson across, have the students respond, and I get a feeling of satisfaction that I have accomplished something other than just 'Turn around,' 'Sit down,' 'Get back in your seat,' 'No, you can't go to the bathroom,' 'Let go of so and so's head.' . . . What also makes me feel good is when a student who wouldn't read out loud suddenly starts volunteering to read . . . even though he is stumbling . . . At least he's reading . . . It's when I see kids' progress.

(Cohn and Kottkamp 1993: 53)

Experiencing the 'psychic reward' of seeing students benefit directly from teaching appears to be the ultimate reward and satisfaction in teaching and derives directly from having developed the kind of relationship with children that makes this possible – despite the fact that 'extrinsic rewards' like remuneration, occupational status and wider feelings of power and influence are reportedly low among teachers as an occupational group. As Johnson (1990) concluded: 'the ultimate reward that teachers seek appears in fact to be quite simple: the opportunity to teach well and to know it matters' (p. 34).

The very essence of teachers is, therefore, closely and inextricably bound up with their perceptions of how the wider circumstances of their work either contribute to, hinder or frustrate this central ideal of their work. There is much in the reform of teachers' work that detracts from this – most noticeably, the low-trust managerial imperatives supposedly aimed at making teachers more accountable for their teaching. These schemes not only undermine the sense of mission teachers have of their own educational purposes but, more importantly, they contribute directly to the construction of 'uncertainties' within the interpersonal relations of teaching. Basically, the work is of such a kind that it continually teeters on the edge of maintaining this 'delicate balance' and, therefore, moves to make schools into more 'restrictive environments' (Cohn and Kottkamp 1993: 185) run the strong chance of interrupting the relational conditions necessary for good teaching. Cohn and Kottkamp (1993) explain the 'fragility' of these relational dynamics both in terms of what can happen inside an individual classroom, as well as in terms of the wider interruptions to teachers' work:

Good days require a delicate interpersonal balance of the teacher and the whole class working together for the teacher to be rewarded more than meagrely. The teacher, a single student or a single interruption may crack the relational dynamic and begin what one teacher described as the 'contagion' that infects the whole classroom.

(p. 67)

Another way this happens is through the 'structural strains' (Cohn and

Kottkamp 1993: 127) accompanying the increased tension created through the artificial, synthetic and distorted expectations of narrowly conceived accountability procedures and their inevitable accompanying increase in 'paperwork' for teachers. As one American teacher expressed it:

> We have like a Gestapo for [lesson plans]. We do a lot of lesson plans. It's almost like a recipe you find on the back of a Campbell's soup can: the objective, the activity, and the assessment . . . [We have] Gestapo agents that come around and sign them. I feel like I'm three years old and I had to be good on the potty or something.
>
> (Cohn and Kottkamp 1993: 133)

Added paperwork, testing, evidence keeping, competency and performance-based approaches, and the general 'tightening of control and the limiting of professional discretion' (Cohn and Kottkamp 1993: 137) have the effect of 'altering purposes [as well as] means' (Cohn and Kottkamp 1993: 136) – which go to the very core of teachers' capacities to make decisions about the nature of the work of teaching. The tenor and tone of these measures is even more damaging, toxic and noxious than the paperwork they generate. Again from the American experience of educational reforms:

> Teachers experienced increasing mechanisms of control through heavy emphasis on testing of basic and limited objectives and through the mandating of particular programs, packages, 'boxes,' and other 'teacher-proof' materials. Paperwork may be seen as 'unprofessional,' demeaning and hurtful, but curricular and instructional control strikes at the very core of how teachers define their work. It limits personal engagement in developing purpose and exercising discretion based on craft experience and minute-by-minute decision-making in the flow of instruction.
>
> (Cohn and Kottkamp 1993: 136)

In a similar vein, and from a European context, Kelchtermans (1996) found that 'teacher vulnerability', expressed in and through questioning teachers moral and professional integrity, occurs most frequently through administrative and policy measures. It produces feelings of 'powerlessness, frustration, disappointment, disillusion, guilt and even anger' (p. 307).

The way competency-based control measures work is that they generate an increased sense of 'vulnerability' (p. 151) on the part of teachers – they feel increasingly exposed and under unnecessary scrutiny, continually experiencing the stress and pressure of having to narrow their focus so as to respond to somebody else's agenda, unable to develop the level of interpersonal relationships with students that is crucial to successful teaching. The American researchers found: 'One assumption behind accountability is that it provides some kind of incentive to improve practice. However, we found nothing encouraging in the ways teachers talked about vulnerability from accountability measures' (Cohn and Kottkamp 1993: 151). But, as these researchers reported, it was not single measures but the cumulative effect of accountability measures that was worst of all for teachers:

> accountability-based vulnerability comes not from a single source. It results from the build-up of successive shock waves assaulting teachers. These waves include changes in student and parent attitudes, assumptions, and behaviours, the increased prescriptions of purposes of education and means for instruction exercised from afar, the imposition of more paperwork, and the clear message of societal distrust.
>
> (p. 152)

> The feelings of vulnerability do not lead to concerted effort to improve practice; they are not carrots. Rather, many teachers experience accountability measures as dysfunctional hammers beating them down even further . . . Teachers feeling these emotions are unlikely to work with more dedication, conviction, engagement, and sense of efficacy. Instead, they are likely to become increasingly cynical, tired, and pawn-like in orientation.
>
> (p. 153)

In Chapter 7 we provide some in-depth insights into how teachers think and experience the kind of exclusions spoken about here, as they encountered a policy initiative that was supposedly for their benefit. But before that, it may be useful to recapitulate on what the AST was about.

ASTs AND THE REMAKING OF TEACHERS' WORK

The concept of the AST in Australian schools can be traced back to the drive towards award restructuring for Australian workers through which the federal governments of the late 1980s and early 1990s sought to increase the economic productivity and international competitiveness of the nation (Bluer 1991; 1993). The concurrent focus of government educational research on the quality of school education (Review Committee on Quality of Education 1985) and the nature of teachers' work (Schools Council 1990), along with those policy imperatives seeking the generic description of work skills and competencies (Australian Education Council 1992), led to a policy climate favourable to the close scrutiny of teaching and learning in schools and other educational organisations (Australian Education Council 1991). This saw teaching practices studied and described in detail, on a scale, and in a political context of labour market reform, that had not been seen before. One outcome of this economic-based reform in the workplace, as it became applied to schools, was a recognition that not all highly experienced class-room teachers end up in school administration and that some system for appraising and rewarding the acquisition of sophisticated skills in the work of classroom teachers was long overdue. Between 1991 and 1993, after lengthy negotiation between teachers, employers and their representatives, all states and territories in Australia introduced an AST scheme to provide recognition of the sophisticated skills held by experienced teachers, some financial reward for those who could demonstrate them, and add legitimacy to the putative connection of the scheme to the enhanced performance of schools as organised workplaces.

Despite its rather impressive and laudable goals the AST scheme received a mixed reception from teachers and policy analysts. Early research on the implementation of the AST scheme by Chadbourne and Ingvarson (1991) questioned whether it could impact on productivity as promised and found many potential problems with the administration of the scheme that led them to wonder if it was, for all, a 'lost opportunity'. Johnson-Riordan's (1995) critical review of the AST process in South Australia found it promoted a reductive view of teaching that limited the possibilities of repre-sentation for highly developed teaching practice to forms conducive to implicit control by employers. In Victoria, Watkins (1994) found that the primacy of the relational nature of teaching practice was lost in the concep-tualisation of skill available within the confines of the selection processes and this required teachers to narrate their skills in unfamiliar and non-preferred ways. Now a few years later, AST schemes in most states are frozen in underdeveloped forms, or, as is the case in Victoria, being phased out and replaced by different kinds of professional recognition and payment patterns.

The introduction of the AST classification to Australian schools was awaited with some measured expectation by Australian teachers. From its conceptual appearance in 1987, the prospect of a designated 'advanced'[1] category for classroom teachers, beyond the usual limits to which they might aspire, was welcomed by teachers, principals, teacher unions and employers alike. There was a uniform chorus of voices endorsing the move towards recognition of the knowledge, ability and professional presence which highly experienced and skilled teachers bring to children in class-rooms and colleagues in schools. However, since that time the specific interests for each of these groups in developing an identified group of

1   The use of advanced as a noun and an adjectival descriptor for a cohort of experienced teachers and certain aspects of teachers' work, such as skills, practice, pedagogies, and the like, will appear as 'advanced'. We choose to place this emphasis because we view the term as highly problematic within our discussion of the AST scheme in the remaking of teachers' work. Indeed, we consider that in its unqualified and over-use in the discussion of the work of experienced teachers it inevitably becomes a weasel-word that vitiates the terms it accompanies.

'advanced' teachers have taken shape in different ways. Concrete definitions of 'advanced' in teaching take on different forms according to the agendas represented. When it comes to specific criteria, similarities strongly present at conception quickly dissipate into generalised notions of 'quality' teaching.

It is fair to say that the articulation of the AST concept, in its nascent stages, took place within an optimistic rhetoric about the cumulative development and diverse level of skill required for successful teaching. Experienced teachers, committed to teaching as a career, and with a record of exemplary teaching were declared deserving of something 'new' to represent their achievements symbolically. Such a move was regarded as simultaneously giving them status in public and peer circles.

The thrust of the arguments presented for establishing a group of designated 'advanced' teachers was positive with a liberal sprinkling of words like 'recognition', 'acknowledgement', 'reward', 'skill', 'leadership' and 'quality' evident in position papers and policy documents. This endorsement of the value of teachers' work can be traced back to the comments on teachers and teaching made in 1990 by the then Federal Minister for Employment, Education and Training, John Dawkins, when he foreshadowed the development of the AST concept in his call for award restructuring in teaching and the development of a 'super teacher' classification: 'The award restructuring process provides the best opportunity for us to achieve enhanced quality teaching, improved career and training opportunities for teachers and more efficient and effective schools' (Dawkins 1990: 2).

Clearly, the federal government saw mutual benefits for teachers and school systems in the restructuring of career paths for classroom teachers. Indeed, this basic assumption resurfaced time and again as the case for award restructuring, the AST concept and the development of the teaching profession was put to the educational community (Schools Council 1990). For the government, it was a way to initiate a national education reform agenda under the rubric of making schools more 'productive' workplaces (Bluer 1991), while linking skills with competency-based standards for teachers' work (Peacock and Bluer 1991), within an attempt to co-ordinate the curriculum (Beazley 1993). Also, the proposed benefits for teachers were not understated. Some prominent players in the push for restructuring claimed that an AST classification would 'provide classroom teachers with greater awards [sic] for demonstrating superior classroom teaching skills, and it embodies a significant career path change for Australia's more than 200,000 school teachers' (Bluer and Carmichael 1991: 27).

Clearly, within the ambit of the revisioning of teachers' work through the AST scheme, teachers were to gain much – for 'the prize is great' (Bluer and Carmichael 1991: 29) – in the form of reward, recognition and skill development through the creation of a 'super teacher' incentive for certain exemplary work practices. Indeed, the literature provided to teachers by employers emphasised the connection between recognition, reward and the demonstration of the higher order teaching skills integral to the AST classification. In Victoria it was stated as:

> the Advanced Skills Teacher category recognises the excellent skills and abilities of experienced teachers engaged in classroom centred work in schools. The AST category will ensure continued quality teaching practice and provide teachers with access to more varied, fulfilling and better paid jobs, thereby assisting in retaining good teachers in the classroom.
>
> (Directorate of School Education Victoria 1992: 9)

In South Australia teachers were advised that:

> the introduction of Advanced Skills Teacher 1 is a new career path to recognise and reward highly skilled teachers wishing to remain in the classroom. The AST 1 classification is a recognition of highly skilled classroom practitioners who share their skills and experience to positively affect the expertise and professionalism of other teachers.
>
> (Education Department of South Australia 1992: 1)

In each case, the recognition of higher order teaching skills and their reward was presented as the rationale for the AST scheme. The connections are plain: if you are an experienced and skilled teacher, then AST provides an avenue for recognition and reward. Teachers in schools understand this skill-recognition nexus very well, but interpret it in a range of ways, as the following selection of comments shows. For example, while not having made application for AST, one teacher understood this to mean a way of gaining some professional kudos, without having to follow traditional promotional-recognition career pathways into school administration:

> I had envisaged that AST would be the beginning of a process of recognising leadership in teaching within the classroom, and a career structure that allowed, in fact encouraged, educators to continue teaching while still being recognised for their value in the profession. In other words, remain practitioners yet still achieve promotion and reward.

It seems many teachers endorsed the importance of recognition for high levels of commitment and leadership in schools which was not tied to positions in school administration. For another, while a career in administration was undesirable, recognition for excellence in classroom teaching was highly valued and sought after:

It's a recognition that we're worth while and we want to stay in the classroom. Well, I have already made that conscious decision — I don't wish to go for any admin. positions. I think it is important that classroom teachers are recognised and rewarded for wanting to stay in the classroom rather than to go into the admin. side of things.

The importance of recognising exemplary classroom teaching practice and providing a reward tied to remaining in the classroom was built into the AST concept from the start. It was an oft-stated objective for award restructuring and the supposed reinvigoration of teachers' work and careers: 'The main justification for this classification is to encourage teachers of high quality to continue their work in the classroom, and in all cases the classification should be framed with this in mind' (Schools Council 1990: 120).

Of course, recognition of the primacy of classroom work in teaching was for many teachers long overdue and readily seen as the sort of recognition that quality practitioners deserved.

Despite having no desire to work in any leadership or administrative role, I have always felt classroom teachers, like myself, deserved some recognition for the work done in schools. Recognition of good classroom teaching practice and recognition of my creativity, adaptability within my profession.

While there are many rewards intrinsic to classroom work, the official nature of the recognition available through an AST award was also understood to be important. Being able to fly the flag for classroom work and wear the campaign ribbons for classroom service was permissible with 'acknowledgement in a formal way . . . verified objectively . . . the system's way of saying how we acknowledge people'. Inevitably, for most teachers their understanding of the importance of AST was grounded in their own circumstances and desire to be seen as doing well at their work. For example, this secondary teacher had long been looking for recognition of a perceived level of quality in his work.

I compared myself to other teachers and I thought I do a pretty good job in teaching, getting organised and doing organisational things around the school, and thought it was about time I got some recognition for that. It's recognition for what I already do. So the AST thing says: 'you're doing it all right, you're teaching well'.

This was a straightforward view common amongst teachers who put themselves up for the AST process, despite the in-built weakness of its generality and reliance on the sentimental principle of 'gratuities for the journey-person'.

The desire to gain some acknowledgement for years of dedication was very often a strong incentive for many who sought to wear the label 'advanced'.

At last I could gain recognition for the extra duties I have been performing over my years of teaching.

I needed some recognition for the work I had done as a teacher.

To me it was the recognition, for all the years of dedication, that I really wanted.

While the notion of recognition of specific forms of teaching ability is seen as important, for many, recognition of exemplary classroom work cannot be disconnected from wider notions of 'advanced' teaching, such as being valued in a school and its community for the extent of contributions made to generations of children over many years of service. This view is equally evident in the comments made by experienced teachers who were unsuccessful in gaining an AST classification. Typically, it goes something like: 'after some success both in the classroom and leadership positions within the school I felt, after 28 years' teaching, I had much to offer'.

Teachers often chose to blur their understandings of recognition to include a range of things other than classroom teaching. In many cases, being an 'advanced' teacher was thought of as a montage of experientially grounded skills and strategies where excellence in classroom teaching was set in relief against other forms of professional (non-administrative) leadership that made for a more complex and inclusive notion of 'advanced' skill in teaching. In general, the common thread present in the weave of teachers' expectations of the AST process was that of long overdue, but very welcome, recognition for good work in classrooms. However, that thread was not uniform in its thickness of conception and understanding and was used in different ways according to the kind of pattern of teaching it was being used to represent. Even though the AST scheme was positively received it proved to be a site of struggle as teachers engaged in various forms of accommodation, contestation and resistance to its remaking of their work.

In Chapter 7 an extensive multi-voiced narrative of the remaking of teachers' work through the AST scheme is presented. It draws upon the voices of teachers, principals and others who have participated in AST application and selection processes and seeks to give a portrayal of the complexity of the scheme and its assimilation into the working lives and career patterns of teachers in Australian schools. In 'Letting the preferred teacher speak' we present an account of the expectations and contradictions that exist within the remaking of experienced teachers through the AST scheme. By recording and critically annotating what teachers had to say about the AST process we provide an up-close examination of how the larger social and

economic forces alluded to so far in this book, which are remaking teachers'
work, impact on the professional lives of those who live, dream and work in
classrooms far from parliaments, boardrooms and conferences. Teachers'
voices are heard about the work of experienced teaching, about teaching skill
as discursive practice, about the merging of skill and policy discourses, and
about the ideological regime of power that the AST scheme has come to
represent for many classroom workers.

Furthermore, in making a link with the arguments found in the first part
of this book and our portrayal of teachers and the AST, we encourage a
reading stance that 'looks both ways'. It has been our intent to connect our
theorising with the case-study material, and *vice versa*. We believe a shut-
tling back and forth should not interrupt the integrity of either part, but
rather add a discursive richness in reading the text as policy ethnography.
Readers may seek connections between the macro and the micro elements
active in the remaking of teachers' work, in a process of 'reviewing' the arguments from earlier text. This, we believe, makes it possible to link the
theorising about the macro forces at work in the remaking of teachers' work,
within the particularity of the AST context, through appropriate revisita-
tions to the earlier arguments in the book.

Chapter 7

Letting the 'preferred' teacher speak

SPEAKING ABOUT THE PAIN OF REFORGING SKILLS INTO WORDS

Huge amounts of time and effort go into getting from the start to the finish of an AST process – from preparing an application, until the stage when the selection panel makes its recommendation. Teachers talk about 'fifty to one hundred hours of preparation', of 'three months' work', and of how the norms of social and classroom life 'collapse' under the sheer intensity of the process. There appears little doubt that the procedure for getting 'advanced' teaching skills articulated and recognised is a huge undertaking for teachers and others co-opted into the process.

> I think it was the most rigorous process I've been through and I was so flat at the end of it. I've never experienced that feeling after other interviews. After the AST interview I felt I was just wrung out. I worked so hard, there was nothing more I could do, or show, yet, I shouldn't have had to do any more than I do normally. But, I felt I did.

One of the more telling observations about this 'intensity-in-process' that teachers and others have noted is the disproportionate amount of time and documentation required for 'advanced' skills accreditation compared to the other forms of teacher recognition which experienced practitioners are likely to engage in as part of career advancement. Surprisingly, teachers learn that promotional opportunities for positions in school administration and other forms of school leadership appear far less intense, in process, than is the case for gaining AST recognition.

> A number of colleagues have said that the AST process is more demanding than applying for promotion positions. It is unrealistically demanding and in need of simplification.

This is evident in the time involved and the kind of documentation of teaching skills required and is poignantly reflected in the nature of the criteria and how they are to be demonstrated. Simply meeting the basic indicators on an AST checklist can be an 'exhaustive' ordeal.

> The criteria are quite exhaustive – in fact I would say that the criteria are more demanding for AST 1 than for a deputy principal's – or even a principal's – position.

By way of illustration, the intensity of the AST process is evidenced in these comments about assessment day by an AST candidate who had experienced other forms of promotional evaluation and inspection.

> We started at 8.30 am and we finished around 4 pm. We did everything in that day: observed lessons, discussed, presented and clarified. We even had lunch together! It was very draining. I've been through assessment under the old system, which was, comparatively, a doddle.

Applicants, while keen to get recognition (on offer) for their experience and level of skill as teachers, were puzzled by how the extensive nature of the criteria and indicators for AST seemed out of all proportion with the financial reward on offer.

> The criteria are mismatched with actual promotion and the salary increase. This enormous amount of work, which took hours, weekends and holidays – a disproportionate amount of time when compared with an executive appointment of any kind – for a $30 a fortnight increase.

Even unsuccessful applicants pondered the question: 'was it worth it?' The pain at missing out, and the acerbic edge it gave to a cynical perspective on the process, provided some insights about the bureaucratic rationale for the AST scheme.

> Ultimately, it was about getting 'cheap' seniors and I wonder why I went through all that [effort and disappointment] for a potential increase in pay of a few hundred a year.

The small nature of the reward – what one teacher referred to as 'just enough for a slab of beer' – for the enormity of the time and effort required to prepare and submit an application, not to mention the level of stress involved, was for many a big disappointment. Indeed, for some, as the intensity of the process became clear in schools, the relatively poor return for effort became a deterrent to continuing with their application. Sadly, for them and the many who chose to continue, the rhetoric of recognition and reward seemed buried beneath an avalanche of paper posturing and skill

construction – lost forever under the crush of accountable detail and manufactured identity.

> Initially I put down that I was going for it, but during term two I
> decided to withdraw my application. Basically, I thought it wasn't
> worth it. I'm finding my job stressful enough, just trying to cope with
> everything. The carrot, that's there in terms of salary increase, doesn't
> seem enough either.

For many teachers, the 'intensity-in-process' was experienced very early in
their engagement with the AST process, through recognition of the exagger-
ated enormity of the thinking, articulation and writing required in making
their AST application. Writing about the qualities of your teaching in the
specific and structured ways necessary to address the AST criteria required a
kind of approach, and discipline, to thinking, translating and representing
your work for which they had, in most cases, little experience. The
comments of independent panel members, who supposedly gave a neutral
'peer' perspective and who relied upon written images of applicants for their
first impressions, underlined the importance of writing skills in getting a
quality, high-impact, application together.

> The person who really does know how to write an application, or who
> has some close friends who know how to write an application for them,
> who know the words to use in these things, they have an advantage.

> We need evidence – signs of things. If people can't write about it, then
> how do we know it's there?

Furthermore, teachers knew and understood the centrality of the written
component of the portrayal they presented of themselves as skilful practitioners in creating vital expectations of skilled teaching in the minds of the
panel members prior to assessment day. It appeared to be very much a case of
written impressions being lasting impressions.

> It seems the whole process, of whether you succeed, or not, rests with
> your application and in addressing the criteria, rather than your teaching
> abilities . . . if you can write a good application – you can get it!

Indeed, there was a feeling that if the written part was not as good as
possible, it would put a lot of pressure on the other phases of the process;
namely, the interview and demonstration lessons. If the first impressions
were not highly positive from the written profiling of skills and abilities,
then there was a huge amount of work to be done on assessment day to 'turn
around' the thinking of the panel members.

> I think a lot rests on the written part. If you don't have it all there, then there is a lot of pressure on your interview.

Predictably, pressure in the latter stages of the process was not easy to handle. However, this was the reality for many teachers – irrespective of their teaching skills – because they found it a daunting task to demonstrate, in written form, how they met the criteria. Inevitably, the final stages of the process – the very part which teachers usually preferred as a venue for 'showcasing' their work – became unreasonably intense under the burden of playing a 'catch-up' game of skill demonstration.

> I have always found it difficult to write to criteria, and to write the amount required, and I was penalised for not being able to write the stated number of pages.

The prospect of this kind of 'early failure' and the threat of self-sabotage pushed people to extraordinary measures in order to get the written application 'very right' before submission. Avoiding the stress of playing 'catch-up' assessment could lead to 'saturation' documentation in an application.

> My written application was developed over two months after researching other people's styles of application. In the end, it was directed to addressing each indicator of each criteria, plus extra indicators, in detail.

In a strange Machiavellian twist to the AST machinery, it could even lead to being taught how to do it properly. Potentially helpful to those seeking to impress was the importance of getting a 'flying start' in the process.

> I had advice within the school. My principal showed me how to do it. It was like a teacher with a child, correcting and saying: 'you still need to put in this, or that'.

Such manipulative interference with the process was probably inevitable when the stakes for schools and teachers were so high. Not only does this tell us something about the fear of getting it wrong and the importance of the written application, but also something about the role that can be played by knowledgeable others, like principals, in the process. Furthermore, there was such a strong sense that the writing stage was so important to a successful application, that this was often enough to 'carry the day', even when other evidence might be missing altogether or otherwise insubstantial and in sparse supply.

Writing the application was an ordeal that took dozens of hours. I am generally at ease with pen and paper, but I did not feel at ease with this. My experience kept telling me that an average teacher with a brilliant written application would win, but a brilliant teacher with average writing skills could lose.

This is a sorry state of affairs and raises many issues about how discourses of 'advanced' skills in teaching are constructed through the rigour of the process, in setting boundaries to admissible evidence, thereby advantaging some, whilst simultaneously disadvantaging others, in ways that ultimately bear little connection to the skills of working with children and adults in caring educational spaces.

SPEAKING ABOUT THE AST AND TEACHERS' WORK

Fossicking for the skill paydirt in AST work

The impact of the newly recognised 'advanced' skills teachers in Australian schools was not immediately apparent. In fact it seemed that there were often different, sometimes contradictory, views about the expectations that teachers had of themselves, and of their colleagues, as AST teachers. Some successful AST candidates believe their success in the process was simply recognition for prior efforts, whilst for others it was an acknowledgement that some form of pedagogical leadership and example setting was required through current, and future, work. However, despite this putatively positive portrayal of AST teachers, many teachers, including potential and unsuccessful candidates, claimed that they saw little evidence of changed work habits, or demonstrable 'advanced' skills, in their AST colleagues.

The attitude of one teacher looking forward to becoming an AST gave a window into the kind of roles which teachers anticipated ASTs taking on after they claim 'advanced' practitioner status. This kind of optimistic response appeared common among potential ASTs and reflects the excitement felt from the affirmative experience of having their teaching skills acknowledged within the professional community of their school.

I think I would feel more responsible for a start. After all, I would be saying that I have advanced skills and therefore it's my responsibility to share and help others more consistently. I feel I would have to put in a lot more than I do.

Furthermore, gaining recognition as an 'advanced' teacher gave many teachers a sense of heightened responsibility about ensuring that the quality of their classroom work remained, and was seen to be, at a nominally 'high' level. If it did nothing else, the expectations and optimism of the AST process developed a more sophisticated gaze, a reflective acuity, in self-understanding about routine teaching work.

> I've become much more conscientious in making sure that all the students are actively engaged in what they're doing. So, that's a benefit of the process. If I hadn't put myself under that scrutiny I might have continued working in the same manner, day in, day out.

Indeed, the experience of self-reflection about teaching practices and work habits which making an AST application required had an important role in focusing expectations about quality classroom teaching. It was not uncommon to find that successful AST teachers expressed a need for a heightened degree of reflexivity in their work.

> It has forced me to reflect on aspects of my teaching. I concentrate more on what I am doing in class.

For many teachers, increased expectations of themselves as exemplary classroom practitioners became translated into a self-imposed form of performance accountability focused on 'desirable' visible traits of the skilful schoolteacher. In its simplest form, it came across as an acute awareness about having your work observed more closely than before; and that this 'new' scrutiny of one's work was a 'natural' part of the AST terrain – it came with the territory, so to speak.

> I'm conscious of the fact that I've now gone up a grade and I can't slacken off. I can't catch myself lingering over a cup of tea anymore in the staffroom and I can't not be thorough in my preparation for lessons.

Notions of AST 'accountability' can vary from the seemingly trivial, like tea-room behaviour, to more substantive demonstrations of leadership. For instance, it might take shape, through tacit expectations, as an acceptance that more involvement at the level of policy development is required, as might occur through overt participation in decision-making structures as a 'visible' pedagogical leader in the school.

> I've been recognised now and I want to live up to that standard. I think it is expected of me as well – and that's fair enough. I find that I'm a lot more involved in committees than I used to be. I feel that I have to be now. And I want to be. This year, I've done a lot more than I did last year.

While this feeling of wanting to demonstrate leadership within the school was common to many newly appointed ASTs, and was an expectation shared by other teachers, there was an indication that some teachers believed ASTs did not always live up to those expectations. A potential AST, who decided not to apply, expressed disappointment about ASTs not fulfilling expectations.

> They are all good teachers who have their own areas of expertise within a subject area, but, it should be shared more than it is. That's certainly not happening anywhere, around here, that I know of.

Indeed, for some, their understanding that ASTs would contribute something special, or new, to the school as (stand-out) pedagogical leaders was not borne out in their observation of AST colleagues.

> I thought that once you become an AST there are certain responsibilities to take on within the school as a subject specialist and leader. But it's not happening like that. In fact, lots of [non-AST] staff in the school are doing things outside of their normal teaching duties.

Furthermore, the perception that ASTs were not taking on anything additional in their day-to-day work was confirmed in comments made by many AST teachers about their roles. Some AST teachers did not recall experiencing any different expectations, or changes, in their work habits; AST, or not, they kept working as they had.

> I don't think what I essentially did in my work changed after I became an AST 1.

> The expectations of what I do didn't change. I thought I was working as an AST according to the criteria and I've just kept at it. In terms of my ordinary working life very little has changed.

However, this did not mean that they felt they were not performing as an AST. In many cases, being appointed an AST meant having already 'got the runs on the board'. For these teachers it was sufficient that they had already demonstrated their 'advanced' skills and leadership abilities before they got their recognition as an AST.

> I'm still the same teacher I always was. I probably do too much and I've always been like that – it's no different to what I was doing before. The expectations aren't any different because I was doing it before, anyway. My own expectations and other people's haven't changed.

More than this, some ASTs chose to claim that AST status was for recognition of past achievements and that it did not, therefore, behold any future commitments to leadership or other expectations of performance. However, the earlier comments from 'recognised' ASTs make the claims about other people's expectations somewhat problematic.

> I don't think I've changed. Not at all, because I figure that if I'm a recognised Advanced Skills Teacher then the things I've been doing, I'll just keep on doing. There's no need to extend myself even further, like I've got something to live up to – it's recognition of what I already do. Most people here have the idea that it's recognition for what you already do. There's nothing extra that people are expecting.

It would seem that the expectations, and subsequent impact, of an AST on the collegiate community of a school exist, and can occur, simultaneously on a number of levels. For instance, from the perspective of AST teachers this happens at a more subtle level than taking on the specific responsibilities or overt forms of leadership which some non-AST teachers seem to expect.

> It didn't change my relationship with other teachers but I've noticed that people treat me differently. A lot of people come to me and ask for advice on things – which astounds me really. Now [as an AST], the questions they ask are more specific. They ask for suggestions about work they can do in class and ways in which it can be presented.

Clearly, in this case, a contribution as pedagogical leader was being (expected from and) made by this AST, which, while at an individual level, was not at a level that was visible to the school's professional community as a whole, but was nonetheless an important act of colleagiate leadership. Therefore, it seems advisable to exercise some caution with the multiple interpretation possible from a non-AST teacher's bald comment, about ASTs, that:

> they should have a role within the school and contribute to it.

The generality of a statement like this does not preclude serendipitous possibilities for leadership that have not been specified in clearly articulated and structured ways. Indeed, whilst ASTs could say that they were not doing anything extra, it may be that at one level this was true, but that at another level they may have been contributing an unobtrusive, but nonetheless significant, form of 'quiet' leadership to their school. This might not always have been planned, as a 'pre-emptive strike' of pedagogical leadership, but likely occurs spontaneously in response to need.

> I work just as hard as I've worked before. I haven't been given anything extra to do, but I am volunteering to do them anyway and I guess I'm doing more at staff meetings.

The evidence suggested that, in this way, there were no clearly visible AST roles to be found in schools. What individual ASTs did as exemplary practitioners varied from school to school, according to the kinds of expertise held by AST teachers and the opportunities for leadership which existed within the school, its programme and its professional community. By and large, ASTs tended to find avenues for sharing their expertise in the local, and inevitably idiosyncratic, circumstances that existed in schools.

> I guess our management structure encourages anybody to be involved in managing a project and it's likely that the ASTs were the ones already doing it, or inclined to want to do it. I think the correlation between who is managing and who is an AST is probably pretty high.

This kind of pragmatic manifestation of AST leadership was confirmed in remarks from a school principal about how the introduction of AST teachers reflected, rather than changed, the way in which leadership occurred in her school.

> It was a hell of a lot of work for me, and for them, but it probably hasn't affected our school very much at all. From my position, we have had a strongly collegiate, collaborative culture for some time and having ASTs has not meant a great deal.

Significantly, this view was an endorsement of comments made by teachers who believed that their work had not changed much and that there were not many additional expectations of them in the school. However, as can be seen from the illustrative comments of teachers above, this is not to say that AST teachers did not make some kind of contribution to the maintenance and growth of a pedagogical culture in schools.

In an overall sense, the return to schools in getting AST teachers recognised and rewarded is not clear. Certainly, those who claimed 'advanced' skill status contributed positively to the professional culture of the schools they worked in, but, at the same time, there was evidence to suggest that it was problematic whether those contributions were any different from what would probably be made by senior, experienced teachers working under circumstances where there was no AST classification. It seems that while a lot of effort was made on the part of teachers and schools to gain 'advanced' skills recognition, there were only marginal returns for this effort in enhanced pedagogical leadership in schools.

Contradictions in remaking highly experienced teachers: AST or not AST

Many long-serving and highly experienced teachers applied for AST classification and many were unsuccessful. For them, this 'failure' was an explicit denial of that official recognition which they sought for their career-long demonstration of teaching expertise, not to mention their professional commitment to schools and children, over many years of dedicated service. For many, the resulting confusion was difficult to understand and produced a range of powerful emotions as they struggled to deal with the frustration and disappointment that came with the simultaneous loss of their goal for 'advanced' status and the mantle of esteemed professional mentor. By the very act of not adequately demonstrating that the pedagogical qualities developed in their accumulated classroom experience matched those set down as 'advanced', these teachers had publicly exposed themselves as made of lesser stuff than their AST-successful colleagues. To their chagrin, they had found that in embarking on their quest for AST status they had entered that territory where long-standing reputations as good operators can explode, the solid bases of high self-esteem can quickly be undermined, and confidence derived from years of positive affirmation could be terminally shattered. For highly experienced teachers who became unsuccessful AST candidates, their engagement with the AST process was not a celebration of their teaching, but, in fact, the direct opposite – the unravelling of their identity as highly competent experienced practitioners. The AST experience left many experienced teachers feeling that their understanding of the level of their competence was not veritable in the way they had assumed it to be.

Consider the following remarks from a group of very experienced teachers who confidently engaged the AST process with an optimism that was not realised. An open reading of the narratives of confidence grounded in experience and localised forms of peer recognition offered in these windows on why teachers apply for AST is very revealing.

I was advised by my principal and fellow colleagues that, in the light of my teaching performance during the last 20 years, I should apply for AST.

After ten years at my last school, I was at a new school where I was English Co-ordinator and Literacy Co-ordinator. I decided to go for AST – after all, I felt comfortable in the school, had a high profile, and was an experienced classroom teacher of 27 years.

After 23 years' teaching, which included Key Teacher leadership, primary and secondary teaching, I knew I had the knowledge, background and a current understanding of educational philosophies and practices. I felt I had the respect of my students and their parents, so I decided to apply.

I saw AST as a reward for 31 years' teaching the students which many other teachers avoided. My colleagues told me I would get it with one hand tied behind my back. I felt confident that anybody could observe my teaching at any time.

Having been a teacher for the last 15 years I decided to apply. Many parents, students and colleagues had labelled me as an honest, hard-working, dedicated teacher who put in for the school community. It seemed that this was what the AST applicant needed, so I applied.

Teaching for 20 years and still having lots of enthusiasm for teaching, I applied. I believed I was an advanced skills teacher and with a high profile, I was happy enough to be the first person in the school to go for it.

What can be read about applying for AST from the words of these teachers? The thing they have in common is that they are highly experienced teachers who, with support from their school communities, exude a strong sense of confidence in approaching the AST process. Not so obvious are the other thing they have in common – they were all unsuccessful. Furthermore, the thrust of these comments conveys a simple message: experience *plus* commitment *plus* status *plus* self-esteem does not equal AST.

By any assessment this is disturbing because it indicates that experienced teachers who had received affirming statements and other endorsement of their competence from school and professional communities did not find any congruence for that in the evaluative landscape of the AST process. There may be many reasons for this, ranging from the submission of poor applications to misinterpretation of the informal feedback from peers and others about their practice. Another possible explanation might be advanced on the grounds that highly experienced, long-serving teachers were disadvantaged in some way by the nature of the requirements for evidencing demonstrable 'advanced' skills in the prescribed ways demanded by the AST process. Experienced teachers saw pedagogical expertise as multidimensional and capable of accommodating many 'readings' evidenced through inductive forms of demonstration.

Clearly, some successful applicants believed this to have been so in their case. Indeed, this was the message in the following rhetorical remark.

I have to ask myself how three experienced classroom teachers, each with more years teaching than all three of the panel put together, could have failed this assessment of their teaching.

Beyond the surface disappointment expressed here, this teacher seems to be saying that something is not ringing true with the AST process when three highly experienced teachers can be judged as non-AST 'deserving' by a group of less experienced peers. Moreover, the point of this expression of incredulity about such an occurrence is meant to challenge directly the veracity of the AST process. It is meant to leave you wondering; how does this happen?

It is, of course, not possible to know for sure, and possibly there are as many reasons as incidences of this kind, all of which warrant some exploration. Perhaps the only way is to explore the things that experienced teachers have to say about the difficulties they encounter in presenting themselves as skilled practitioners in AST selection profiles. In following this line of inquiry, the teacher-storied evidence suggests that one possible answer might be found in the important task of compiling a portfolio of compelling supporting documentation. One teacher thought that failure to retain paper evidence over the years prevented them from documenting in detail many of the things they were claiming (as self-evident) about their experience as a competent teacher.

> Over my years of teaching I have undertaken so many professional development activities and courses that I cannot remember when, where and what many of them were. I always undertook them to improve my skills as a teacher but didn't keep reference details as I didn't think I would ever need them – therefore, I was unable to detail these in my written application.

While having pieces of paper to show that particular courses were attended, ideas met and training programmes engaged does not demonstrate 'advanced' teaching skills, the actual process of recording one's own developmental history as a teacher, through being a pedagogical archivist for oneself, is recognisably a crucial resource in creating a persuasive portrayal of the 'advanced' skill teacher. Older teachers felt that the less competitive nature of teaching as an occupation in the previous couple of decades meant they were less inclined to keep the formal documentary evidence of their developmental experiences as a teacher which now appears mandatory for the official, and simplistically symbolic, demonstration of teaching competencies. Consequently, having a different window, or 'headset', on how to describe the complexity of their work – one which did not find recourse to incontestably demonstrative documentation – left them at a disadvantage in a process that relied so heavily upon written forms of documentation in the portrayal of 'advanced' teaching skills.

This convergence of evidence with documentation led to anger when teachers instinctively knew that the evidence of the required skills is found in everyday practice, for the astute classroom connoisseur to see, but for some reason is not able to be captured and conveyed in the way demanded by the process. A discursive slippage of some magnitude seems implicit when this occurs and it is this point of contradiction in the process which generates a lot of emotive reaction.

> I was very disappointed when I was told that I did not get AST because to me it was the recognition for all the years of dedication that I had really wanted. A few days later, when the Deputy came in to a lesson of mine in full swing, he said: 'now I see the evidence I didn't have for the AST' – I found that particularly galling. How did he not have that evidence if part of the feedback said I had been an asset to the school? Since not getting it I feel resentful, angry and bitter and I have given up investing outside of a dutiful commitment only. I have lost a lot of confidence through the process.

For many of these teachers, conversing about their teaching in ways that required the dismantling of their experience into 'bits' which could be convincingly shown to be congruent with AST criteria left them feeling uncomfortable about the process and uneasy about how it could capture the essence of what they saw as the complex nature of their skill base as experienced teachers. Again, at base, a discursive slippage between discourses of skill for experienced teachers and the AST criteria seems to be the source of the problem. The complete removal of skill from the context of practice is seen as fundamentally flawed, axiologically and discursively, by many experienced teachers.

> At no time did I feel comfortable with any aspect of the process. I felt it to be artificial and contrived. I did not put on any special lessons. I just wanted the panel to observe my normal day-to-day work. I felt the process required me to be boastful about my teaching. It ignored what I am – as a good and conscientious teacher.

The need to manufacture the evidential process was something which did not sit well with many experienced teachers who were reluctant to get involved with any evanescent staging that did not reflect for them the integrity of the complex character of their day-to-day work. Vainglorious boasting about teaching prowess fell outside the pedagogical ambits of most long-serving classroom teachers. Falsely attractive displays of skill for the satisfaction of AST selection procedures were seen as unscrupulous exercises in self-grounded displays of teacher expertise.

> Many teachers are put off applying and disagree with the process. It is geared to the eloquent and those who are able to 'put on a show'. This makes it very inconsistent in its outcomes. It is not what it was proposed to be. As an experienced classroom teacher of 27 years:

English Co-ordinator, [Language] Co-ordinator, [Senior Secondary [Moderator] – I failed! I still can't accept that judgement. I have to question the expertise of the panel who assessed me. I feel cheated when I hear of others I consider less able, less experienced from other schools getting AST.

The anguish and pain of the experienced teacher who failed the AST process was very real. The reasons are unlikely to be simple, and the testimonials presented here from experienced teachers who were also unsuccessful with their AST applications reflect the complex intersection of experience, skill and discursive practice in teachers' work. Inevitably, the complexity of a process like that set up for selecting 'advanced' skill teachers meant that problems arise for some who engage it. Human beings and their works are far too complex to be fully inscribed by a grab-bag of criteria for establishing one or another set of traits, behaviours or attitudes. Some things will always be emphasised more than others, some included and others not; the consequences of which will be exciting and opportunistic for some, whilst frustrating and devaluing for others.

There will always be some aspects of any selection process which will advantage some applicants, either individually or collectively, over others through prior knowledge, experience or proclivity with some important part, or requirement, of that process. Applicants from smaller and isolated schools, as well as applicants from non-mainstream curriculum areas, found it more difficult to negotiate the AST process beginning to end than many other teachers. The evidence from the narratives of optimism and loss, of confidence and despair, presented here from a montage of experienced teachers' words suggests that this may also be the case for those long-serving experienced teachers not used to promoting themselves competitively against set criteria as 'advanced' classroom practitioners, and who were reluctant to become proselytised to new performance management articulations of their work.

SPEAKING ABOUT THE DISCURSIVE FORMATION OF SKILL IN TEACHERS' WORK

Official AST discourses on teaching skill

The introduction of the 'advanced' skills classification into Australian schools has played an important role in the formation of new ways of discussing and understanding the work of experienced teachers. It has been important in framing a discourse on skilful teaching through structures fabricated for the recognition processes teachers must engage with when articulating their 'advanced' teaching skills for a peer audience. The

selection of one set of processes, over other possibilities, framed for the exposition of teaching skills in written form privileges a discourse about teaching
that requires literal constructions of teaching skill. Aspects of teachers' work
which do not lend themselves to succinct demonstration in literalistic styles
embedded in the criteria are made marginal to the discussion of 'advanced'
skill in teaching. Given that 'the form of representation we choose to use is
constitutive of the understanding we acquire' (Eisner 1992: 12), when it
comes to the articulation of skill in the work of experienced teachers, the
framing of the discursive boundaries limits the ways in which that skill can
be presented and understood. Indeed, privileging a written discourse of skill
in the AST process makes influence from similarly framed educational
arenas, such as policy discourses, highly likely through a discursive
synchronicity.

Once established, the criteria come to dominate how skilful teaching can
be articulated and demonstrated. Aspects of teaching which can be used to
illustrate criterion points become highly relevant, whilst teaching experiences that demonstrate other skills and abilities become irrelevant. The
forms of inductive reasoning about skill indigenous to schools, grounded in
the experience of teaching practice, are displaced by more technical, deductive forms suited to definitive assessment by 'context-free' observers of
teaching.

> It seems the whole process of whether you succeed or not rests with your
> application and in addressing the criteria rather than in your actual
> teaching abilities. I've heard stories from teachers who are very good
> teachers, and are told by others that they are very good teachers, but
> because they didn't properly address the criteria in the way they wrote
> their application, they failed.

This was a sentiment expressed by others in various ways. The way in which
the criteria, as written indicators, point the applicant toward particular
representations of their teaching can be seen in the remarks below. Implicit
judgements about the relevancy of experiences to a discussion of skilful
teaching are present in how the criteria are worded.

> I touched on different aspects of my teaching and used those different
> episodes and incidents to illustrate how I met the criteria. If those
> criteria weren't there I probably would have written a different appli-
> cation.

For this teacher the criteria made him look at his teaching, for evidence of
a particular kind, from one perspective above others. Necessarily focusing
in a selective way on his work made some aspects less 'visible' in the
collection process. This slant on the nature of his 'advanced' skills as a

teacher led him to focus less on his classroom skills than he would have liked.

> I would have placed far more emphasis on what I do in the classroom. I feel that's where I do my job. They wanted to know a lot more about the peripheral issues of being a teacher, which are important, but I think I would have preferred to concentrate more on what I do in my classroom. If it hadn't said these are the criteria you must address, I would have given more prominence to my classroom skills.

This kind of remark encapsulates how the methods of representation of 'advanced' skill in teaching structure the kind of understanding that is possible. From this teacher's view, the most desirable representation of his classroom skills was not possible because the criteria point him towards collecting evidence about other kinds of skills and, therefore, under-emphasised what he saw as 'advanced' classroom-based skills in his work.

Nevertheless, not all teachers saw the criteria as unhelpful. Some saw the criteria as an organisational frame in which to work when presenting a portrayal of themselves as 'advanced' teachers.

> When I read the criteria, I wasn't put off by them at all. It was simply a matter of organising my thoughts under those headings and thinking about what I did and which of the criteria it actually addressed.

However, for other teachers the restriction of information in applications to that which could be matched to the set-down criteria meant that 'word-games' could be played with them to maximise the likelihood of success. In these games, skill in literal articulation of the convergence of belief and action became important.

> Sure, I can satisfy all of the criteria, but it's the actual expression of ideas which is important. If you can't write about equality, inclusion, and things which you might not have experienced, or confronted, in your teaching, you will still have to present a philosophy that is acceptable. I have seen applications for AST that have been 'put together' and they don't represent the views of the person who is applying. Now, that's worrisome.

The reference to 'acceptable philosophies' indicates how the formulation of the criteria embodied a specific position and an accompanying set of values about how 'advanced' teachers work and what 'advanced' teachers should know about teaching and learning. The kind of language and metaphors used in the criteria carry with them an axiological position about how teaching is to be described and accounted for. These comments from a peer assessor confirmed this.

> The criteria have values. Teachers who show the values get the money – teachers who can engage in conversation with others and convey those values. It is about teachers being able to say: 'this is what I believe I am doing and this is the evidence'. That is what the criteria are about – about teachers articulating a view on teaching. However, you can be a good teacher and not be able to converse about it in that way.

The caveat at the end of these remarks highlights a major problem with privileging certain forms of expression for skill in teaching. There can be no guarantees about any correspondence between talking about teaching skills and putting them into practice. Indeed, this was a concern expressed by those teachers who believed that it was difficult for them to engage in the kind of discourse about their work which required careful use of policy terminology.

> I'm not a person who has got the gift of the gab in that way. A lot of teachers know how to present, and have got the right answers, but it doesn't necessarily mean that they are good teachers. It just means that they can talk their way around the criteria.

This presented an ethical dilemma for many teachers. Teachers faced the challenge of a choice between presenting a view of oneself as an experienced and skilful practitioner, as they believed it to be, or, presenting a view of themself as a teacher, with 'acceptable philosophies', in a way that successfully demonstrated the criteria.

> I've written many applications in my life for all sorts of things, but I don't believe in writing things that aren't true. I'm not going to make them up because when it comes to an interview situation I am not going to be able to lie about them – and that's when the crunch comes. So yes, I can satisfy the criteria, but when it comes to writing it in the correct terminology, expressing views that are expected of me as an AST teacher, then I might not be able to express it the way the Department wants.

The artificiality of this was a concern for many teachers because it closed windows on a whole range of ways of looking at skills in classroom teaching. Applying the principle that 'you see what you know how to say' meant that the terminology which was presented in the criteria both enabled and disabled certain kinds of evidence. It might include discussion of policy implementation, but simultaneously exclude a lot of evidence from classroom work because it cannot be adequately channelled into a written application.

> I tried to make my application as honest as I could, yet I found the jargon in the criteria, and the way everything had to be classified according to it, to be fairly intimidating. The only way I could deal with it was to give examples of myself working in particular situations. The way you have to channel everything according to those seven criteria meant that you had to breathe and sleep them. That was artificial. In the classroom, when I was thinking about my application, I wasn't thinking 'I do this well' but, rather, 'what could I tell them that's going to fit criteria number 5'. It's like trying to get all the ducks in a row.

A comment like this reflects the epistemic struggle faced by many teachers in replacing preferred inductive description of their work with illustrative support for deductive criteria about teaching. Under such conditions teaching as complex work gets hacked down to a shape where it fits the mould set by the limits imposed by the criteria because the discourse narrows the representation of skill to just a small part of what teachers do in classrooms. What must be recognised is that criteria-focused rhetoric on teachers' work is a different contradictory kind of work-discourse on teaching to that privileged by teachers because it fetishises general over specific forms of knowledge and technicist over narrative forms of representation in the portrayal of teachers' work.

> You're writing in an, almost, academic way – you can't just put in little notes because if we're going to look at classroom practices then we've got to go beyond the bounds of what the criteria are for AST. I'm not criticising the criteria, but I think you've got to look at the whole person.

As the criteria narrowed down the kind of discourse permissible about skilled teaching, it became more difficult for some teachers to translate their experiences into a form that would enable them to participate in the kind of discussion of skill necessary for meeting the requirements of the process. Unfortunately, despite the best intentions, careful framing of criteria did not necessarily lead to flexible options, nor multiple possibilities, for teachers to demonstrate the teaching skills they possessed. A person with an insight into how the criteria were put together explained how this was lost in making the process more demanding.

> When the criteria were formed, they tried very hard to come up with criteria that encapsulated good progressive teaching and to articulate it

in a way that might be useful to people. But I think it has got lost in the ruck a bit . . . the rigours of the process dissuades some people from applying.

This was experienced by a number of teachers, particularly those who did not teach in the mainstream areas of a school's activity. When you do not fit the usual patterns of teaching experience, specific criteria can be difficult to meet in predictable ways. An entirely pragmatic, seemingly neutral, decision for a methodological solution like increased rigour in the process could shut down opportunities for some teachers to bring forward unusual, yet possibly sophisticated, examples of the application of 'advanced' skills in their work.

> While the criteria can give you something to hang your ideas on, they can be a problem when you have to demonstrate working with others in curriculum initiatives because some subjects do not lend themselves too readily for teachers to work outside of their normal areas of expertise. For example, music teachers quite often get caught up with band rehearsals and their time at lunch and after school is taken up in that way. They can't get involved in the same way as other teachers.

Similar problems were faced by teachers of specialist subjects. The kind of work they did, the skills which were simultaneously required and developed, and the sophisticated nuances within specialist pedagogical work, are invisible to the wider community of peers.

> Some people couldn't see how what I do at this school covers all of the criteria and I had to challenge that attitude and say: 'well read out any of the criteria and I will find something that I do which fits'. While I knew I could fit them, the person who came into the school to evaluate me couldn't get their head around the fact that a gymnastics teacher might fit all the criteria. I felt challenged and said: 'I do other things in the school than teaching gymnastics and I do fit the criteria'.

That a pre-formed attitude by a peer assessor had to be challenged and reversed by this gymnastics teacher reflects a significant problem that arises when discourses about 'advanced' skill are narrowed in such a way that certain kinds of experience in the work of teaching seem to be, at best, unlikely or, at worst, inadmissible as exemplars of skilful work in teaching. The comments below from a peer assessor reinforce these insights into how there can sometimes be an ontological slippage between written discourses about skill and demonstrated skill in teaching practice.

After reading an application you sometimes get a feeling about the applicant which could be quite wrong. You go into a school having already formed some kind of judgement. On the other hand, the person may really know how to write an application, or has friends who know how to write their application, and knows the words to use. Again you get a feeling for the person, but think: 'I hope this is what I'm going to see in practice'.

Clearly, initial impressions formed from the written application presented problems for those assessing teachers in the AST process. How much correspondence there was between the successful negotiation of a written discourse on skill in teaching and the demonstration of that in classroom work was an important problematic, of the process, for AST panel members. The two things are very different and reflect at a basic level the potential contradictions between written and practical – predominantly oral – discourses about skill in teaching. Teachers understood this ontological problem at a fundamental level as the comments below show.

> You can empathise with a policy, or have an understanding about it as a broad issue, because it's very easy to be theoretical and to use jargon, but the crux of being a good teacher is about what happens in the classroom – how you adapt your teaching as a response to student needs and interpret the policy at school and classroom level.

> I can see that teaching is not just about what happens in the classroom, but what you're doing outside of the classroom must all come back to your effectiveness in class. You can grandstand as much as you like, but it comes down to how you teach those kids.

Inevitably, reliance on narrow literalistic descriptions of 'advanced' teaching skill provide only a shallow, largely predictable, exposition of the diversity and breadth of skills which teachers can possess and develop to sophisticated levels. Teachers understand this well because of their understanding of the complexity and diversity of classroom work and the range of pedagogical skills required to perform at high levels of competence.

The establishment of a discourse about teaching skill has an important impact on how teachers can present themselves as 'advanced' practitioners. There are advantages and disadvantages in developing the kind of written discourse about 'advanced' skill in teaching that occurred with the AST process. In a positive sense, it challenges teachers to reflect upon their work in different ways and present themselves as teachers in a way that is accessible to non-teachers. At the same time, dangers lie in connecting 'advanced' skill in teaching to the restricted notion of 'teacher as litterateur' because of the wealth of modes for expression of skill which are shut down when that occurs.

Intersecting policy and skill discourses

It is not altogether surprising that the introduction of the 'advanced' skills classification into Australian schools has privileged a written discourse about skill and teaching. For some time teachers have recognised their need to develop more sophisticated ways of articulating what it is that they do in their work; but, at the same time, its conterminous linkage with policy discourse may have other less desirable associations for teachers in how their work can be proscribed. For example, the specification of indicators for 'advanced' skill in teaching that incorporates policy jargon which requires evidence of policy implementation for their demonstration may link conformist pedagogies to definitions of skill and, simultaneously, cause the exclusion of other kinds of construction for exemplary teaching practice. Put succinctly, the written discourse excludes as it includes.

In this sense, the creation of a legitimising nexus between adherence to policy, its efficient implementation and career advancement implies the manipulation of the skill discourse in an ideological manoeuvre that can lock teachers into implementing government objectives in schools through the offer of reward and status for commitment to policy. Astute social commentators recognise how the literalisation of work and culture has increased formalised state control over public life (Marin 1995); and in this same way the written skill discourse facilitates the tighter control of teachers' work. For many teachers, its crudest manifestation, in a process like AST verification, occurs in a push–pull scenario where if you can demonstrate the acceptable pedagogical values, then you get the kudos (and the money) for being an 'advanced' teacher. It is pertinent to recall the comments of a peer assessor:

> the criteria have values. Teachers who show the values get the money . . . that is what the criteria are about.

Initially, concerns about the criteria being too easily met and, consequently, the scheme being too expensive led to the criteria being used as a means of making the selection process difficult, so that a *de facto* quota system came into effect, through incorporating policy values. A person associated with the development of AST criteria recalls how this happened:

> as the Department came to realise that the AST would be a personal classification based on merit, it decided that to keep the cost down it would toughen the criteria as much as possible and try to control the selection process.

The merging of skill and policy discourses in this way became an effective way of making the process more rigorous and, therefore, of installing a 'negative potential' which might discourage some teachers from applying. At the same time, teachers and principals believed that the focus of most criteria were directed towards the demonstration of those skills which employers wished to encourage because of the significant role they can play in the implementation of organisation policy.

> Some criteria in particular don't address teachers' work but are a systemic way of saving money by getting teachers to do more than class-room teaching.

These comments from a peer assessor endorse this view and give an insight into how this synchronisation of policy and teaching practice takes shape in the specification of preferred ways of working in schools. As a case in point:

> what's most important, as reflected in the criteria, is teachers working collaboratively with each other.

The push towards collaboration among teachers is usually presented as indicative of teacher professionalism, independence, self-help and empowerment, but is, now, increasingly being seen as a form of post-Fordist influence in the organisation of teachers' work where flatter management structures mean that classroom teachers have more accountability for their own performance and that of colleagues (Smyth 1991; Dow 1996). Teachers are well aware of the ideological nature of this process where AST status is joined to organisation-ally preferred ways of working and delineated forms of accountability.

> The central ideology – by ideology I mean the philosophy of the whole thing – says let's orchestrate some type of system, which isn't wanted, so we'll have some type of status [in place] which will separate staff. I don't think it's about being developmental or a learning process for teachers.

If they had a choice, the preference for many teachers would have been to omit any consideration of success in policy implementation from the description of their 'advanced' skills. Teachers understand that the more criteria and indicators focused upon the requirements of the employer, through things like work patterns and policy implementation, the less they are focused on these higher order, often idiosyncratic, pedagogical skills important in work with children in classrooms. Such an understanding is implicit in the comment below.

> Some of the things I would put down are things that I know I'm natu-rally good at as a teacher, others would be things that I have had to

learn to survive, and others would be things that the Department has forced me to be good at: adapting quickly, teaching on the run, giving the impression that I'm an expert in areas where I'm not. I'd leave out a whole lot of things that have been forced on us from the outside, flexibility, change, and policy stuff.

In addition to preferred work practices like collaboration, AST panel interviews also tended to focus on knowledge of policy and its implementation in schools. When describing the focus of their interviews concerned teachers often spoke about the specific ways in which this was enacted.

The questions were about trends, or new developments, in education and how I see them affecting the way I teach.

I had to give more evidence that I understood social justice policy and how I evaluate programmes which the school has set up.

I had addressed poverty, but I hadn't addressed students with disabilities, ESL students, or how I teach girls and I had to talk specifically about those issues. You can have a good rapport with students, and a very productive classroom, but if you don't show an awareness of these things, then you'll probably miss out.

The centrality of showing a knowledge of policy initiatives is confirmed by one principal's comments about the role played by the 'outside' panel member during that phase of the interviews where a policy agenda seemed to be most strongly pushed.

The applicant has to satisfy the independent peer [assessor] who wants to hear about social justice and other policy matters in a broader than 'in my classroom' context.

This seemed to be the major stumbling block for many teachers and principals in accepting the legitimacy of this kind of orientation for the selection processes. The problem was not so much that an awareness of policy was important, nor that the reformist directions of a lot of policy were unwarranted, but that its connection to classroom practices and the grounding of 'advanced' teaching skills there, rather than in broad terms expressed in ideological posturing through the use of 'correct' terminology, was getting lost in a process generated in this way.

It's very easy to be theoretical and to use jargon, but I think the crux of being a good teacher is what happens in the classroom. How you adapt your teaching as a response to student needs and an awareness of policies and a willingness to interpret policy at school and classroom level is what makes a good teacher.

We want to make it clear that teachers were not saying that policy was not a 'good thing', or that in many instances they did not productively enact these policies in their classroom work – for example, 'social justice' – but rather, that they objected to the belief, which people outside of school workplaces sometimes seem to hold, that policy was something to be mindlessly spot-welded onto teaching. Teachers had a much more nuanced reading of how policy was integrally embedded into their teaching.

Indeed, the alienating nature of the written discourse was painful for many teachers because it was seemingly so distant from the extant world of skill they experienced in their work. There was a kind of ontological slippage between these expressions of skill and its execution in real teacher's work – it was becoming unrecognisable.

> I found it too clinical and overladen with a kind of bureaucratic legalese and too remote from my experiences as a classroom teacher.

The constant return of the skill discourse to classroom work was what teachers wanted – not the elimination of reference to policy. Furthermore, it seemed to them that the most sensible way to frame policy and skill was through attentiveness to the plurality of interpretations (of both) that were possible in the classroom context.

> Something like social justice has to be interpreted because it's one of those jargon terms that means different things to different people – and that has to be addressed.

However, the remarks below from a principal suggest that this was not the way AST selection panels operated. Panel discussions tended to disconnect interpretation of policy from individual action in classrooms by seeking evidence of generic, abstracted understanding of policy from applicants.

> The panel has to collect sufficient evidence to be convinced that the applicant has demonstrated a global connotation; which is not a part of the teacher's classroom work – which is problematic in this context.

Understandably, many teachers found this difficult to accept when they held firm beliefs that evidence of successful policy implementation needs to be grounded in classroom practice, and not in politically expedient regurgitation of the correct words.

> Good teaching is evidenced in good teaching practice, which is what it should be based on – not politically motivated inquiry about whether the teacher conforms to the latest doctrines and knows all of the latest jargon for things.

Furthermore, this tacit understanding that there were 'right' answers to linking policy with teaching skill was experienced in various ways by teachers who engaged the AST process. Most often this was accentuated at the interview stage where policy agenda was visibly displayed through the questions asked by employer representatives.

> I was bombarded with questions from the peer assessor and made to feel very uncomfortable as if I was not hitting the 'right' buttons.

When this occurred, as pointedly as expressed here, the process became very artificial and, inevitably, word spread among teachers that there were 'ways' to handle the agenda pursued at panel interviews. These remarks from a principal indicate that only too clearly:

> we need to make sure that they know how to jump through the right hoops because I think that the AST process is very false and superimposed from outside with very little thought to what already exists inside the school. There's a certain amount of what I'd call sewer-rat-cunning. It means you know how to stuff the system.

While the resistance of teachers to the disconnection of policy knowledge from classroom practice may be considered positively, as a form of defence which allowed teachers to circumvent the agenda of those controlling the skill discourse, another, unfortunate outcome of this manipulation of the selection process occurred when some teachers withdrew from the process altogether. For many of these teachers, in simple terms, it came down to a choice of playing along with the rules of the game, or refusing to play at all.

> I do actually teach my classes very well, but I am not good at prostituting myself and, therefore, I will never be an AST person – nor can I recommend any real classroom teacher to waste their time and heartbreak with this process.

This principled statement about not tangling with the political games inherent in the selection process was a significant vote of no-confidence in the AST criteria and their assessment by this teacher. Clearly, for some, adopting an amoral attitude of going along with the process to get the desired goal of AST recognition was not something they were prepared to do.

The connection of the criteria for AST classification to a policy discourse invited an ideological framing of the discourse of 'advanced' skill in teaching. Teachers sensed this in how the criteria were put together and how the panel process required demonstration of adherence to policy in ways that sought separation from interpretation in a classroom context. While most were unhappy about this, and aware of its limitations in getting to the heart of the connection between skill and policy in teachers' work, many were prepared to 'go along with the charade' in order to gain AST status. However it is looked at, the intersection of skill and policy discourses in the remaking of 'advanced' teachers' work is productive of a complex and politicised arena filled with narratives of accommodation, contestation and resistance.

SPEAKING ABOUT THE SKILL AND THE IDEOLOGICAL WORK OF TEACHING

Competing definitions of skill in teaching

The AST process has become a way of describing 'advanced' skill in teaching which performs a significant legitimising function in the occupational recognition of experienced classroom teachers. Its introduction and development, from idea to policy, charts the evolution of a vision of the highly skilled classroom practitioner, as championed by teacher advocates who value classroom work in schools. This was given visible shape in the documentation of criteria which circumscribe that vision and a set of accompanying indicators which seek to define the manifestation of exemplary teaching skills. Importantly, what is at the base, fundamentally informative of those criteria and the associated indicators, is a choice, an agreed position, on how to describe and identify 'advanced' teaching skills; one given expression in bureaucratic and professional spaces through the negotiation of employer and teacher visions of 'advanced' teaching. As a choice, some things have been included and others left out. That which appears, written down, in the AST criteria and developed in the particular statement of indicators constitutes one formation of 'advanced' teaching among many. By their inclusion, some teaching skills are therefore privileged over others in gaining formal recognition as 'advanced'. Many teachers are aware of this legitimation of some elements of their teaching and the simultaneous non-admission of others. For some teachers, their difficulty in meeting AST criteria is located in the inadmissibility of those manifestations of their skill which they regard as demonstrative of *their* activities as 'advanced' classroom teachers. A deconstructive and resistant reading of the AST process and the discourse of teaching skill which it enables can be found in the accommodating and contesting narratives of teachers' understandings of how the process works to define, limit, legit-imise and exclude some pedagogical skills as 'advanced' over others.

The political history of the AST process, so often rendered invisible to teachers, is revealed in the recollections of one individual who participated in the negotiation between employer and teacher representatives that even-tually developed the broad thrust of the criteria as they presently exist.

> There was a long drawn-out debate between the Department and the Union which often stalled. The Department resisted all the way; some bureaucrats couldn't accept that the quality of one's teaching should be grounds for career advancement and higher salaries. Their whole strategy was to neutralise it as much as possible; both to control it and reduce expenditure.

These comments reflect the struggle over the specification of 'advanced' teaching skills that lies beneath the seemingly given and neutral criteria which appear in the version of the AST process teachers encounter. A highly politicised process of negotiation between the competing interests of employers and teachers was an important determinant of what ended up in the AST selection criteria, what was left out, and what was presented as objective, complete and fixed. Again, the negotiated nature of what is now AST text is emphasised by the same person.

> We had to negotiate the criteria and processes. The Department were reasonable in trying to describe characteristics of good teaching that teachers could aspire to. If all teachers were doing that sort of stuff, then our schools would be very good.

The feeling expressed here is that the criteria – as they were negotiated – did capture some of the essence of an agreed position on 'advanced' teaching, and that it gave teachers a valuable perspective on how to assess and improve their work; but at the same time, because it was a choice of some things over others, within the complexity of describing, choosing and writing down, the final statements of skill as found in the criteria were not as encompassing as might be desired in an ideal world. In other words, something was lost in the translation. It is this loss that leads to the kind of ontological slippage evident in the teacher narratives presented in the earlier part of this chapter. This same sense of loss in diverse veracity is expressed in the comments about contestability of selection indicators made by a peer assessor.

> It took two years to negotiate the final form of the criteria. They are quite good, but there could be other ones. While the criteria are fairly wide; having to make sure all indicators are 'ticked off' was contested –

a real sticking point – because there are other indicators which we could accept.

The clear sense that what was contained within the AST criteria was but one selection from many, in a rich source of ways of describing 'advanced' teaching skill, has also been recognised by many AST applicants. For one teacher, that was evident in the teachers' reaction to having to focus the application on only some parts of their work, which they thought they might not have used in their own preferred portrayal of 'advanced' teaching skills.

> I touched on *some* aspects of my teaching and used those episodes and incidents to illustrate how I met the criteria. If those criteria weren't there I probably would have written a different application. I would have placed far more emphasis on what I do in the classroom. I feel that's where I do my job. They wanted to know a lot more about the peripheral issues of being a teacher, which are important, but I think I would have preferred to concentrate a lot more on what I do in my classroom.

The point being made by this teacher is that whilst there are many things which 'advanced' practitioners might do in their work and which draw upon their expert skills, the individual choice by teachers as to what is most important in the context of the challenge of their classroom will vary from person to person. Others see it similarly and, like the teacher below, instinctively know that what matters most is how those skills impact upon the success of their own practice.

> If it hadn't said these are the criteria you must address I think I would have given more prominence to my classroom skills. For me, it's the other things you do instinctively: ring parents, discuss a student's progress, you see them at BBQs – all the things you do in developing relationships with people.

This teacher is making several points that are important in a discussion of the discursive boundaries implicit in the AST process. Firstly, classroom skills are not represented highly enough in the 'advanced' criteria and involvement in activity primarily located in teacher work outside the classroom is over-represented. Second, the relational skills important in the development of quality teaching in classrooms where children and adults coexist are not emphasised enough in the criteria. Third, and implicit in the statements above, the idea that an application which successfully addresses the selection criteria may be possible to *construct*, even when effective classroom teaching is considered problematic from a perspective that chooses to emphasise a different set of teaching and relational skills.

In this sense, the preparation of an application becomes a matter of conforming to the required pattern of elucidation of the criteria (through the satisfaction of the indicators) in the most effective way possible. The most effective way is to converse about your work as a teacher using the patois of the AST discourse. Its ultimate grounding in classroom practice becomes secondary to the task of participating in the kind of discussion of teaching skills that is contained within the discursive frame set out in the textual artefact known as the AST criteria. An understanding of that is implicit in the remarks below made by a teacher who chose not to apply for AST because it seemed too much like a game.

> Certainly a great deal of garbage is written just to satisfy the terminology and to cover the criteria. They may not even be applicable to the people who are applying but they have to cover them, so they do. I just find that wrong. It's about playing the game. Personally, I can't be bothered with it.

Another teacher put in similar terms the central importance of knowing what the rules of the skill discourse game were in successfully negotiating the selection process. Perhaps paradoxically, this was seen as more difficult than actually self-assessing the suitability of one's experience as a potential AST.

> My concern was not whether I was AST material, but that I didn't know what the game was. I didn't know whether I was going to play by the right rules. I didn't know whether the process was going to try and trip people up, to find some area where they weren't too competent, or didn't have the appropriate knowledge, or whether it in fact was an assessment of what people are doing, or have done as teachers.

Teachers recognised that the satisfaction of the AST criteria, even when they have a tenuous connection to the actual experience of the person writing the application, was mostly about playing the discourse game that was embedded therein. Furthermore, implicit in this was a recognition that playing by the discursive rules of the AST skill game separates the satisfaction of criteria from actual teaching skills, as they exist in the relational world of classrooms. In such a process it became possible for highly regarded classroom practitioners to be unsuccessful in their engagement with the process; a result that was discursively possible but experientially nonsensical – the ultimate bizarre outcome of the ontological slippages discussed earlier.

> I've developed this cynicism, and it's not outrageous, shared with other friends outside of my school. People who I considered as outstanding professionals missed out totally in their schools. There was a guy who

set up a whole LOTE [Language Other than English] programme – a most successful programme in the eyes of language teachers – yet he missed out.

Storied accounts of this kind were widely repeated and were often the source of much disquiet about the slippage between the AST skill discourse and alternative perceptions of skilful teaching that eventually undermined the confidence of many teachers in the AST selection process. It needs to be recognised that this putatively gross inconsistency can occur because many teachers find it difficult to enter the skill discourse set up by the AST criteria. The way in which teaching was described in the criteria, including the kind of words used in those descriptions, was not something that many teachers were familiar or comfortable with in discussing their work. This discursive gulf between quotidian and bureaucratic forms of talk about teaching led to frustration and intense pressure as teachers felt compelled to (re)interpret their understandings of skill in their work so as to make a case for their AST applications. Moreover, having to talk about your work in classrooms in someone else's language, one which is alien to classroom and staffroom talk, was not easy, or eagerly embraced.

> When I first started doing it, it seemed very difficult. I thought I'll never get through this. It seemed a completely overwhelming task; unless you break it down into bits and look at what's required. Try to understand the wording that's used, have a clear idea or definition of words; for example, 'collaboration'.

For this teacher, one who was ultimately successful in getting AST, gaining an understanding of the unfamiliar terminology used in the selection criteria was the key to playing the AST skill discourse game by matching classroom experience to the kind of demonstrable evidence required by the AST criteria. Clearly, it was overwhelming and intimidating for many teachers. Finding that participation in the AST skill discourse was possible was only the first challenge. It was also necessary to be able to render unique experience from working in classrooms into a portrayal of skill that was legitimately admissible into the skill discourse of the selection process.

> My experiences as a teacher are very different from those of many other teachers. I've spent most of my working life going from school to school as a contract teacher – more than 20 schools over 10 years. It was difficult to demonstrate that I was competent and skilled because my experience didn't match up with what most people do in schools. So, when I saw the criteria some of them frightened me, as I didn't feel they addressed what I was most strong in.

A similar kind of 'normality-gap' situation for teaching experience must be confronted by teachers who work in specialist curriculum, or classroom support, areas within schools. Those criteria which are most easily represented through mainstream forms of interaction and skill demonstration in schools may present difficulties for some teachers, as this teacher-librarian found out.

> One member of my panel said that the things I missed out on would have been far more easily achieved in a classroom situation than in the library. I felt these comments reflected a lack of understanding of the role of teacher-librarian and lack of prior knowledge of my work. For teacher-librarians, AST only looks at the teaching role of our jobs, little emphasis is given to the other half of our work.

For this disappointed candidate, the AST skill discourse privileged certain forms of teachers' work through how skills are presented in the selection criteria. In such cases gaps in experience or work practices, which existed primarily from the nature of the work carried out, made it difficult for those teachers to overcome the discursive limitations built into the AST process in their presentation of evidence for some of the criteria. Sometimes the work just did not seem to lend itself to doing the things that many other teachers do in schools.

Another problem faced by many AST candidates centres on a belief that the criteria do not give any prominence to the ordinary, daily work which teachers do and in which a multitude of relational skills are demonstrated by highly experienced classroom practitioners. This concern was often expressed as a difference between generality and particularity that privileges certain discursive forms. One unsuccessful candidate put it like this:

> I see it overly dependent on a willingness from people to comply with a process very focused on verbal ability, and those performance skills which are far removed from the day-to-day teaching life.

Another teacher, a successful AST candidate, saw it much the same way. Management skills of a high order were required to operate as an effective and reliable collegial team member in schools, and teachers found it difficult to understand how these quotidian realities of school-life came to be left out of the AST criteria.

> I think the process just doesn't take into account the management of the myriad of things that occur in a school in a given day. The criteria do look at things that teachers do, but we don't look at each of those criteria each day because we're concerned about things like what's going to happen next lesson. I think that somewhere in the process you've got

to address the day-to-day issues and convince people, as an AST, that your daily management is a very skilful part of your work. In keeping the school running, and you sane, if you don't have strategies available for the things which might occur, then you're down the gurgler.

Comments of this kind indicate a belief that the AST discourse selectively focused on those aspects of a teacher's work which could be easily written down but which avoid the more ineffable aspects of that work. Often it is the things that are hard to pin down which experienced teachers see as the hallmarks of the good classroom operator and collegiate guru. Inevitably, the absence of the contextual leads to limited portrayals of teachers' work that fail to capture many of the truly evocative essences of the classroom life of a teacher. Teachers were often left thinking that the criteria did not connect, concretely, to what teachers did in classrooms.

Some of the criteria are a long way from classroom teaching, which was what I thought was supposed to be at the heart of the AST.

I would question the extent to which the process emphasises the applicant's ability to articulate what they do and be explicit about *some* aspects of their work. I don't see it as an accurate test of good classroom teaching because while some criteria are central, others are more peripheral to classroom teaching. Overall, I think it's a pseudo-judicial process with a lot of gobbledegook that makes it hard for classroom teachers.

There is a recognition here that only some of the criteria were about classroom work and that there was a bureaucratic subtext, of how teaching skill is to be represented, in the criteria as they appear at present. Necessarily, the presence of others peripheral to classroom work was seen as a reflection of the political reality of how the AST skill discourse has, at base, come out of the negotiation between teacher and employer representatives and the interests of each constituency. Another school principal speaks knowingly about how this came to take place.

I have a cynical view personally; but I do believe some criteria are excellent and are important parts of the craft, art, technique and skill of good teaching. However, given the structure of the criteria it is very important that we ensure that teachers are able to show others that they work within the framework designated by these criteria; i.e. that they are worthy of the status of AST.

Clearly, the bureaucratically endorsed discourse on teachers' work and skill as it existed in the form of official documents which attempted to chronicle the things that competent and highly skilled teachers did as part of their work in schools, had an important role in setting the discursive boundaries for a legitimised recognition process like the AST scheme. As is suggested above, there was no choice – teachers had to find ways to discuss and portray their work within the discursive boundaries found in the AST process if they were to gain the benefits from an official recognition of their 'advanced' teaching skills.

The AST process for recognising highly skilled classroom teaching established a discourse of skill which defined an occupationally legitimised way in which teachers and others were able to converse about the classroom skills possessed by teachers. At the base of that discourse were the AST selection criteria, which articulated a specific set of written indicators for skilled teaching which has embedded within it a choice about what is admissible and what is not. An excavation of the authorial intent for those criteria is important for identifying the selectivity implicit in some kinds of pedagogical skill being recognised as reflective of the 'advanced' practitioner whilst, simultaneously, other kinds of highly developed classroom skills are not. The linking of occupational rewards to descriptions of teaching practice that are congruent with the skill discourse advantages some teachers and politicises the development of pedagogical skills. The preferred valuing of those skills in relation to policy initiatives prevents many teachers from being able to demonstrate productively their pedagogical skill, in ways that are acceptable and satisfying (for them), within the boundaries of the AST discourse.

Universal skills and ideology conduits

The AST process recognised a specific set of skills in teaching as 'advanced' and in doing so has encouraged their development in the many experienced teachers who eagerly sought 'advanced' status. Furthermore, it legitimised, possibly even mandated, their acquisition by the cohort of soon to be experienced teachers who seek long, productive and well-paid high-status careers in the classroom. As already discussed, this took shape in the establishment of a skill discourse which set the parameters for the discussion of 'advanced' levels of skill in teaching and formalised a process for the documentation and verification of 'advanced' skills. A common complaint of the AST process by some teachers and principals was that the criteria had too general a focus on classroom work which allows an emphasis on skills which were often peripheral to working with children in classrooms. At the base of such complaints about selection criteria was a belief that those skills which assisted teachers in the implementation of policy initiatives and demonstration of commitment to bureaucratically endorsed preferred ways of working in schools were seen as being more important in the decision making about whether teachers qualify to be labelled as 'advanced' practitioners. If this is the case then the skill discourse is open to significant influence by the latest formations in educational policy and the selection processes will tend, therefore, to advantage the candidates who have close identification with, and in their practice commitment to, those kinds of teaching experiences which are likely to be rich in things which can support that vision of teaching. Under such circumstances, there is likely to be a rapid growth in the presence of those kinds of pedagogical skill which are conducive to the implementation of policy objectives from what is best described as 'discursive stirpiculture' in teachers' work. That is, a process where certain descriptions of teachers' work are selected, while others are simultaneously weeded out, through the construction and reward of particular skills for the preferred teacher. The discursive borders of the skill discourse describe a pedagogical terrain which favours those teachers who are prepared to be proselytised to new policy and school reform by becoming school-site conduits for the latest educational ideology.

Many teachers, both successful and unsuccessful, believed that the required view had to express values which were congruent with those implicit in the latest policy imperatives. The most recent reform initiatives conveyed a set of priorities about the purpose and operation of schools which affected how the work of teaching was judged. Inevitably, 'advanced' teachers become those who quickly assimilate the 'new' through their flexibility as learners and show an ability to demonstrate the efficacy of innovations in curriculum and pedagogy through their skill as communicators. This ability to communicate the implementation of the 'new' was conflated with their qualification as pedagogical leaders.

> This year it's the National Curriculum and the standardised testing that the Government is bringing in. You need to sympathise with policy and have an understanding about it as an issue and to use the policy jargon.

An articulation of policy assimilation and implementation in teaching practice was clearly a core value of the AST process. This had to be done substantively and comprehensively. More pragmatically, the importance of expressing an awareness of policy was integral to participating in the AST skill discourse. With little knowledge of policy development the chances of being able to negotiate the basic features of the AST application became greatly diminished. The challenge for potential AST candidates was to develop their practice, and a supporting world view, which took on board the directions advocated by policy. The way to present an 'acceptable philosophy' was to follow the discursive example set in those official documents which connected policy initiatives to the work which teachers did. The interpretation of policy is often a reliable guide to what are considered relevant and up-to-date forms of teaching practice.

> I knew I could meet the criteria but I knew evidence was necessary. I went about my task of collating evidence and I looked at the . . .

[official] working document and used it as a guide when preparing my application.

Indeed, this appeared to be a good way to ensure that none of the latest initiatives were missed and that correct terminology was used. Most teachers recognised that directions for policy do change and that what was once 'in' may not be anymore and that a favourable focus for an AST application cannot rely upon past knowledge of policy or even commonplace triumphs with established practice. More often than not, the successful applicants seemed to be those who identified and understood that pattern in the process.

> Which issues are the flavour of the year, or the decade, have changed several times in the fifteen years I have been teaching. After a heavy burst of the ESL things, we're now getting into the poverty thing, and social justice is the current push. It has to be carefully interpreted because it's one of those jargon terms. To me, social justice means gender issues, kids with disabilities education; people who are disadvantaged through no fault of their own.

Some teachers saw this emphasis on policy implementation as leading to the separation of classroom context from the skill discourse and its replacement by competence conformity; a situation where the satisfaction of selection criteria could be more easily obtained through the demonstration of an understanding of policy discourses, than through the demonstration of teaching experiences. It found expression in a number of ways when teachers talked about the AST process.

> Jargon and current ideologies can over-ride common sense.

> I have seen applications which neatly represent policy views, yet they're not the views of the person who is applying.

The underlying distrust of this apparent invasive inclusion of policy jargon into the skill discourse was worrisome for many teachers. The richness and diversity of individual manifestations of pedagogical skill became devalued and uniformity in how one's work could be portrayed as skilful became more likely. In their experience of the AST process some teachers felt the sharp end of the privileging of policy discourse in trying to satisfy the selection criteria. In particular, the articulation of 'old ideas' proved a significant disadvantage.

> Things I thought would be pluses in my application, turned out to be minuses. Things which had always worked brilliantly for me, are now a

no-no. As I tried to push what I thought were still valued educational tenets, I was unknowingly 'digging my own grave'.

Similarly, the other side of the coin, where policy discourse informed the definition of appropriate versions of 'advanced' pedagogical skill, was one that saw the non-articulation of the latest ideas also turning out to be a major obstacle in gaining AST. When one teacher admitted not being influenced by an important policy document, he believed that the strong disapproval shown to that revelation deleteriously affected his rating.

> I spoke to my application and expounded on some areas which I believed showed where I met the various criteria but the interview revealed that I believed my teaching practices had not been influenced by the document [names policy document].

In another twist on the same theme, teachers who worked in schools where important policy issues were ignored, or not allowed to influence school-based practices, could also be disadvantaged as AST applicants. If you did not become aware of policy developments and make your teaching practice reflect them, then your ability to demonstrate the skills privileged as 'advanced' became highly problematic. One teacher found that out, to his cost, at the end of the process during his panel interview.

> The day itself went well, but as I was not aware of some issues that were obviously important to the AST process, such as 'Girls in Education', I failed. In my school, that issue had been pushed under the carpet [sic]. That attitude, and my ignorance, blocked a lot of the channels in the process that were open to teachers in other schools.

Many teachers faced a similar problem when their experience did not neatly match that with which the panel was familiar or expected to be demonstrated. Getting it right meant having to convince the panel about things which bear only an indirect connection to the kind of classroom work being undertaken by the applicant. Criteria which reflected policy about preferred ways of working could lead to teachers having to demonstrate their skills 'hypothetically'. Not all teachers were able to carry that off, despite being highly expert in the skills required for successful work in the area under question.

> For my assessment, I generally felt things had gone reasonably well. In the end, it seems, I passed in all areas except my knowledge of current policies and programmes. Having been highly focused about literacy, having found resources to teach students with a deficit, having convinced the school it needed a literacy course if serious about students

with deficit, and students with behaviour problems, I couldn't really see why I was questioned about literacy programmes for kids at a level far above those for whom I had a concern.

A colleague who applied for AST and teaches PE was asked to show how to incorporate co-operation with TAFE [Technical and Further Education] – we have a TAFE campus on site – in his programming. Now, given that both the questioner and the applicant knew that the TAFE neither ran, nor planned to run, any fitness type courses, what was the relevance to his classroom teaching?

In situations like these it was no wonder that teachers felt that policy imperatives were the dominant factor in how teaching skills were meant to be represented. Their work in classrooms fell into line behind policy. Sadly, for most teachers there seemed little room for manoeuvring around such things and many ended up becoming unsuccessful AST applicants who carried away a lot of cynicism from their experience with the AST process.

These teacher narratives about the AST skill discourse indicate that it is also a policy discourse; one in which AST applicants must be proficient if they are to demonstrate their 'advanced' teaching. Familiarity with policy, its jargon and the imperatives it contains for practice, was clearly important when the selection criteria necessitate the demonstration of the latest pedagogical trends in teaching practice.

SPEAKING ABOUT GENDER

There were also some not-so-well-disguised gender undertones at work behind the organisation and evaluation of AST criteria. While many of the teachers interviewed did not reference their critique of the AST process explicitly in terms of gender politics, it was nevertheless clear in their repeated reference to masculinist language, implicit in the managerialist discourses within and against which their teaching was being evaluated, that gendered hierarchies were at work in the AST process. It seemed that preferred language was an important relay through which gender politics got played out in successive stages of the AST scheme.

A deficit view of women in the promotion process is implicit in these reflections on the AST process by a school principal:

AST is very much about recognising your own skills and being able to sell them. Teachers, especially women, have never really learnt the requisite, in our competitive age today, to state clearly what they believe in, who they are, what they can do, and how they can use those skills. That's part of the AST process – to debunk that old culture stuff of putting yourself down instead of saying quite unemotionally and objectively 'I possess these skills, this is how I use them and this is what motivates me'.

Furthermore, women often have to 'prove themselves' in ways that are different, and sometimes descriptively more exhaustive, than is the case for men (Clark 1990). When AST candidates observe that the intensity of the selection process is greater than that for senior administrative positions in schools, they are identifying the gendered hierarchies of power and privilege that Jackson (1991) describes. It underlies the simplicity of describing advanced teaching skills in purely technical ways and points convincingly to the gendered construction of the work of classroom teachers and school administrators.

'Lived' career patterns described by women teachers often do not 'fit' models like the AST where continuities in work histories and school experiences seem implicit to the demonstration of advanced skill. Women teachers are less likely to make long-term plans in their jobs and are more likely to have worked in a succession of short-term and/or contract appointments. Women teachers, especially older, more experienced women, often blame themselves for the fragmentation of their teaching careers (Acker 1995a) and find the evidential demands of the AST process intimidating. Indeed, the likelihood of these, and other forms of gender-bullying, or gender-exclusion, as work-site experience for promoted women in schools, may be a real deterrent for seeking higher-status positions in and beyond classroom teaching (Clark 1990).

Chapter 8

Conclusion

REJECTING ECONOMIC PALIMPSESTS OF TEACHERS' WORK

Teachers' work is neither innocent nor neutral in its relation to the economic forces and social movements at work in society at large. Throughout this book we have tried to 'look both ways' in order to get an up-close view of the changing narratives of teachers' work and at the same time map the social and economic terrain to give a broader, more global, view of the ideologies, policies and practices involved in remaking teachers' work. In doing this through continuous links between our theorising about globalisation, the structural adjustment of economies, social change through moral panic, managerialism and economic rationalism, workplace competencies and the marketisation of public life – within the empirical richness of a case study about the Advanced Skills Teacher scheme – we have sought to bring critical illumination to the overlap between ideology, policy and practice in the remaking of teaching. Our success, or otherwise, in putting those links in place, in ways that enable the reader to maintain some 'stereoscopic discursive-vision' with our reasoning, and at the same time keeping our text 'writerly' with continuous opportunity for interpretation, will be evident by now. It remains for us to revisit our arguments, theorising and portrayals about the remaking of teachers' work from our own experience of 'writing both ways'; to capture the essences of those dramatic, profound and far-reaching changes being visited on schools worldwide that have their genesis a long way from classrooms and playgrounds, but are impacting upon teachers and their work.

We should reiterate that an Australian context is not assumed here, even though we obviously draw from that in pulling together the gist of our arguments about what is happening to teaching in a wider global context. Our Australian case study is posited rather as being highly indicative of what our reading of the literature tells us is happening elsewhere.

Those who work in, or with, schools and who interact with the educational lives that are shaped, constructed and enacted there have in recent times become well acquainted with the benefits of efficient management of schooling based on economic criteria. As the commodification of our lives continues at great pace – to the point where anything of value or desire can potentially be traded and subjected to the rules of exchange even in areas previously regarded free from the economic rigours of the market, like sport, health and schooling to name a few – it becomes likely that the discourses of economic management and the marketplace will have significant influence over the reorganisation of taken-for-granted positions about the work performed in those 'public' activities.

The globalisation of the world economy sees the shifting of capital and production across geographical and political boundaries in search of cheap labour and low-cost resources for the manufacture of goods for world markets. The drive for a competitive edge pushes business, industry and government constantly to seek innovative use of resources and technologies in production, more efficient ways to organise workers in the pursuit of cost-effective output, and the creative formation in new and expanded markets of demand for new, bigger and better goods and services. The kinds of economically and technically rationalist discourses that go with the trend towards economic globalisation carry powerful metaphors and conceptual apparatuses for the revisioning and organisation of social relations and their links to work and production. Such discourses are not confined to 'big' business and transnational industries; they 'reach down' and 'act at a distance' informing the way schools are constructed as places of learning and the way teachers work and students learn.

We see this occurring in the proliferation of terms like productivity, restructuring, self-management, and the like, applied to the reform of schools and the remaking of teachers' work in Australia and elsewhere. Shrinking public expenditure, as governments concentrate on the politically specious issue of 'debt management' and pursue an agenda of 'privatisation', witnessed in an increasing commodification of all sectors of state-provided education, has ensured that economic rationalist thinking has replaced educational thinking as the preferred way in which schools are to serve the interests of students and communities. As this occurs, and schools are subjected to reform based on new visions for the organisation of education, teachers' work is 'structurally adjusted' accordingly to suit the kinds of teaching required in self-managing schools. For us, this explains the shift towards post-Fordist forms of organisation in teachers' work where much of the supervision and administration of classroom workers lies within schools themselves through devolved responsibility for performance management and quality assurance of programmes and teachers. Additionally, this occurs in the erosion of the creative aspects of teaching when the management of things like curriculum and assessment retreats from schools to more central locations. In the AST scheme, the work of experienced and highly competent classroom workers undergoes 'structural adjustment' in its tighter prescription through criterion-referenced assessment of skills and competencies for working pedagogically and collegially. Teachers who engaged the AST process were overwhelmed by the detailed way in which the work of the supposedly 'best' classroom teachers is specified.

We find that schools are now expected to do more with less and at the same time submit to 'muscular forms of supervision' which place the work of teachers and students under closer scrutiny through centrally controlled mechanisms like standardised testing, performance management and criterion-referenced determinants of status such as the AST scheme. Indeed, as our examination of the AST scheme revealed, teachers find the structural readjustment of their work through award restructuring anchored in notions of increased productivity and the linkage of teachers' work to national economic priorities for competitive production, an arena of contestation over the definition of teaching as work. Increasingly, the assertion of preferred ways of working that are embedded in the discourses of collegiality, performance and skill are seen by teachers as a struggle over the admission and exclusion of what are legitimate ways to represent the imperatives and limits of their work. AST candidates were often torn between the requirement to tell some things about their work and their desire to tell it in other ways.

In our analysis this reaching down of economic rationalism takes shape in what has been aptly described as 'policy hysteria' (Stronach and Morris 1994) and a consequent intensification of prescription in teachers' work at the school level. The expansion of central policy development into pedagogy and curriculum means tighter control over what is considered to be good practice in teaching and a subsequent narrowing of what encompasses exemplary teaching typical of the highly competent classroom worker. We believe that this represents a tendency to see the work of teaching as generically descriptive and ultimately articulated through a 'one size fits all' template which devalues difference and creative idiosyncrasy. Those things that are centrally important to the pedagogic flexibility valued by experienced teachers in coping with the inherent messiness and unpredictability of classroom work, which inevitably have an ineffable character, are lost in the tighter prescriptions of what teachers do. Within our portrayal of the AST process we found that teachers regarded the invasion of policy imperatives into the criteria for 'advanced' teaching as an effective limitation on how skilful teaching can be represented. They found that the complexity of the relational qualities necessary for the very best classroom teaching cannot be adequately described in work-criteria which are strongly linked to the outcomes of policy implementation.

The structural adjustment of teachers' work which we see occurring through criterion-referenced assessment of skills and competencies for working pedagogically and collegially is about the revisioning, reconstrual and reconstruction of teaching according to economic understandings about the purpose and value-loci of school education. Often associated with this is an assumption that schools must accept some blame for the downturn in production and the competitiveness of economies. Poor performance by business, industry and government is traced back to poorly skilled workers and the failing of educational systems in fulfilling their national responsibilities in delivering appropriately motivated and educated people ready to enter the workforce. In delivering commonsense articulations of the links between national economic well-being, lifestyles, productivity, work skills and schooling, the reformist discourses of economic rationalism and managerialism portray schools as being 'at fault' in the deterioration of living standards, as costly and ineffective in their social function and service to the national 'good'.

We see this as about 'manufacturing a crisis' of confidence in schooling through the representation of its shortcomings in ways that simultaneously make connections between schoolwork and economic prosperity and affect a disguise for the larger forces at work on the social fabric of which schools are a part. In our view, once the myths and lies about the connections between the pedagogical work of schools and effectiveness of business in responding to declining and changing markets for manufactured goods are reasonably accepted as associative, then it becomes possible to argue for the expiated reform of schools and teachers' work. It is this kind of school reform, which seeks the instrumental connection of school and economic activity, that we find so objectionable because of the effect on teachers' work that such means–ends thinking permits. When teachers' work becomes a conduit for harnessing learning to the rectification of non-educational problems, the process of structural adjustment has moved a long way towards the reconstruction of teaching in the service of the economy. This is why so many teachers are non-plussed by their engagement with new arrangements, like the AST scheme, for their work; the new demands for detail appearing to come 'out of left field'.

To see teaching in this way allows for the close prescription of what counts as good or effective teaching and, as a direct result, the removal of those things which are not easily described in ways that are amenable to technical and nominally 'objective' forms of observation and appraisal. This in turn enables teaching to be fragmented into smaller and more tightly defined tasks which are easily accounted for and reviewed by those in managerial roles and positions of external authority. As a trend this leads to 'routinisation and proletarianisation' in teachers' work which makes it suitable for the kind of closer supervision and management that an economically rationalist perspective demands. As we saw in the concept of the 'evaluative state' (Neave 1988), the emergence of policy implementation as a fundamental part of teachers' work allows for the transference of more responsibility for the enactment of systemic policy imperatives to individual teachers at the same time as allowing for greater external monitoring of the 'effectiveness' of the work of individual teachers. In the evaluative mode of an economically rational state, the work of teachers is controlled, and linked to the bigger picture, through 'silk glove' forms of accountability that are built into the policies informing the fundamental imperatives of schooling. We see this illustrated in how teachers react to the criterion-referenced description of skill for advanced teaching in the AST process. Teachers found that the selection of 'advanced' teachers from the cohort of experienced teachers was located primarily in the identification of that narrow range of pedagogical skills which were demonstrable most readily through evidence about the implementation of policy. For them, this was a bureaucratic endorsement of the link between preferred ways of working and official measures of accountability; and for us, it reflected a firmer link between the informant economic and managerialist ideologies and teaching as represented through policy limitations of what counts as skilled work in classrooms.

We have viewed this reconstruction of teaching as economic work as a 'moral panic' (Cohen 1972) over the decline in productivity and loss in profits from industry and business. It is mistakenly connected to the apparent deleterious work of social institutions like schools, rather than the flight of capital to new low-cost, high-return feeding grounds. As we argued, moral panics are often convincing without evidence through the portrayal of catastrophic consequences to established ways of life that are cherished or have some fundamental essence. The moral panic that schools are failing the nation, business and workers through inefficient teaching practices and lack of success in preparing students for an economy that needs skilled workers, sees the wholesale displacement of those educational discourses about schooling steeped in the relational nature of teaching and learning. In their place are posited economic rationalist discourses which have more to do with getting value for money at the lowest optimal costs than with the discursive practices of teaching. Factors which inhibit this kind of value in schooling require drastic restorative action in order that cost effectiveness is attained. In something like the AST scheme, teachers see it as: 'teachers who show the values, get the money'.

This leads to policy discourses about schooling and teaching which bring into policy the language of business and conceptual frames which allow for the kinds of hard-nosed economic accountability found in the cut-throat world of competitive business. Accordingly an enterprise culture that commodifies schooling quickly asserts itself as a new organising form for the reorganisation of the work of schools and teachers. It is a way of thinking about the work of teachers and pupils which devalues the complex nature of the learning relationships between teachers and students, and students and other students, by carrying the discourse about teaching and learning through ontologically loose notions of skill and competency that appear simply transferable between individuals in a learning process. Individual teachers and students are seen as possessing skills and competencies acquired and shed through suitable processes of learning and training. That this is not an adequate way of understanding how learning occurs as social activity is disguised by aerosol words like 'quality' which act to cover up the unsuitability of the synthetic discourses for the description of the messiness and relational complexity of teaching as work. Teachers who engaged the AST process testified to the pedagogic meaninglessness of the fragmentation of teaching skill to criterion-referenced descriptions of classroom work. The reductionist thinking about teaching skill found in the AST scheme denied the existence of multiple-value positions for assessing a range of sophisticated practices for teachers' work accomplished within particular contexts and with particular sets of children and colleagues.

Throughout our theorising and analysis of the AST scheme, we have been eager to adopt a 'reading position' on teachers' work that permits the possibility for interruption of the discourses serving to remake teaching. We see economic rationalist and managerially discursive frames providing new hegemonic constraints on the way in which teaching can be represented in official spaces such as the AST process. We consider it important that teachers have the opportunity to access discourses about their work which counter the constraints by drawing upon language and conceptual apparatuses different to those that see teaching as primarily economic work. The indigenous occupational discourses in teaching, which celebrate the creatively idiosyncratic nature of teaching and acknowledge the contextual complexity of the teaching event, are one source for discursive possibility counter to the new hegemonic forms of enterprise culture. When AST applicants bumped up against the unfriendly aspects of the AST process, and the selection criteria, they often expressed their frustration about how the process restricted them from presenting themselves as skilled workers in the ways they would have preferred. For some, this was poignantly shaped into a refusal to participate despite the hallmarks of 'advanced' being obviously present in their work.

We used the distinction between 'readerly' and 'writerly' text (Barthes 1975) to enable a perspective on the discursive possibilities within what we see as hegemonic and counter-hegemonic discourses on teaching. The economic rationalist and managerialist discourses on teaching, and we see the AST scheme as an example of them, are a 'readerly' text on teaching because they are highly definitive about what counts, how it is organised, how it is identified, and what the presence/absence of certain indicators of teaching means for assessing individual teaching competence. It offers very little, if any, opportunity for critical and reflective engagement with the text because of its reification of the teaching qualities and attributes coded as 'advanced'. In our case study of AST candidates many teachers complained about the 'rigidity' of the process and the criteria because of a perceived exclusion of unusual or non-mainstream versions of skilful teaching; as a limiting consequence of the bureaucratic influence for tighter prescription and accountability in teachers' work. On the other hand, the more flexible and inclusive indigenous practitioner discourses about the work of experienced teachers admit the possibility of many pedagogical 'faces' for the highly skilled classroom worker. In this kind of 'writerly' text it is possible for individual teachers to 'rewrite' the conceptual frames of advanced skill according to their own contextual circumstances in ways that enable them to represent the richness of their work. We found this tension between 'readerly' and 'writerly' qualities to be congruent with that tension between synthetic and authentic discourses and considered it indicative of the struggle over representation and exclusion that lies at the heart of the remaking of teaching going on in apparently innocent processes like those of the AST scheme.

For us, teaching must be 'writerly' text because of the language-rich nature of teaching, the way it is lived as a 'narrative event' and described in practitioner discourses as a 'narrated event' (Bauman 1986), where multiple versions and interpretations of teaching as work exist simultaneously. This is precisely what many of the AST applicants, successful and unsuccessful alike, referred to in claiming that the AST selection criteria were too narrow in focus and that they prevented the multiple expression of teaching skill. Teaching as 'writerly' text enables teachers to give voice to their own definitions of what counts as experienced classroom work and how it might be best portrayed to capture the pedagogical essences embedded contextually in the relationships found in schools. The interests informative of the synthetic and authentic discourses are in competition over the demarcation of what can count as 'advanced' teaching and who gets to control the accounting processes. Teaching as 'writerly' text keeps that in flux – whilst as 'readerly' text it becomes fixed. Teachers constantly struggled to maintain 'writerly' possibility in their work through various forms of accommodation, contestation and resistance to the closure of narrative windows provided by the indigenous discourses of teaching. This occurred in the AST process when teachers learnt the jargon to 'play the game', insisted upon describing their policy knowledge through reference to specific classroom events, and when they refused to engage the process because of its artificiality.

We have regarded the 'readerly' text of teaching skill found in the AST process to be about breaking down the complex and sophisticated nature of the work of the 'advanced' teacher into manageable sections that require teachers to see their work as fragmented and technical rather than wholistic and contextually responsive. This is indicative of 'low-trust' in the competency of teachers beyond that which can be tightly proscribed through criterion-referenced performance indicators as suited to business-style accountability. Inevitably, this fragmentation of pedagogical work leads to intensified working conditions for teachers and imposes a technical rationality which prepares the work of teachers for the kind of fast-track adaptability required in market-driven and customer-responsive organisations. The economic rationalist agenda behind the restructuring of teachers' work which led to the introduction of the AST scheme required schools to become market-focused in pursuit of maximum return. Necessarily, this filters down to classroom workers in order that 'productivity' can be connected in a discursive feedback loop to provide those educational commodities demanded by the paying customer. As we see it, the most effective way of achieving this is through discursive simplification and intensification of teachers' work; and the congruity of this discursive concentration of teaching with market forces occurs through the close connection of teaching skill with policy implementation. As policy changes, so does the work of teachers; discursive manipulation with technical precision.

The characteristics of the 'good' teacher within economic rationalist and managerial discourses reduce the multidimensional nature of teaching to the kind of technical description found in a list of competencies. More than anything else, this requires from teachers a capacity, and an acquiescence, for the abstraction of the essences of teaching as work from the contextual meanings in which that work finds its maturity. It requires a willingness to submit the self-construction of one's own teaching to the kind of enforced discipline inscribed in the authorship of some aspects of teaching over others. In the case of the AST process, the 'policy-saturated' nature of the selection criteria and the inevitable linking of 'advanced' teaching to the discipline of policy implementation was something of which teachers were only too well aware. Our case study reveals how this sat in contradiction, starkly, to the construction of teachers as autonomous and self-managing professionals.

Throughout we have emphasised the rhetorical potency of the skill discourse found in the AST process for the creation of 'preferred meanings' about 'advanced' teaching. Individuals in possession of the right kind of knowledge about their work, who understand the nuances of the managerialist control of teachers' work, and who are able to render the complexity of classroom work into the narrower discursive forms contained within criterion-referenced descriptions of teaching, are likely to be advantaged in something like the AST process. The rhetorical focus of the skill discourse takes an individualistic position on the acquisition of teaching skills through its emphasis on individual demonstration of competence and the award of individual badges of 'advanced' teaching. This is disturbing on two counts. Firstly, because it grounds the articulation of skill and 'advanced' teaching in a mode of representation suitable to technical forms of accountability; and second, because it is an attempt to 'spot-weld' an individualist vision of experienced classroom work onto what is predominantly a collegiate occupational culture. Competence at all levels in teaching exists within shared understandings of the relational primacy of the work and is developed as social practice within a community of teachers and students. Individualism has a lot in common with isolation and stand-alone portrayals of experienced classroom work. Cut free from the shared culture in which they were nurtured, individually claimed teaching skills are unlikely to ring true in any convincing sense except for the 'maverick' or 'loner' teachers.

Once individualist cultures of teaching and skill are in place it becomes possible to construct visions of school reform which rely upon the individually malleable and adaptive teacher. In such visions teachers are calculable, flexible, accountable, entrepreneurial, manageable, marketable and responsive to the customer-driven wants from the educational system. The entrepreneurial teacher is one who can individually take on board the 'failures' of school(s) and respond quickly to policy initiatives, which are developed away from the contamination of school, with the express intention of 'fixing' the school. In the AST scheme, individuals possessed of 'advanced' teaching skills were those who showed the right amount of 'policy gloss' and demonstrated their flexibility for proselytisation to the latest school reform package. Economically rationalist visions of teachers as individuals within the corporate culture of the school are more easily supported through the remaking of teachers as independent repositories of competence who work in isolation from colleagues. Indeed, this is how the AST version of the 'advanced' teacher was constructed – as an individual pedagogical warrior – and despite the nominal importance of collaboration in some parts of the AST process, it smacked of dangerous 'contrived collegiality' (Hargreaves 1994) as long as it was conterminous with individual locations of skill within a market-driven discourse of reform.

We have tried to argue strongly throughout our belief that there are many ways of representing the work of teaching and that any conceptual limitations to ways of constructing teaching are likely to promote conservative views of what counts as desirably skilful classroom work. We see teaching being remade as technical activity where teachers in possession of appropriate competencies are able to perform individually the tasks required to make teaching and learning efficient and productive. This is a very different version of teaching as work than if teaching is seen as craft or bricolage, or moral, intellectual and political activity. In those cases teaching is more readily observed as idiosyncratically relational, responsive, collective and ethically grounded in a heritage of schooling that has little to do with commodities, consumers and markets. We see this as the difference between 'low-trust' and 'high-trust' forms of accountability that exist between teachers and their employers. The teacher as technician is important in the construction of teaching as a 'readerly' text, whilst other forms of viewing teachers variously permit some energising capacity for a contextually grounded responsiveness in a 'writerly' version of teachers' work.

It is our view that teaching has moved to a set of ideologies, policies, practices and discourses where consumerist, contractualist, managerialist and marketised values and beliefs are what counts most in shaping teaching. We see this as a fundamental shift away from those educational values which have sustained education in the post-war era and we are alarmed by the decline in those discourses which have supported the expansion of educational provision as a legitimate form of public activity. This reshaping of teaching takes place through initiatives like the AST scheme where particular ways of viewing the work of teachers and schools, in this case the skills of experienced teachers, are presented as authoritative and non-negotiable rather than as one choice among many. Furthermore, we are disturbed that genuine discourses about the practice of teaching are being replaced by pedagogically synthetic, economically rational, kinds which embed teachers in subordinate positions, especially with regard to the processes of definition and control, in their work.

The voices of teachers are largely missing in the remaking of teachers' work occurring through processes of structural adjustment from the policy-driven reform of teaching informed by economic priorities. This is reflected in the disappointment teachers expressed about the way this reform has its genesis far from the immediate problems of the classroom and in their anger about its impositional presence in their working lives. Our case-study account of skilled teachers and the AST credentialling process was an attempt to hear what teachers had to say about the ideologies, policies and practices at work in the remaking of teaching. They told of the struggle over the discursive construction of their work through the competitive tension between indigenous and policy narratives in teachers' work. We suggested that readers connect our account of this struggle to our arguments about the economic forces at work through a continuous reading process of 'previewing' and 'reviewing' in order to give a narrative vibrancy to the account from 'looking both ways'. In this way the ideologies, policies and practices of remaking teachers' work can be seen as integrated and whole. It shows that teachers are not 'failing' in their work, but are engaged in a fight over its definition which sees them contesting and resisting the leaching of the educational integrity from their day-to-day work.

It is worth briefly revisiting the heuristic of palimpsest that we started out with – the notion of writing over something that has been erased. We still believe this to be a helpful way of conceiving of the forces operating upon the indigenous culture of teachers' work, even though we believe the expunging to be far from complete. There was evidence, for example, in the case study of some of Gunter's (1997) 'listening schools and listening practitioners' (those who were prepared to acquiesce to the policy imperative), but there were also significant numbers of 'vocal teachers and vocal schools' prepared to assert their professional voices; we were enormously heartened by the stories of these teachers.

In this book we have sought to show how teaching is being remade by global economic forces which have little to do with the relational world of teaching and learning inhabited by children and teachers. In our view the schoolworld has become a site of production linked to the pursuit of capital with the work of students and teachers structurally adjusted to the demands of economic productivity and the construction of adaptable workers. We are concerned that economic well-being has become a pedagogical imperative of such huge proportions in teaching that the work of teachers is being remade to serve the economy through the edicts of policy. We believe that the reaching down of the economy into teachers' work through the formalisation of a narrow vision of the efficient, entrepreneurial and productive 'preferred teacher' should be seen for what it is – the loss of the pedagogical primacy of the relational in teaching. Despite our concerns about the trends witnessed here we reassert the integrity of teachers to construct teachers' work through practitioner discourses which celebrate teaching in its many versions without resort to managerialism.

Bibliography

Acker, S. (1995a). Gender and teachers' work. In M. Apple (ed.): *Review of Research in Education* (vol. 21, pp. 99–162). Washington, DC: American Educational Research Association.

—— (1995b). Carry on caring: the work of women teachers. *British Journal of Sociology of Education*, 16(1): 21–36.

Agger, B. (1990). *The Decline of Discourse: Reading, Writing and Resistance in Postmodern Capitalism*. London: Falmer Press.

Ainley, P. (1993). *Class and Skill*. London: Cassell.

Alford, J. (1993). Towards a new public management model. *Australian Journal of Public Administration*, 52(2): 135–48.

Angus, L. (1993). The sociology of school effectiveness. *British Journal of Sociology of Education*, 14(3): 333–45.

Apple, M. (1986). *Teachers and Texts: A Political Economy of Class and Gender Relations in Education*. New York and London: Routledge & Kegan Paul.

—— (1996a). *Cultural Politics and Education*. Milton Keynes: Open University Press.

—— (1996b). Power, meaning and identity: critical sociology of education in the United States. *British Journal of Sociology of Education*, 17(2): 125–44.

Arnold, M. (1996). The high-tech post-Fordist school. *Interchange*, 27(3 & 4): 225–50.

Arnstine, D. M. and McDowell, J. (1993). Unfair rewards: merit pay, grades and a flawed system of evaluation. *Teacher Education Quarterly*, 20(2): 5–21.

Ashenden, D. (1989). Chucking the chooks: restructuring the education industry. *Education Australia*, no. 7: 9–10.

Aucoin, P. (1990). Administrative reform in public management: paradigms, principles, paradoxes and pendulums. *Governance: An International Journal of Policy and Administration*, 3(2): 115–37.

The Australia Institute (1996). *What Should Governments Do? Auditing the National Audit Commission* (Discussion Paper no. 8). Canberra.

Australian Education Council (1991). *Young People's Participation in Post-Compulsory Education and Training (The Finn Report)*. Canberra: Australian Government Publishing Service.

Australian Education Council and Ministers for Vocational Education Employment and Training (1992). *Putting General Education to Work: The Key Competencies Report (The Mayer Committee Report)*. Melbourne: Australian Education Council.

Bacharach, S., Conley, S. and Shedd, J. (1990). Evaluating teachers for career awards and merit pay. In J. Millman and L. Darling-Hammond (eds), *The New Handbook of Teacher Evaluation* (pp. 133–46). Beverly Hills, CA: Sage.

Ball, S. (1988). Staff relations during the teachers' industrial action: context, conflict and proletarianisation. *British Journal of Sociology of Education*, 9(3): 289–306.

—— (1990). *Politics and Policy Making in Education: Explorations in Policy Sociology*. London and New York: Routledge.

—— (1993a). Education policy, power relations and teachers' work. *British Journal of Educational Studies*, 41(2): 106–21.

—— (1993b). Culture, cost and control: self-management and entrepreneurial schooling in England and Wales. In J. Smyth (ed.), *A Socially Critical View of the Self-Managing School* (pp. 63–82). London: Falmer Press.

—— (1994). *Education Reform: A Critical and Post-Structural Analysis*. Milton Keynes: Open University Press.

—— (1997). Good school/bad school: paradox and fabrication. *British Journal of Sociology of Education*, 18(3): 317–36.

—— and Bowe, R. (1990). Where the garment gaps: policy and ethnography as practices. Unpublished paper, King's College, London.

—— and —— (1992). Education, markets and professionalism: some recent reflections on recent policy developments in England and Wales. *Melbourne Studies in Education*, 56–62.

Barnet, R. and Cavanagh, J. (1994). *Global Dreams: Imperial Corporations and the New World Order*. New York: Simon & Schuster.

Barnett, R. (1994). *The Limits of Competence*. Milton Keynes: Open University Press.

Barrow, R. (1987). Skill Talk. *Journal of Philosophy of Education*, 21(2): 187–95.

Barthes, R. (1975). *S/Z: An Essay* (trans. R. Miller). New York: Hill & Wang.

Barzelay, M. (1992). *Breaking through Bureaucracy: A New Vision for Managing in Government*. Berkeley: University of California Press.

Batsleer, J., Davis, T., O'Rourke, R. and Weedon, C. (1985). *Rewriting English*. New York: Methuen.

Bauman, R. (1986). *Story, Performance, and Event: Contextual Studies of Oral Narrative*. Cambridge: Cambridge University Press.

Beazley, K. (1993). *Teaching Counts: A Ministerial Statement*. Canberra: Australian Government Publishing Service.

Berliner, D. and Biddle, B. (1995). *The Manufactured Crisis: Myths, Fraud and the Attack on America's Public Schools*. Reading, MA: Addison-Wesley.

Beyer, L. and Liston, D. (1992). Discourse or moral action? A critique of postmodernism. *Educational Theory*, 42(4): 371–93.

Biklen, S. (1995). *School Work: Gender and the Cultural Construction of Teaching*. Albany: SUNY Press.

Bizzell, P. (1992). What is a 'discourse community'? In P. Bizzell (ed.), *Academic Discourse and Critical Consciousness* (pp. 222–37). Pittsburgh: University of Pittsburgh Press.

Blackmore, J. (1992). The gendering of skill and vocationalism in twentieth-century Australian education. *Journal of Education Policy*, 7(4): 351–77.

—— (1995). Breaking out from a masculinist politics of education. In B. Limerick and B. Lingard (eds), *Gender and Changing Educational Management* (pp. 44–56). Rydalmere, NSW: Hodder Education.

—— (1996). Doing 'emotional labour' in the education market place: stories from the field of women in management. *Discourse: Studies in the Cultural Politics of Education*, 17(3): 337–50.

Bluer, R. (1991). Reforming schools – the Australian way. *Unicorn*, 17(2): 67.

—— (1993). The origins and dimensions of the Advanced Skills Teacher classification. In M. Gaffney and F. Crowther (eds), *Advanced Skills Teaching: A Demonstration of Professionalism or Opportunity Lost?* (vol. 19, pp. 1–5). ACEA Monograph Series: Australian Council for Educational Administration.

—— and Carmichael, L. (1991). Award restructuring in teaching. *Unicorn*, 17(1): 24–9.

Bottery, M. and Wright, N. (1996). Cooperating in their own deprofessionalisation? On the need to recognise the 'Public' and 'Ecological' roles of the teaching profession. *British Journal of Educational Studies*, 44(1): 82–98.

Bowe, R., Ball, S. and Gold, A. (1992). *Reforming Education and Changing Schools: Case Studies in Policy Sociology*. London and New York: Routledge.

Brandt, R. (1990). *Incentive Pay and Career Ladders for Today's Teachers: A Study of Current Programs and Practices*. Albany: SUNY.

Brecher, J. and Costello, T. (1994). *Global Village or Global Pillage: Economic Reconstruction from the Bottom Up*. Boston: South End Press.

Carlson, D. (1995). Making progress: progressive education in the postmodern. *Educational Theory*, 45(3): 337–57.

Carnegie Forum on Education and the Economy (1986). *A Nation Prepared. Teachers for the 21st Century: The Report of the Task Force on Teaching as a Profession*. Washington, DC: Carnegie Forum on Education and the Economy.

Carr, W. and Hartnett, A. (1996). *Education and the Struggle for Democracy: The Politics of Educational Ideas*. Milton Keynes: Open University Press.

Casey, K. (1992). Why do progressive women activists leave teaching? Theory, methodology and politics in life history research. In I. Goodson (ed.), *Studying Teachers' Lives* (pp. 187–208). London and New York: Routledge.

Castells, M. (1989). *The Information City: Information Technology and the Urban-Regional Process*. Oxford: Blackwell.

Ceroni, K. (1995). Promises made, promises broken: a literary criticism of the Pennsylvania lead teacher experience. Unpublished Doctoral Dissertation, University of Pittsburgh.

—— and Garman, N. (1994). The empowerment movement: genuine collegiality or yet another hierarchy? In P. Grimmett and J. Neufeld (eds), *Teacher Development and the Struggle for Authenticity: Professional Growth and Restructuring in the Context of Change* (pp. 141–61). New York and London: Teachers College Press.

Chadbourne, R. and Ingvarson, L. (1991). *Advanced skills teacher – 1: lost opportunity or professional breakthrough (Seminar Series: Report no. 9)*. Melbourne: IARTV.

Chossudovsky, M. (1997). *Globalization and World Poverty: Impacts of IMF and World Bank Reforms*. London and New Jersey: ZED Books.

Clark, M. (1990). *The Great Divide: Gender in the Primary School*. Melbourne: Curriculum Corporation.

Coffield, F. (1990). From the decade of the enterprise culture to the decade of the TECs. *British Journal of Education and Work*, 4(1): 59–78.

Cohen, S. (1972). *Folk Devils and Moral Panics: The Creation of the Mods and Rockers*. London: MacGibbon & Kee.

Cohn, M. and Kottkamp, R. (1993). *Teachers: The Missing Voice in Education*. Albany: SUNY.

Cole, M. and Hill, D. (1996). Between postmodernism and nowhere: the predicament of the postmodernist (a reply to Nigel Blake). Unpublished MS, University of Brighton.

Conley, S. and Odden, A. (1995). Linking teacher compensation to teacher career development. *Educational Evaluation and Policy Analysis*, 17(2): 219–37.

Connell, R. (1989). The labour process and the division of labour. In B. Cosin, M. Flude and M. Hales (eds), *School, Work and Equality* (pp. 123–34). London: Hodder & Stoughton.

—— (1995). Transformative labour: theorizing the politics of teachers' work. In M. Ginsburg (ed.), *The Politics of Educators' Work and Lives* (pp. 91–114). New York and London: Garland.

—— (1996). *Prepare for interesting times: education in a fractured world* (Inaugural professorial address): University of Sydney.

Conti, R. and Warner, M. (1993). Taylorism, new technology and just-in-time systems in Japanese manufacturing. *New Technology, Work and Employment*, 8(1): 32–42.

Cookson, P. (1994). *School Choice: The Struggle for the Soul of American Education*. New Haven: Yale University Press.

Cooley, M. (1980). *Architect or Bee*. Sydney: Transnational Co-operative.

Costello, T. (1996). Whatever happened to the common good? *The Age*, 20 August: 13.

—— (1997). Some values are free. *The Age*, 16 January: 15.

Croft, S. and Beresford, P. (1992). The politics of participation. *Critical Social Policy*, 35: 20–44.

Darrah, C. (1992). Workplace skills in context. *Human Organization*, 51: 264–73.

Davies, B. and Harre, R. (1990). Positioning: conversation and the production of selves. *Journal for the Theory of Social Behaviour*, 20(1): 43–63.

Dawkins, J. (1990). *Quality of Teaching – An Issue for All*. Canberra: Australian Government Publishing Service.

Deever, B. (1996a). Is this radical enough? Curriculum reform, change and the language of probability. *Interchange*, 27(3 & 4): 251–60.

—— (1996b). If not now, when? Radical theory and systemic curriculum reform. *Journal of Curriculum Studies*, 28(2): 171–91.

Delbridge, R., Turnbull, P. and Wilkinson, B. (1992). Pushing back the frontiers: management control and work intensification under JIT/TQM factory regimes. *New Technology, Work and Employment*, 7(2): 97–106.

Dillard, J. and Nehmer, R. (1990). Metaphorical marginalization. *Critical Perspectives on Accounting*, 1(1): 31–52.

Dinham, S. and Scott, C. (1997). The Advanced Skills Teacher – a missed opportunity? *Unicorn*, 23(3): 36–49.

Directorate of School Education Victoria (1992). *Advanced Skills Teacher 2 and 3 Selection Training Manual*. Melbourne: Directorate of School Education Victoria.

Dow, A. (1996). Collaboration and resistance at Gallipoli highschool: the work of teaching in a post-Fordist era. Unpublished Doctoral Dissertation, The Flinders University of South Australia.

Dwyer, P. (1995). Foucault, docile bodies and post-compulsory education in Australia. *British Journal of Sociology of Education*, 16(4): 467–77.

Eagleton, T. (1983). *Literary Theory: An Introduction*. Oxford: Blackwell.

Education Department of South Australia (1992). *Advanced Skills Teacher Procedural Manual*. Adelaide: Education Department of South Australia.

Eisner, E. (1992). Objectivity in educational research. *Curriculum Inquiry*, 22(1): 9–15.

Fairclough, N. (1992a). *Critical Language Awareness*. New York: Longman.

—— (ed.) (1992b). *Language and Power*. London: Longman.

Fine, M. (1991). *Framing Dropouts: Notes on the Politics of an Urban Public High School*. Albany: SUNY.

—— (1993). [Ap]parent involvement: reflections on parents, power and urban public schools. *Teachers College Record*, 94(4): 682–710.

Finegold, D., McFarland, L. and Richardson, W. (1992). Something borrowed, something blue? A study of the Thatcher government's appropriation of American education and training policy, Part 1. *Oxford Studies in Comparative Education*, 2(2).

——, —— and —— (1993). Something borrowed, something blue? A study of the Thatcher government's appropriation of American education and training policy, Part 2. *Oxford Studies in Comparative Education*, 3(1).

Firestone, W. (1994). Redesigning teacher salary systems for educational reform. *American Educational Research Journal*, 31(3): 549–74.

—— and Pennell, J. (1993). Teacher commitment, working conditions, and differential incentive policies. *Review of Educational Research*, 63(4): 489–529.

Foucault, M. (1977). *Discipline and Punish: The Birth of the Prison* (trans. A. Sheridan). Harmondsworth: Penguin.

Freeland, J. (1985). Australia: the search for a new educational settlement. In R. Sharp (ed.), *Capitalist Crisis and Schooling: Comparative Studies in the Politics of Education* (pp. 212–36). Melbourne: Macmillan.

—— (1992). Education and training for the school to work transition. In T. Seddon and C. Deer (eds), *A Curriculum for the Senior Secondary Years* (pp. 64–88). Melbourne: Australian Council for Educational Research.

Gavey, N. (1989). Feminist poststructuralism and discourse analysis. *Psychology of Women Quarterly*, 13: 459–75.

Gee, J., Hull, G. and Lankshear, C. (1996). *New Work Order: Behind the Language of the New Capitalism*. St Leonards: Allen & Unwin.

Gee, J. and Lankshear, C. (1995). The new work order: critical language awareness and 'fast capitalism' texts. *Discourse: Studies in the Cultural Politics of Education*, 16(1): 5–20.

George, S. and Sabelli, F. (1994). *Faith and Credit: The World Bank's Secular Empire*. Harmondsworth: Penguin.

Gewirtz, S. (1997). Post-welfarism and the reconstruction of teachers' work in the UK. *Journal of Education Policy*, 12(4): 217–31.

Gewirtz, S., Ball, S. and Bowe, R. (1995). *Markets, Choice and Equity in Education*. Milton Keynes: Open University Press.

Giddens, A. (1994). *Beyond Left and Right: The Future of Radical Politics*. Cambridge: Polity Press.

Gillett, J. (1996). The making of the preferred principal – changes in the nature of the work of principals and implications, especially re. union membership. Unpublished MS, Adelaide.

Giroux, H. (1993). *Living Dangerously: Multiculturalism and the Politics of Difference*. New York: Peter Lang.

Goode, E. and Ben-Yehuda, N. (1994). *Moral Panics and the Construction of Deviance*. Cambridge, MA, and Oxford: Blackwell.

Goodman, J. (1994). External change agents and grassroots school reform: reflections from the field. *Journal of Curriculum and Supervision*, 9(2): 113–35.

Goodson, I. and Hargreaves, A. (eds) (1996). *Teachers' Professional Lives*. London: Falmer Press.

Gordon, L. (1992). Educational reform in New Zealand: contesting the role of the teacher. *International Studies in the Sociology of Education*, 2(1): 23–42.

—— (1995). Reflections on the social market: an investigation of school choice in a social policy context. Unpublished MS, University of Canterbury.

Grace, G. (1997). Politics, markets and democratic schools: on the transformation of school leadership. In Halsey, A.H.; Lauder, H.; Brown, P. and Stuart Wells, A. (eds), *Education: Culture, Economy, Society* (pp. 311–19). Oxford: Oxford University Press.

Gramsci, A. (1971). *Selection from the Prison Notebooks*. New York: International Publishers.

Greene, M. (1982). Education and disarmament. *Teachers College Record*, 84: 128–36.

Gunter, H. (1997). *Rethinking Education: The Consequences of Jurassic Management*. London: Cassell.

Haberman, M. (1991). The pedagogy of poverty versus good teaching. *Phi Delta Kappan*, December: 290–4.

Hall, S. (1980). Encoding/Decoding. In S. Hall, D. Hobson, A. Lowe and P. Willis (eds), *Culture, Media, Language: Working Papers in Cultural Studies, 1972–79* (pp. 128–38). London: Hutchinson with Centre for Contemporary Cultural Studies, University of Birmingham.

—— (1992). The question of cultural identity. In S. Hall, D. Held and T. McGrew (eds), *Modernity and its Futures* (pp. 297–316). Cambridge: Polity Press.

Hamilton, C. (1996). 'Misotely' and the National Commission of Audit. In The Australia Institute (ed.), *What Should Governments Do? Auditing the National Commission of Audit* (pp. 26–39) (Discussion Paper no. 8). Canberra.

Hargreaves, A. (1994). *Changing Teachers, Changing Times: Teachers' Work and Culture in the Postmodern Age*. London: Cassell.

—— and Dawe, R. (1990). Paths of professional development: contrived collegiality, collaborative culture, and the case of peer coaching. *Teaching and Teacher Education*, 6(3): 227–41.

Harmon, M. and Mayer, R. (1986). *Organization Theory for Public Administration*. Boston: Little, Brown & Co.

Harre, R. and Gillett, G. (1994). *The Discursive Mind*. Thousand Oaks, CA: Sage.

Hartley, D. (1992). *Teacher Appraisal: A Policy Analysis*. Edinburgh: Scottish Academic Press.

—— (1997). *Re-schooling Society*. London: Falmer Press.

Hatcher, R. (1994). Market relationships and the management of teachers. *British Journal of Sociology of Education*, 15(1): 41–61.

—— and Troyna, B. (1994). The 'policy cycle': a Ball by Ball account. *Journal of Education Policy*, 9(2): 155–70.

Head, S. (1996). The new, ruthless economy. *New York Review of Books*, February: 47–52.

Herzfeld, M. (1983). Looking both ways: the ethnography in the text. *Semiotica*, 46(2–4): 151–66.

Hess, G. (1992). Chicago and Britain: experiments in empowering parents. *Journal of Education Policy*, 7(2): 155–71.

Hodge, B. (1993). *Teaching as Communication*. London and New York: Longman.

—— and Kress, G. (1993). *Language as Ideology*. 2nd edn, London and New York: Routledge.

Hoggett, P. (1996). New modes of control in the public service. *Public Administration*, 74: 9–32.

Hollway, W. (1989). *Subjectivity and Method in Psychology: Gender, Meaning and Science*. London: Sage.

Hood, C. (1995). Contemporary public management: a new global paradigm? *Public Policy and Administration*, 10(2): 104–17.

—— and Jackson, M. (1991). *Administrative Argument*. Aldershot: Dartmouth.

hooks, b. (1989). *Talking Back: Thinking Feminist, Thinking Black*. Boston: South End Press.

Hutton, W. (1995). *The State We're In*. London: J. Cape.

Hyland, T. (1994). Silk purses and sow's ears: NVQs, GNVQs and experiential learning. *Cambridge Journal of Education*, 24(2): 233–43.

Ilon, L. (1994). Structural adjustment and education: adapting to a growing global market. *International Journal of Educational Development*, 14(2): 95–108.

Ingvarson, L. and Chadbourne, R. (1996). *Reforming teachers' pay systems: the advanced skills teacher in Australia*. Paper presented at the American Educational Research Association, New York.

Jackson, N. (1989). The case against 'competence': the impoverishment of working knowledge. *Our Schools/Our Selves*, April: 78–85.

—— (1991). *Skills formation and Gender Relations: The Politics of Who Knows What*. Geelong: Deakin University Press.

Jacobs, M., Munro, P. and Adams, N. (1995). Palimpsest: (re)reading women's lives. *Qualitative Inquiry*, 1(3): 327–45.

Janks, H. (1991). A critical approach to the teaching of language. *Educational Review*, 43(2): 191–9.

—— and Ivanic, R. (1992). Critical language awareness and emancipatory discourse. In N. Fairclough (ed.), *Critical Language Awareness* (pp. 305–31). New York: Longman.

Johnson, S. (1984). Merit pay for teachers: a poor prescription for reform. *Harvard Educational Review*, 54(2): 175–85.

—— (1990). *Teachers at Work: Achieving Success in Our Schools*. New York: Basic Books.

Johnson-Riordan, L. (1995). AST1 in South Australia: a critical review. *South Australian Educational Leader*, 6(1): 1–8.

Jones, K. and Williamson, K. (1979). The birth of the schoolroom. *Ideology and Consciousness*, 6: 59–97.

Junor, A. (1988). Australian education reconstructed. *Arena*, 84: 133–40.

Keegan, W. (1992). *The Spectre of Capitalism: The Future of the World Economy after the Fall of Communism*. London: Radius.

Keep, E. (1992). Schools in the market place? Some problems with private sector models. *British Journal of Education and Work*, 5(2): 43–56.

Kelchtermans, G. (1996). Teacher vulnerability: understanding its moral and political roots. *Cambridge Journal of Education*, 26(3): 307–23.

Kelsey, J. (1995). *Economic Fundamentalism: The New Zealand Experiment – A World Model for Structural Adjustment?* London: Pluto Press.

—— (1996). In New Zealand its . . . back to the nineteenth century. *Frontline*, 39(October): 15–16.

Kenway, J., Bigum, C., Fitzclarence, C. and Collier, J. (1993). Marketing education in the post-modern age. *Journal of Education Policy*, 8(2): 105–22.

——, ——, —— and Tragenza, R. (1994). The rise and rise of markets in education. *Changing Education*, 1(1): 1 and 6–7.

Keyman, E. (1997). *Globalization, State, Identity/Difference: Toward a Critical Social Theory of International Relations*. New Jersey: Humanities Press.

Kickert, W. (1993). Steering at a distance: a new paradigm of public governance in Dutch higher education. Unpublished MS, Erasmus University, Rotterdam.

King, B. (1994). Locking ourselves in: national standards for the teaching profession. *Teaching and Teacher Education*, 10(1): 95–108.

—— (1995). Disciplining teachers. *Education and Society*, 13(2): 15–29.

Kramer-Dahl, A. (1995). Reading and writing against the grain of academic discourse. *Discourse: Studies in the Cultural Politics of Education*, 16(1): 21–38.

Kremer-Hayon, L. (1994). The knowledge teachers use in problem solving situation: sources and forms. *Scandinavian Journal of Educational Research*, 38: 63.

Kress, G. (1985). *Linguistic Processes in Sociocultural Practice*. Geelong: Deakin University Press.

Kumar, K. (1995). *From Post-Industrial to Post-Modern Society: New Theories of the Contemporary World*. Oxford: Blackwell.

Kupferberg, F. (1996). The reality of teaching: bringing disorder back into social theory and the sociology of education. *British Journal of Sociology of Education*, 17(2): 227–47.

Lacey, C. (1977). *The Socialisation of Teachers*. London: Methuen.

Lakoff, G. and Johnson, M. (1980). *Metaphors We Live By*. Chicago: University of Chicago Press.

Lather, P. (1991). *Getting Smart: Feminist Research and Pedagogy with/in the (Post) Modern*. New York and London: Routledge.

Lawler, E. (1990). *Strategic Pay: Aligning Organisation Strategies and Pay Systems*. San Francisco: Jossey Bass.

Lawn, M. (1988). Skill in schoolwork: work relations in the primary school. In J. Ozga (ed.), *Schoolwork: Approaches to the Labour Process of Teaching* (pp. 161–76). Milton Keynes: Open University Press.

—— (1990). From responsibility to competency: a new context for curriculum studies in England and Wales. *Journal of Curriculum Studies*, 22(4): 338–400.

—— (1995). Restructuring teaching in the USA and England: moving towards the differentiated, flexible teacher. *Journal of Education Policy*, 10(4): 347–60.

—— (1996). *Modern Times? Work, Professionalism and Citizenship in Teaching*. London: Falmer Press.

Lawton, D. (1992a). *Education and Politics in the 1990s: Conflict or Consensus?* London: Falmer Press.

—— (1992b). Why restructure? An international survey of the roots of reform. *Journal of Education Policy*, 7(2): 139–54.

Levin, H. and Rumberger, R. (1983). The low-skill future of high tech. *Technology Review*, Aug./Sept.: 19–21.

Limerick, B. and Lingard, B. (eds) (1995). *Gender and Changing Educational Management*. Rydalmere, NSW: Hodder Education.

Lingard, B. (1995). Gendered policy making inside the state. In B. Limerick and B. Lingard (eds), *Gender and Changing Educational Management* (pp. 136–49). Rydalmere, NSW: Hodder Education.

—— (1996). Educational policy making in a postmodern state: an essay review of Stephen J. Ball's 'Education Reform: A Critical Post-Structural Approach'. *The Australian Educational Researcher*, 23(1): 65–92.

——, O'Brien, P. and Knight, J. (1993). Strengthening Australia's schools through corporate federalism. *Australian Journal of Education*, 37(3): 231–47.

McDonald, J. (1992). *Teaching: Making Sense of an Uncertain Craft*. New York: Teachers College Press.

McIntosh, G. (1995). *The Schooling Revolution: Too Much, Too Fast?* Canberra: Parliamentary Research Service.

McLaren, P. (1994). *Critical Pedagogy and Predatory Culture: Oppositional Politics in a Postmodern Era*. London and New York: Routledge.

McMurtry, J. (1988). The history of inquiry and social reproduction: educating for critical thought. *Interchange*, 19(1): 31–45.

—— (1991). Education and the market model. *Journal of Philosophy of Education*, 25(2): 209–17.

Macan Ghaill, M. (1991). State-school policy: contradictions, confusions and contestation. *Journal of Education Policy*, 6(3): 299–313.

—— (1992). Teachers' work: curriculum restructuring, culture and power in comprehensive schooling. *British Journal of Sociology of Education*, 13(2): 177–99.

Macedo, D. (1994). *Literacies of Power: What Americans Are Not Allowed to Know*. Boulder, CO: Westview Press.

Maguire, M. and Ball, S. (1994). Discourses of educational reform in the United Kingdom and the USA and the work of teachers. *British Journal of In-Service Education*, 20(1): 5–16.

Mahony, P. and Hextall, I. (1997a). *Teaching in the managerial state*. Paper presented at the Annual Meeting of the Australian Association for Research in Education, Brisbane.

—— and —— (1997b). Problems of accountability in reinvented government: a case study of the Teacher Training Agency. *Journal of Education Policy*, 12(4): 267–83.

Malen, B. and Hart, A. (1987). Career ladder reform: a multi-level analysis of initial efforts. *Educational Evaluation and Policy Analysis*, 9(1): 9–23.

Marginson, S. (1995). Markets in education: a theoretical note. *Australian Journal of Education*, 39(3): 294–312.

—— (1997). *Markets in Education*. Sydney: Allen & Unwin.

Marin, P. (1995). *Freedom and its Discontents: Reflections on Four Decades of American Moral Experience*. Vermont: Steerforth Press.

Mihevc, J. (1992). The changing debate on structual adjustment policies in Sub-Saharan Africa: Churches social movements and the World Bank. Unpublished Ph.D., University of St Michael's College, Toronto.

Milligan, S., Ashenden, D. and Quin, R. (1994). *Women in the Teaching Profession* (Commissioned Report 32). Canberra: National Board of Employment, Education and Training.

Mitchell, D. (1996). Social policy and the National Commission of Audit: old whines in new bottles? In The Australia Institute (ed.), *What Should Government Do? Auditing the National Audit Commission* (pp. 17–28). Deakin, Australian Capital Territory: The Australia Institute.

Mohrman, A., Mohrman, S. and Odden, A. (1996). Aligning teacher compensation with systemic school reform: skill-based pay and group-based performance awards. *Educational Evaluation and Policy Analysis*, 18(1): 51–71.

Moore, A. (1996). 'Masking the fissure': some thoughts on competencies, reflection and 'closure' in initial teacher education. *British Journal of Educational studies*, 44(2): 200–11.

Moore, R. (1987). Education and the ideology of production. *British Journal of Sociology of Education*, 8(2): 227–42.

Muetzelfeldt, M. (1995). Democracy, citizenship and the problematics of governing production: the Australian case. In R. Jureidini (ed.), *Labour, Unemployment and Democratic Rights* (pp. 33–48). Geelong: Centre for Citizenship and Human Rights.

Murgatroyd, S. and Morgan, C. (1993). *Total Quality Management and the School*. Milton Keynes: Open University Press.

Murnane, R. and Cohen, D. (1986). Merit pay and the evaluation problem: why most merit pay plans fail to survive. *Harvard Educational Review*, 56(1): 1–14.

Murphy, J. and Hallinger, P. (eds) (1993). *Restructuring Schooling: Learning from Ongoing Efforts*. Newbury Park, CA: Corwin Press.

National Commission on Excellence in Education (1983). *A Nation at Risk; the Imperative for Educational Reform*. Washington, DC: US Government Printing Office.

Neave, G. (1988). On the cultivation of quality, efficiency and enterprise: an overview of recent trends in higher education in western Europe 1986–88. *European Journal of Education*, 23(1–2): 7–23.

Neumann, W. (1979). Educational responses to the concern for proficiency. In G. Grant (ed.), *On Competence* (pp. 66–94). San Francisco: Jossey Bass.

Nias, J., Southworth, G. and Campbell, P. (1992). *Whole School Curriculum Development in the Primary School*. London: Falmer Press.

Nicholls, P. (1995). *Manufacturing consent through the market: the case of the service sector.* Paper presented at the Research Seminar Series, Murdoch University.

Nickerson, N. (1984). Merit pay – does it work in education? *NASSP Bulletin*, 68: 65–6.

Noble, D. (1994). Let them eat skills. *The Review of Education/ Pedagogy/Cultural Studies*, 16(1): 15–29.

OECD (1983). *Compulsory Schooling in a Changing World*. Paris: OECD.

OECD (1989). *Schools and Quality: An International Report*. Paris: OECD.

OECD (1990). *The Teacher Today*. Paris: OECD.

OECD (1995). *Governance in Transition: Public Sector Management Reforms in OECD Countries*. Paris: OECD.

O'Neill, J. (1997). *Teacher Appraisal in New Zealand: Beyond the Impossible Triangle*. Palmerston North: ERDC Press.

Ozga, J. (ed.) (1988). *Schoolwork: An Introduction to the Labour Process of Teaching*. Milton Keynes: Open University Press.

—— (1990). Policy research and policy theory: a comment on Fitz and Halpin. *Journal of Education Policy*, 5(4): 359–62.

Peacock, D. and Bluer, R. (1991). Competency-based standards and the teaching profession. *Independent Education*, 21(4): 20–1.

Polanyi, M. (1969). *Personal Knowledge: Towards a Post-Critical Philosophy*. London: Routledge.

Pollitt, C. (1996). *Managerialism and the Public Services: Cuts or Cultural Changes in the 1990s?* 2nd edn, Oxford: Blackwell.

Porter, R., Rizvi, F., Knight, J. and Lingard, R. (1992). Competencies for a clever country: building a house of cards? *Unicorn*, 18(3): 50–8.

Power, S. (1992). Researching the impact of education policy: difficulties and discontinuities. *Journal of Education Policy*, 7(5): 493–500.

—— (1995). The detail and the bigger picture: the use of state-centred theory in explaining education policy and practice. *International Studies in Sociology of Education*, 5(1): 77–92.

Pring, R. (1996). Editorial. *British Journal of Educational Studies*, 44(2): 139–41.

Proudford, C. and Baker, R. (1995). Schools that make a difference: a sociological perspective on effective schooling. *British Journal of Sociology of Education*, 16(3): 277–92.

Queensland Department of Education (1996). *Learning and Working Together* (1, 2, 3). Brisbane: Queensland Department of Education.

Reid, I. (1996). *Higher Education or Education for Hire? Language and Values in Australian Universities*. Rockhampton: Central Queensland University Press.

Review Committee on Quality of Education (1985). *Quality of Education in Australia: Report of the Review Committee.* Canberra: Australian Government Publishing Service.

Robinson, P. (1993). The strange case of the bechemal sauce. In Centre for Skill Formation (ed.), *After Competence: The Future of Post-Compulsory Education and Training* (vol. 2, pp. 136–41). Brisbane: Griffith University.

Rose, N. (1988). Calculable minds and manageable individuals. *History of the Human Sciences,* 1(2): 179–200.

Rosenholtz, S. (1986). Career ladders and merit pay: capricious fads or fundamental reforms. *Elementary School Journal,* 86(4): 513–29.

Rumberger, R. (1988). *Conceptual and Methodological Issues in Assessing Work Skills: A Multi-Disciplinary Analysis.* Santa Barbara: University of California.

Sachs, J. (1997). Gender and the cultural construction of teaching. A review of 'School Work: Gender and the Cultural Construction of Teaching' by Sari Knopp Biklen. *Curriculum Inquiry,* 27(1).

Said, E. (1994). *Representations of the Intellectual.* London: Vintage Books.

Sampson, S. (1991). Women teachers' careers. In P. Hughes and P. McKenzie (eds), *Australian Teachers' Careers* (pp. 121–37). Hawthorn: Australian Council of Educational Research.

Santa Ana, J. (1992). Sacralization and sacrifice in human practice. In World Council of Churches' Commission on the Churches' Participation in Development (ed.), *Sacrifice and Humane Economic Life* (p. 20). Geneva: World Council of Churches.

Sawada, D. and Caley, M. (1985). Dissipative structures: new metaphors for becoming in education. *Educational Researcher,* 14(3): 13–19.

Sayer, A. (1986). New developments in manufacturing: the just in time system. *Capital and Class,* 30: 43–72.

Schon, D. (1983). *The Reflective Practitioner: How Professionals Think in Action.* New York: Basic Books.

Schools Council (1990). *Australia's Teachers: An Agenda for the Next Decade.* Canberra: Australian Government Publishing Service.

Seddon, T. (1990). On education and context: insights from the first Monash University forum on the VCE. *Australian Journal of Education,* 34(2): 131–36.

—— (1994). Reconstructing social democratic education in Australia: versions of vocationalism. *Journal of Curriculum Studies,* 26(1): 63–82.

Sedunary, E. (1996). Neither new nor alien to progressive thinking: interpreting the convergence of radical education and the new vocationalism in Australia. *Journal of Curriculum Studies,* 28(4): 369–96.

Self, P. (1993). *Government by the Market.* London: Macmillan.

Sewell, G. and Wilkinson, B. (1992). 'Someone to watch over me': surveillance, discipline and the just-in-time labour process. *Sociology,* 26(2): 271–89.

Shor, I. (1996). *When Students Have Power: Negotiating Authority in a Critical Pedagogy.* Chicago and London: University of Chicago Press.

—— and Freire, P. (1987). *Pedagogy for Liberation: Dialogues on Transforming Education.* Westport, CT: Bergin & Garvey.

Sinclair, A. (1996). Leadership *in* administration: rediscovering a lost discourse. In P. Weller and G. Davis (eds), *New Ideas, Better Government* (pp. 229–44). St Leonards, NSW: Allen & Unwin.

Smyth, J. (1991). International perspectives on teacher collegiality: a labour process discussion based on teachers' work. *British Journal of Sociology of Education*, 12(4): 323–46.

—— (1992). Teachers' work and the politics of reflection. *American Educational Research Journal*, 29(2): 267–300.

—— (ed.) (1993a). *A Socially Critical View of the Self-Managing School*. London: Falmer Press.

—— (1993b). *A Study of Participation, Consultation and Collective Bargaining in the Teaching Profession in Australia* (Report). Geneva: International Labour Organization.

—— (1995a). Devolution and teachers' work: the underside of a complex phenomenon. *Educational Management and Administration*, 23(3): 168–75.

—— (ed.) (1995b). *Critical Discourses on Teacher Development*. London and Toronto: Cassell/Ontario Institute for Studies in Education Press.

—— (1995c). Teachers' work and the labour process of teaching: central problematics in professional development. In T. Guskey and M. Huberman (eds), *Professional Development in Education: New Paradigms and Practices* (pp. 69–91). New York: Teachers College Press.

—— (1995d). What's happening to teachers' work in Australia? *Educational Review*, 47(2): 189–98.

—— (1996a). Evaluation of teacher performance: move over hierarchy here comes collegiality! *Journal of Education Policy*, 11(2): 185–96.

—— (1996b). The socially just alternative to the 'self-managing school'. In K. Leithwood, J. Chapman, D. Corson, P. Hallinger and A. Hart (eds), *International Handbook of Educational Leadership and Administration Part 2* (pp. 1097–131). Dordrecht, Boston and London: Kluwer Academic Publishers.

—— (1996c). *What's happening to teachers' work in an era of curriculum statements and profiles?* Paper presented at the National Workshop of the Health and Physical Education Learning Area of the National Statements and Profiles, Melbourne.

—— (1998a). Teaching and social policy: images of schools and classrooms for democratic change. In B. Biddle, T. Good and I. Goodson (eds), *International Handbook of Teachers and Teaching* (pp. 1081–1143). Dordrecht, Boston and London: Kluwer Academic Publishers.

—— (1998b). Some global forces affecting school supervision. In G. Firth and E. Pajak (eds), *Handbook of Research on School Supervision* (pp. 1173–1183). New York: Macmillan.

Soucek, V. (1995). Public education and the post-Fordist accumulation regime: a case study of Australia. *Interchange*, 26(2): 127–59.

Spann, R. (1981). Fashions and fantasies in public administration. *Australian Journal of Public Administration*, 40: 12–25.

Spratt, D. (1995). Beyond the gloss. *Frontline*, 26(July): 2.

Stewart, J. (1994). *The Lie of the Level Playing Field*. Melbourne: Text Publishing.

—— and Ranson, S. (1988). Management in the public domain. *Public Money and Management* (Spring–Summer): 13–19.

Strain, M. (1995). Autonomy, schools and the constitutive role of community: towards a new moral and political order for education. *British Journal of Educational Studies*, 43(1): 4–20.

Stretton, H. and Orchard, L. (1994). *Public Goods, Public Enterprise, Public Choice: Theoretical Foundations of the Contemporary Attack on Government*. London: Macmillan.

Stronach, I. and Morris, B. (1994). Polemical notes on educational evaluation in the age of 'policy hysteria'. *Evaluation and Research in Education*, 8(1 & 2): 5–19.

Sullivan, K. (1992). The myth of partnership: educational reform and teacher disempowerment. *New Zealand Annual Review of Education*, 2: 151–65.

—— (1994). The impact of educational reform on teachers' professional ideologies. *New Zealand Journal of Educational Studies*, 29(1): 3–20.

Taylor, S., Rizvi, F., Lingard, B. and Henry, M. (1997). *Educational Policy and the Politics of Change*. London and New York: Routledge.

Taylor-Gooby, P. (1994). Post modernism and social policy: a great leap backwards? *Journal of Social Policy*, 23(3): 385–404.

Threadgold, T. (1988). The genre debate. *Southern Review*, 21: 315–30.

Thurow, L. (1996). *The Future of Capitalism*. St Leonards, NSW: Allen & Unwin.

Vickers, M. (1994). Cross-national exchange, the OECD, and Australian education policy. *Knowledge and Policy*, 7(1): 25–47.

Vidal, G. (1995). *Palimpsest: A Memoir*. London: Abacus.

Walker, J. (1991). A general rationale and conceptual approach to the application of competency based standards to teaching. Unpublished paper, Sydney.

Wallace, M. (1993). Discourse of derision: the role of the mass media within the education policy process. *Journal of Education Policy*, 8(4): 321–37.

Walter, J. (1996). *Tunnel Vision: The Failure of Political Imagination*. St Leonards, NSW: Allen & Unwin.

Warton, P., Goodnow, J. and Bowes, J. (1992). Teaching as a form of work: effects of teachers' roles and role definitions on working to rule. *Australian Journal of Education*, 36(2): 170–80.

Watkins, P. (1994). Advanced skills teachers: progress and problems in their establishment in Australia. *International Journal for Educational Management*, 8(4): 1–8.

Watson, K. (1996). Banking on key reforms for educational development: a critique of the World Bank Review. *Mediterranean Journal of Educational Studies*, 1(1): 43–61.

Watts, T. (1993). Connecting curriculum to work: past patterns, current initiatives and future issues. In J. Wellington (ed.), *The Work Related Curriculum: Challenging the Vocational Imperative* (pp. 40–53). London: Kogan Page.

Weber, S. (1996). The future campus: virtual or reality. *The Australian* (18 September).

Weiler, H. (1989). Why reforms fail: the politics of education in France and the Federal Republic of Germany. *Journal of Curriculum Studies*, 21(4): 291–305.

Welch, A. (1996). *Australian Education: Reform or Crisis*. St Leonards: Allen & Unwin.

Wellington, J. (ed.) (1993). *The Work Related Curriculum: Challenging the Vocational Imperative*. London: Kogan Page.

West Africa (1988). IMF found guilty. *West Africa* (17–23 October): 1942–3.

Westoby, A. (ed.) (1988). *Culture and Power in Educational Organizations*. Milton Keynes: Open University Press.

Wiseman, J. (1995). Globalization is not Godzilla. *Frontline*, 26(July): 5–6.

Woods, P., Jeffrey, B., Troman, G. and Boyle, M. (1997). *Restructuring Schools, Reconstructing Teachers: Responding to Change in the Primary School*. Milton Keynes: Open University Press.

World Bank (1994). *Adjustment in Africa*. Washington, DC: Oxford University Press.

World Bank (1995). *Priorities and Strategies for Education*. Washington, DC: A World Bank Review.

Yeatman, A. (1996). The new contractualism: management reform or a new approach to governance? In G. Davis and P. Weller (eds), *New Ideas, Better Government* (pp. 283–92). Sydney: Allen & Unwin.

Young, J. (1971). The role of the police as amplifiers of deviance, negotiators of drug control as seen in Nottinghill. In S. Cohen (ed.), *Images of Deviance* (pp. 27–61). Harmondsworth: Penguin.

Zaida, A. (1996). The Rochester Renaissance Plan: a corporate farewell to the imagination. Unpublished MS, University of Rochester, New York.

Index

abstract instrumentalism 17
accommodation 30, 54, 92
Accord 7
accountability 82, 98
action at a distance 15
adding value 45
admissible evidence 93
Advanced Skills Teachers (ASTs) 3, 29, 93, 95
adversarial type 92
aerosol word 81
agency 27, 28, 42
annexes of industry 11
anti-language 86
appendages to industry 44
application of criteria 92
appraisal 20
arenas of formation and implementation 30, 54
Advanced Skills Teacher: criteria 93, 94, 167, 168, 169, 170, 171, 172, 173, 174, 184, 185,186, 197, 198 199; discourse genre 181, 182, 183, 198; failure 163, 164; gender politics 190, 191; ideology 186, 187, 188, 189, 190; implementing policy 174, 175, 176, 177, 178, 179, 186, 187, 188, 189, 190, 194, 196, 199; merit pay 123, 124; process intensity 154, 155; responsibilities 159, 160, 161, 162; showing-off 166, 167; skill documentation 165, 166; South Australia 148, 150; Victoria 148, 150; written applications 156, 157, 158
auditing 20
autonomy 16, 22
award restructuring 7

back to the basics 32
bad schools 45
basic skills 34, 44, 36
basic skills tests 114, 194
benchmarking 34, 68, 21, 50
best practice 68
betrayal of professional competence 99
black box of the classroom 97
Bretton Wood Conference 57
bureaucratisation of goodwill 99

calculative compliance 129
career: structures 83; change for teachers 31
carrier of ideology 3, 93
centralisation and regulation 103
changing technologies 14
chief executives 99
choice 15, 16, 23, 48, 56, 62, 83, 97, 100, 101, 102, 103, 104
client-focused 68, 69
co-producer of knowledge 9
collaboration 23 94, 103
collegiality 23, 73, 94, 103, 105
commodification 19
common sense 45, 74, 81, 86, 95
community 40, 96
competencies 3, 6, 20, 31, 45, 56, 80, 92, 95; competency approaches 83
Competency Based Training 108
competency frameworks 136, 137, 146, 149, 198
competency movement 52
competency syndrome 38
Competency-Based Standards (CBS) 53
competent technicians 56
competition 62

competitive individualism 105
complexity 87
compliant labour 22, 24, 44
constructed educational market 102
consumer sovereignty 135
consumerist behaviour 99
consumerist policies 100
consumers 97
consumption 27
consumption-led economy 16
contestation 92, 95
contours of the political world 86
contracting out 68
contrived: colleagiality 95; collegiality
    200
core skills 79
corporate capital 12
corporate compradors 27
corporate managerialism 3, 21
corporate predators 61
corporatisation 68
Council for the Accreditation of Teacher
    Education (CATE) 136, 137
counter discourse 87
counter hegemonic 7, 28, 87
crisis of legitimation 32
critical evaluation 40
critical literacy 86
critical sensibility 40
critique the canon 27
culture of continuous improvement 17
curriculum audits 23
curriculum prescription 64
customer's gaze – discipline 105
customers 20, 69

de-professionalisation 73, 76
decentralisation 18, 20, 103
decision-making 22
decisions at a distance 15
decolonising 14
deficits of individual teachers 99
delegated supervision 55
depoliticising teaching 55
deregulated global economy 70
deregulation 18, 19, 59
deskilling 104
devolution 21, 23, 25, 33, 56, 96, 102
differentiation 16
disciplinary technologies 112, 128
discipline 91
discourse: authentic 141, 198, 201;

commodity production 71; derision
    69; emancipatory 143; governing-at-
    a-distance 16; managerial 138, 139,
    140, 143, 197, 199; reification 5;
    synthetic 141, 142, 197, 198, 201;
    synthetic and dependent 66; the
    market 100; transformation 5;
    vocationalist 4; aspiring 3;
    competencies 8; enactment 3;
    ideological 14; managerialist 34, 66,
    76; official 3, 85; social regulatory
    16; counterhegemonic 5; indigenous
    10, 27, 66, 86, 92; teachers' resistant
    95
discursive – tradition of teaching 95
disintegration 13
dismantling of educational
    bureaucracies 24
dismantling of teaching 95
displacement 66
docile bodies 107, 108
dominant: discourses 16, 37, 84, 86;
    metaphor 49; viewpoints 86
duality of meaning 50
dumbing down 93

economic: competitiveness 34, 72;
    fundamentalism 2; imperatives 2, 3,
    22, 33, 49, 62, 65, 69, 82;
    restoration 6; restructuring 17;
    tectonic plates 11, 21; work 6, 20
educated citizenry 20
education-business partnerships 80
educational: leaders 99; markets 100;
    policy borrowing 81; reform 2, 46,
    48, 77; restructuring 5
Educational Review Office 99
educational values 21
educative values 27
effect of markets 97
effectiveness 7, 86
efficiency 7, 83, 86
emancipatory 28, 37
emasculated views of teaching 55
empowerment 17, 103
enhanced career pathway 8
enterprise culture 76, 77, 80, 85, 105
enterprising skills 80
entitlement to the basics 83
entrepreneaurial teacher 200, 202
ethical space 14
ethnic diaspora 14

evaluative state 50, 195, 196
everyday reality of teaching 87
evidence 95
excellence 12, 21, 85
explicit contracts 98

failing the system 71
fear of failure 94
federalisms, changing 4
feminisation 76
feminisation of teaching 73
fiscal crisis of the state 22
flat management structures 77, 105
flexibility 7, 16, 23
for profit activity 71
Fordist 16, 77
Foucault 107, 111, 114
fragmentation 16

gaze of self-regulation 93
gender-blindness 72, 75
generic: competencies 33, 34; skills 32,
    36; teaching competencies 27
global integration 3, 13, 14
globalisation 13, 15, 17, 67, 68, 78, 89,
    193
great policy leap backwards 24
guilt 93

health-and-safety standards 15
hegemony 6, 48, 58, 60, 79, 80
hermetically sealed moments 29
high-quality entrants 8
high-tech skills 71
high-trust 98
homework 83
homogenising of markets 18
horizontal violence 95
human capital 3, 5, 20, 36, 72, 74, 82
Human Resource Management 105
hybrid identities 14
hypotactic 90

identity/difference 14
ideological: lineage 48; manoeuvre 93;
    warehouse 63; innocent 86
ideology: 105; carriers of 89
image and impression management 16,
    77, 94, 104
imaginative space 2
inappropriate prescriptions 2

individual rewards 94
individualisation 32, 56, 103
individualism 11
individualist: cultures 119; emphasis 64
industrial: ethnographies 36; model of
    management 46
industry, interests 44
inscribed identity 109
integration 13
intellectual satisfaction 64
intensification 129, 198, 199
intensification of work 17
international: best practice 21; capital
    16; clearinghouse 81;
    competitiveness 2, 3, 7, 18, 22, 74,
    78, 82; division of labour 17;
    marketplace 12
International Monetary Fund 39, 57, 60
internationalisation 15, 18
interview: game 94; process 94
invisibility 75, 93
invisible carriers of systems policy 96

just and compassionate society 41
just-in-time 17

labour market flexibility 3
labour process 5, 18, 25, 43, 73
language games 93
lead teachers 17, 83, 126, 127
leadership 83
learning community 95
legitimising policy 86
level playing field 25
line management 21, 96
listening practitioner 5
listening school 5
locally managed schools 48
logics of industrial production 96
looking both ways 29
low-trust 8, 98, 99, 100

macro-forces 6
macro-micro problem 29
making transparent 32
management by hierarchy 99
managerialism 7, 19, 20, 27, 50, 64,
    72, 98, 104
managerialist: ideology 5, 56; incursions
    5
manufactured crisis 46

manufacturing of consent 105
mapping the discourses 3
market competition 96
market: forces 16, 97; discipline 61;
    ideology 103; liberalisation 64;
    relationships 97
market-driven forms of educational
    policy 102
market-led reforms 97
marketisation 51, 83, 96, 97, 98, 101,
    102, 104, 105
marketplace 25
markets 86, 97
masked 95
mechanistic 49
mental labour 54
merit pay 123, 124, 125, 126
methodological individualism 79
micro-economic reform 2, 6, 7, 40, 91
monetarist economics 58
monolithic capitalism 31
moral panic 65, 68, 71, 73, 196
mouthing the rhetoric 93
muscular political posturings 21

narrowing down teaching 93
Nation at Risk 19
nation states 14
National Council for vocational
    Qualification 136
National Curricula 20, 21
national: disintegration 14;
    fragmentation 13; priorities 50, 64
National Professional Qualification
    (NPQ) 128
National Vocational Qualifications 52
Natural Board for Professional Teaching
    Standards 136
naturalised 45, 86
neo-classical economics 54, 59
networking 23
new management regimes 55, 96, 97,
    104
new public administration 8, 116, 127
New Right 2, 48, 56, 77
new vocationalism 77, 78, 79
new work order 78
New Zealand 97
Newtonian Machine 49

OECD 61, 68, 72, 81
OCD 106

Ofsted 128
one-dimensional approaches 38
oppositional reading 85, 89, 106
ordeal by representation 94
orientation 49
orthodox economics 58
outcomes 7, 20, 23, 25, 27, 33, 34, 49,
    56, 64, 83, 86
outsourcing 77

palimpsest 4, 5
palimpsest 201
paratactic 90
partnerships 17, 23
pedagogical: engagement 121;
    technicians 20
pedagogocial spaces 120
pedagogy: of liberation 114; of poverty
    115
performance: appraisal 23; facade 94;
    indicators 21, 49
Performance Management 21
performance standards 83
personal classification of skill 94
policy: assimilation 93; borrowing 72;
    conformity 93; disjuncture 91;
    disseminators and legitimators 81;
    ethnography 29, 30; frameworks and
    guidelines 23; gloss 93; hysteria 31,
    194; sociology 96; text 4, 30
political: imagination 6, 27, 85;
    reassurance 21
politics of appropriation 10
populist debate 32
possessive individualism 78, 79, 98
post-Fordist 7, 16, 40, 77, 130, 175,
    193
post-modernism 28, 31
postcolonial criticism 14
power 14, 27, 43, 68, 86, 91
predatory culture 27
preferred: individualist remedies 64;
    policy options 82; principal 116;
    teacher 99, 116, 118, 120, 122, 133,
    196, 202
principal-teacher relations 99
private: education 19; enterprises 23;
    sector 12, 24
privatisation 18, 19, 59, 62, 68
producer capture 97, 135
producers 20
productivity 3, 7, 18, 33, 38, 86

professional: autonomy 54; development 8; view of teaching 103
profiling 20
progressive: pedagogy 55; politics 51
proletarianised 20, 50, 100
public: education 19; imagination 12; misinformation 47; sector performance 68; spaces 2; sphere 22, 27

quality: 45, 76, 77, 85; assurance 21, 23; audits 34
quasi-judicial process 92
quasi-managerial function 104
quasi-markets in education 103
quasi-privatised environment 100

re-gendering of educational policy 76
re-masculinisation 76
readerly 88, 89
reading: and writing against the grain 86; position 84
recentralisation 16, 20, 21, 22
reclaiming voice 27
recognition and reward 8
recurring waves of reform 32
reducing role of government 17
reflective practice 34, 87, 88
reform/change fatigue 33
regulation of pay and promotion 102
relational nature: of teachers' work 8; of teaching 6, 52, 93, 95
relay of the wider restructuring 3
relevance 79
resistance 5, 30, 54, 85, 86, 90, 92, 95
resistant forms of reading 37
reskilled 73
responsibility 16, 56
responsiveness 23
restructuring 4, 6, 8, 22, 26
rigour 83
ruthless economy 2

school: charters 21; development plan 105
School Development Planning 128, 129
school effectiveness 83
school reform 6
school-based management 23, 48
scientific management 49
scripted performance 88

self-imposed performance accountability 93
self-management 23, 24, 97
self-managing school 48
self-monitoring 64
self-promotion 94
self-worth in teaching 94
selling the school 99
settlement 29, 92, 100
shared experiential construction 96
shrinking tax bases 24
silenced subjectivity 14
site-based management 48, 87
skill in teaching 91
skills: formation 3, 6, 18, 19, 27, 33, 34, 37, 51, 56, 70, 74; modules 79
slogan system 81
social: atomisation 62, 81; benefits 18; capital 62; control 17; dislocations 44; justice 11, 50, 93; pathology 27; social, political and moral deficits 63
sociology of education 29
speaking the changes 2
standardization, frenzy of 52
standards 37, 45, 56, 87
steered education market 102
strategic profiling 51
stratified education system 20
structural adjustment 17, 19, 20, 42, 60, 62, 69, 193, 194, 195, 201
structural efficiency 39
struggle 91
subservient 83, 86
surveillance 17, 20, 27, 50, 64

teacher: appraisal 27; burnout 2; professionalism 55, 103; proofing 103
Teacher Training Agency 127
teacherese 90
teachers' preferred ways 92
teachers' voices 3, 4, 5, 8, 9, 14, 28, 85, 89, 91, 119, 144, 153, 198 201
teaching: as gendered work 73; as moral, intellectual and political activity 131, 132, 133, 200; as technical activity 130, 131, 200; never innocent 91
team work 17, 23, 55, 105
technical rationality 21, 68, 87, 88, 92,
technology of control 49
temporarily negligent 93

testing 20
the state 18
theoretical capital 9
Total Quality Management 17, 21, 52, 105, 128, 129
trade unions 18
transnational: capital 27; corporations 68; economic forces 17; economic interests 44; economies 15

uncertainty 16, 22
unmasking 32
unveiled 89

user pays 23, 62, 71

value: added 86; for money 99
vocal: school 5; teacher 5
vocationalism 19, 20, 51, 76
vulnerability 95

work-related: competencies 53; skills 40
workers 44
World Bank 39, 57, 58, 59, 60, 61, 62, 63, 83
world best practice 2, 70
writerly 88, 89, 90